QUEERING MESOAMERICAN DIASPORAS

TRANSFORMATIONS: WOMANIST, FEMINIST, AND INDIGENOUS STUDIES

Edited by AnaLouise Keating

A list of books in the series appears at the end of this book.

QUEERING MESOAMERICAN DIASPORAS

REMEMBERING XICANA INDÍGENA ANCESTRIES

SUSY J. ZEPEDA

UNIVERSITY OF ILLINOIS PRESS
Urbana, Chicago, and Springfield

1 2 3 4 5 C P 5 4 3 2 1
♾ This book is printed on acid-free paper.

Parts of chapter 1 originally appeared in "Decolonizing Xicana/x Studies: Healing the Susto of De-indigenization," *Aztlán: A Journal of Chicano Studies* 45, no. 1 (Spring 2020): 225–41.

Parts of chapter 3 originally appeared in "Queer Xicana Indígena Cultural Production: Remembering through Oral and Visual Storytelling," *Decolonization: Indigeneity, Education & Society* 3, no. 1 (2014): 119–41.

Library of Congress Cataloging-in-Publication Data
Names: Zepeda, Susy J., 1977– author.
Title: Queering Mesoamerican diasporas : remembering Xicana indígena ancestries / Susy J. Zepeda.
Description: Urbana : University of Illinois Press, [2022] | Series: Transformations: womanist, feminist, and indigenous studies | Includes bibliographical references and index.
Identifiers: LCCN 2022003385 (print) | LCCN 2022003386 (ebook) | ISBN 9780252044533 (cloth) | ISBN 9780252086601 (paperback) | ISBN 9780252053535 (ebook)
Subjects: LCSH: Mexican American women—Ethnic identity. | Mexican American women—Spiritual life. | Mexican American arts. | Hispanic American lesbians—Psychology. | Central American Americans—Ethnic identity. | Indian gays—Intellectual life. | Feminism—United States. | Decolonization—Social aspects—United States. | United States—Civilization—Indian influences.
Classification: LCC E184.M5 Z47 2022 (print) | LCC E184.M5 (ebook) | DDC 305.48/86872073—dc23/eng/20220207
LC record available at https://lccn.loc.gov/2022003385
LC ebook record available at https://lccn.loc.gov/2022003386

Para todas mis abuelitas, empezando con
Rosario Sánchez Benítez y Gregoria Yañez.
Doy gracias por las bendiciones y su iluminación.
Son flores en la tierra y estrellas en los cielos.

To my ancestor nephew Orion,
tlazohcamati for illuminating our pathways to Mictlan and the cosmos.

For Maria Carmen Tavitian and Sylvia Villa,
and all the mothers, life givers, abuelitxs, elders, and relatives
who left this dimension too soon during transformational pandemic times.
We remember you. We honor you.

CONTENTS

FOREWORD

ANALOUISE KEATING

What roles can scholarship (including academic publishing) play in effecting progressive transformation, at both individual and collective levels? How can we use writing, reading, publishing, and other research-related activities to foster progressive change? How do we produce scholarship that does not simply replicate the status quo but, instead, transforms it—making it more inclusive, expansive, and revolutionary? How do we use our research and writing to enact physical-material change? And what roles might Spirit (define it how you will) play in these transformations? Can we develop Spirit-inflected epistemologies, ontologies, and methods?

Transformations: Womanist, Feminist, and Indigenous Studies emerges from these and related questions. Grounded in the belief that radical progressive change—on individual, collective, national, transnational, and planetary levels—is urgently needed and in fact is possible (although typically difficult to achieve), this book series functions as invitation into radical change. It offers new venues for transdisciplinary scholarship informed by women-of-colors theories and post-oppositional approaches to knowledge production and social change.[1] *Transformations* invites authors to take risks (thematically, theoretically, methodologically, and/or stylistically) in their work—to both build on and move beyond disciplinary- or interdisciplinary-specific academic rules; and, through these risks, to invent new (transdisciplinary) perspectives, methods, and knowledges.

This series is especially interested in supporting work that offers alternatives to the spirit-phobia dominating much U.S. academic scholarship. As I use the term, "spirit-phobia" refers to the overreliance on logical thought, narrow definitions of what constitutes empirical evidence, avoidance of nonphysical ontologies, and erasure of metaphysical speculation found in much contemporary scholarship. I coined the term "spirit-phobia" to describe scholars' avoidance of Gloria Anzaldúa's politics of spirit (or what Anzaldúa sometimes theorized as spiritual activism); this avoidance had prevented scholars from exploring some of Anzaldúa's riskiest, most innovative theories.[2] Like whiteness (from which, in part, it emerged), spirit-phobia functions to keep people safely contained within preexisting structures and logical, mechanistic frameworks. As I explained previously, these mechanistic educational systems train us "to rely almost exclusively on rational thought, anti-spiritual forms of logical reasoning, and empirical demonstrations." Not surprisingly, then, we condemn "references to spirit, souls, the sacred, and other such spiritually inflected topics . . . as essentialist, escapist, naive, or in other ways apolitical and backward thinking."[3] But this condemnation locks us into the status quo and, thus, inhibits our ability to envision radical change.

Susy J. Zepeda's *Queering Mesoamerican Diasporas: Remembering Xicana Indígena Ancestries* boldly challenges spirit-phobia. Zepeda explores a variety of spirit-infused tactics, techniques, and methods including prayer, ceremony, ritual, and altar making. She uses scholarly apparatus and language but also exceeds them. Take, for example, how empirical evidence functions in her investigation of re-membering as academic healing praxis. To be sure, memories are not empirical, if by "empirical" we refer to conventional western scientistic standards and definitions; however, memories *are* empirical when we define the term more broadly to encompass collective experiential wisdom. Or take, for another example, Zepeda's innovative engagement with Anzaldúa's Indigenous ancestral spiritual traditions (important components in Anzaldúa's esoteric spiritual mestizaje and spiritual activism). As Zepeda implies, Anzaldúa's decades-long struggle to bring her Indigenous-informed, mestizaje spirituality into secular feminist, Chicanx, and other academic venues played a contributing role to her premature demise. For this reason (as well as many other reasons), I'm especially delighted by Zepeda's interpretation of *Borderlands/La Frontera* as an "altar, an *ofrenda* that remembers and honors the ancestors of decolonization, those that guide the process of being whole again." Inspired by Anzaldúa and others, Zepeda enacts what she calls "methodologies of transformation (e.g., spirit research)." To sit with the altar pieces from Anzaldúa's house, to use prayer, imagination, and deep thought as investigative techniques: this is a brave path, one fraught with dangers. I applaud Zepeda's bravery in making her way through this challenging terrain, and I'm excited to see how others (*including, perhaps, you, dear reader*) will build on her work.

ACKNOWLEDGMENTS

This book is a seed that was watered, nourished, and cultivated by many loving souls. Far too many to name here. *Estoy muy agradecieda*. I am so grateful to everyone who inspired, guided, listened, prayed, contributed and encouraged me along the transformational path of writing and birthing these pages. I thank my mother, Adela Zepeda, for birthing me and raising my sisters and me, and now co-raising my nephew Nova, while supporting my writing and journey over the years. I am grateful to my father, Armando Zepeda, who later in life has offered a healing relationship that guides the tracing of my own ancestry. *Gracias a mi Tío Alvaro, Tía Elva, Tía Arcelia, Tía Angelina, Tío Fernando, Tía Gris, Tía Rosie, Tío Ignacio, Tío Luis, Tía Maria, y todxs mis tías y tíos, los quiero a todos, y gracias por creer en mí. Somos familia.* To my amazing cousins, their respective partners, and beautiful children, this is for you. To my sisters, Zulma and Denise Zepeda, you are blessings in my life that I count daily. Your support of my writing and life's path is immeasurable. To my nephew, Nova, and next generations, your blessed smile, laughter, and hugs sustain me on my journey. To Spencer, thank you for loving my sister and being a part of our lives. *Tu presencia sana.* The same can be said of Pablo Alvarez, *gracias por todo mi hermano de la Luz*.

I offer my sincere gratitude to the original peoples, *pueblos originarios*, in the various *tierras*, sacred tlalli, land where I did my work. I offering my sincere thanks to the four directions (the east, *Tlauiztlampa lugar de Quetzalcoatl*; the west, *Cihuatlampa lugar de Xipetotec*; the north, *Mictlampa lugar de Tezcatlipoca*; and the south, *Huitzlampa lugar de Huitzilopochtli*), the cosmos, and *madre tierra*, the Earth. I thank *Creador/Creadora* and my ancestors with my whole heart, and all the *abuelas, abuelos, abuelxs*, elders, ancestors, and relatives who have guided a pathway for this work of remembering. *Doy gracias por los cantos y los cuatro elementos: tierra, agua, viento, fuego*.

This book is possible only because of the profound visionary artwork of Laura Aguilar, Gina Aparicio, Dalila Paola Mendez, and Celia Herrera Rodríguez. I am indebted to these artists and their ancestors for their creative productions that have guided my spirit research and consciousness. In addition, I had the great fortune to interview Laura Aguilar, Gina Aparicio, Lillian Castillo-Speed, Pamela Chavez, Jeanne Cordova, Nicolette Czarrunchick, tatiana de la tierra, Aurora Guerrero, Osa Hidalgo de la Riva, Dalila Paola Mendez, Claudia Mercado, Juanita Ramos, Irene Reti, Yolanda Retter, and Carla Trujillo; those dialogues provided a foundational basis from which to weave artistic, cultural, and political expression. Your presence, friendship, artwork, and reciprocity provided me with a sense of rootedness to create and write through expansion and without fear. All my gratitude. I also thank Margaret "Quica" Alarcon, Maritza Alvarez, Adelina Anthony, Jesus Barraza, Melanie Cervantes, Karla Legaspy, and Lilia "Liliflor" Ramirez, who continue to create inspirational transformative art.

On my *camino* I have been blessed with circles that have held me on my journey and allowed me to grow, to release my *susto* and step in fully to whom I am meant to be on this Earth. I thank Estela Román, who opened my pathway to traditional medicine through her *temascal*. Gracias, Pablo Alvarez, for your sacred friendship that was the catalyst to travel to meet maestra Estela. My gratitude to Patricia Cardenas, who facilitated a blessed connection with the National Comadres Network. *Gracias, queridas comadres* Susanna Armijo, Debra Camarillo, Alicia Chavez-Arteaga, Rosa González, Lauren Padilla-Valverde, Ysenia Sepulveda, Laura Tinajero, Citatli Arvizu, Sandra Flores, Sara Haskie-Mendoza, Pamela Marquez, Alma Vasquez, Sarah Villa, and Marcia Rincon-Gallardo. I sincerely thank *maestro* Jerry Tello, Héctor Sánchez-Flores, Mario Ozuna-Sanchez, Valerie Garcia, Nelda Olvera, Leo Chavez, and all the amazing staff and board of the National Compadres Network. It is my honor to serve and be in relation with you all. Jerry, *tlazohcamati* for your teachings about the fourth round—they sustained me to complete this work. I also want to offer my sincerest gratitude to Doña Enriqueta Contreras, *su hija Norma, y familia por abrir las puertas y camino de sanación*. All my love to *mis hermanas* who held me while doing such intense *trabajo* over the years: Melusina Gomez, Alejandra Olguin, Atava Garcia Swiecicki, Batul True Heart, Candice Valenzuela, among many other siblings and teachers. *Gracias infinitas* to my spirit sistars Berenice Dimas, Felicia Montes, Maria

Teresa Rivera, Claudia Rosales, Reyna Toledo, and Maria Villamil. This sisterhood has been life aligning. Tía Rocky Rodríguez, Iriany Lopez-Hernandez, Ana Ruth, Raquel, Susana, Tema and Adilia, and all those I have been blessed to sit in circle with, I am beyond grateful for what I have learned and experienced in ceremony with you. Tlazohcamati Angela Mictlanxochitl Anderson Guerrero *por guiar mi camino con Nana Metzli*. My sincerest heart-centered *agradecimiento a todas las abuelas, hermanas, y familia* Huitzilmeztli. Tlazohcamati Abuela Rosa Tupina Yaotonalcuauhtli, Abuela Bea Ilhuicatlahuili Villegas, Amanda Lopez, Diana Barragan, Erica Hooper-Arana, Leticia Aparicio, Pilar Roqueni, Silvia Chivis Tlahuilli Macuilxochitl, Susana Ramírez, Mikizollin, Ana Isabel y *todas las danzantas de la luna*. I also am thankful for the medicinal support offered by RaheNi González I'naru, Gabe Calderón, Victor Jose Santana, Nam-Thu Tran, and other blessed souls during the *danza*. Zamora, thank you for your work with the Wakan Wiya Two Spirit Drum. Tlazohcamati Temachtiani Patricia Chicueyi Coatl for the profound ancestral *enseñanzas*. Trudy Robles, your unconditional love, brilliance, and spirit guidance has been an amazing blessing in my life.

At the University of California, Davis, I am indebted to the department of Chicana/x studies, all my gratitude to my colegas for welcoming me to the professoriate—thank you, Angie Chabram, Clarissa Rojas, Ofelia Cuevas, Sergio de la Mora, Maceo Montoya, Yvette Flores, Natalia Deeb-Sossa, Lorena Marquez, and Michael Singh. A special note of gratitude to our chair, Carlos Francisco Jackson, for believing in my research and vision without hesitation. My work as a professor would not be possible without the support of our staff, Alyssa West and Alma Martinez as well as the student staff. I am also deeply grateful to the lecturers and adjunct faculty who hold up our department and teach our students with integrity. To my *colega* Patricia Quijada, thank you for the writing retreats and for guiding my work with your fierce prayers. My gratitude to Marcela Cuellar, Susan Kaiser, Amina Mama, Beth Rose Middleton, Bettina Ng'weno, Gloria Rodriguez, Robyn Rodriguez, Julie Sze, Sunaina Maira, Rana Jaleel, and Ryan Cartwright, among many other colleagues who have provided guidance and friendship for me to land well at UC Davis. Thank you to the students I have had the great fortune to work with over the years, have opened my heart to walk with immense courage. I am grateful to each person I am honored to call my student and co-learner. Among the many I appreciate and hold in esteem, I name here Bee Curiel, Andrea Dominguez, Alejandro Espinoza, Ofelia Ferreyra, Briana Garcia, Mayra Garza, Sarita Maritza Hernandez, Magda Jimenez, Ana Maciel, Marlené Mercado, Ix'chel Osmara Martinez Moreno, Esmeralda Raya, Maria Salazar, Vanessa Segundo, Monica Velazquez, and George Villa. Your presence and spiritual *trabajo* on this Earth are fiercely illuminating the path for the next generations. Tlazohcamati to Cuauhtemoc Quintero Lule, Daniel Ahuicapahtzin Cornejo, Mirka Dirzo, Rebeca Figueroa, Hector Gamero, Hector Guzman, and Betsy Muñoz Romo for Náhuatl study that truly facilitated a profound connection with the Náhuatl language on my journey. Melissa Moreno, Adelita Serena, Jennifer YaYa Porras, and Diana Almendariz, I am grateful for your trust and community-centered collaborations. Maria Esther Fernandez, Carlos Jackson, and the artists of the *Xicanx Futurity* exhibition—Celia Herrera Rodríguez, Gina Aparicio, Margaret "Quica" Alarcón, Felicia "Fe" Montes, Melanie Cervantes, and Gilda Posada—you have all my respect and gratitude for walking into the fire for our peoples. Suzy Hernandez, Luke Turner, and your twin daughters, your healing presence and talents arrived in cosmic timing.

To my academic sisters, Pascha Bueno Hansen and Sandra Alvarez, thank you for the container we have created to hold one another through our respective journeys. Roya Rastegar, thank you and the Santa Cruz Feminist of Color Collective for nearly a decade of diligent writing and dreaming. I am forever indebted to the Research Cluster for the Study of Women of Color in Collaboration and Conflict at UC Santa Cruz that created a space of intellectual growth and resonance for my path. During my time on Ohlone land, I had the honor of building with visionary scholars, and femtors/mentors, including Cindy Cruz, Angela Y. Davis, Herman Gray, Rosa Linda Fregoso, Amy Lonetree, Olga Nájera-Ramírez, Marcia Ochoa, Catherine Ramírez, Russell Rodríguez, and Felicity Amaya Schaffer. For this rigorous training, I am forever grateful. Sara M. Benson, thank you for being the most amazing editor and friend. Rosalee Cabrera, Irene Reti, and Valerie Chase, your guidance and gifts are incredible medicine. Cindy Bello, Xóchitl Chávez, Soma de Bourbon, Sarita Gaytan, Derrick Jones, Claudia López, Nick Mitchell, Steve Nava, Eric Stanley, Jasmine Syedullah, Heather Turcotte, and Travis Williams, among others, thank you for walking the journey of graduate school with me.

Over the years, friendship has sustained me by reflecting back to me who I am. At the risk of missing many loved ones, here I thank Pablo Alvarez, Antonio Camacho, Alicia Carroll, Michelle Castor, Pamela Chavez, Sandi Escobar, Yvonne Estrada, Linda Gardner, Laura Gomez, Aurora Guerrero, Jamila Guerrero-Cantor, Susan Luevano, Dalila Paola Mendez, Eve Oishi, Dana Olwan, George Villa, and Terry Wolverton for believing in me as an intellectual, teacher, and writer. I sincerely appreciate your unconditional support. Xamuel Bañales, Yrenia Cervantes, Maria Figueroa, Santiago Andres Garcia, Martha Gonzales, Roberto Hernandez, Irene Lara, Jennie Luna, Cindy Martinez, Lara Medina, Marcelo Garzo Montalvo, Cherríe Moraga, Sandra Pacheco, Laura Pérez, Cueponcaxochitl Moreno Sandoval, Cristina Serna, Michelle Tellez, and Yolanda

Venegas, among others, thank you for your visionary spirit-rooted intellectual and creative contributions that have inspired me stay focused and determined in my work. Much gratitude to the *compas* of Xicana Tiahui, Joel Calixto, Gustavo Garcia, Maritza Geronimo, Kimberly Miranda, Natalia Toscano, and Kristian Vasquez for your work to create alternative knowledge formations, including the Eagle and Condor Liberation Front. The presence of Sacred Circles (Whittier), Taller Arte de Nuevo Amancer (TANA) at UC Davis (Woodland), Las Maestras Center for Xicana[x] Indigenous Thought, Art and Social Practice at UC Santa Barbara, Sol Collective in Sacramento, as well as Casa Tia Luna in San Francisco and the Latinx Research Center at UC Berkeley have been generative spaces of intellectual spirit growth. I am grateful. Thank you, Kathleen Taylor-Fillebrown and Myrna Tellez, for generously opening your homes to me, to retreat, create, and write. Thank you, Susan James and the Pacifica family.

My gratitude to AnaLouise Keating, who believed in my book project from the inception and offered formative guidance. At the University of Illinois Press, I thank acquisitions editors Dawn Durante, Alison Syring Bassford, and Dominique Moore, and all the staff who were instrumental in moving the book forward to completion. I wholeheartedly thank the reviewers of my manuscript. Various grants and fellowship funded the research in this book, including the UC Davis Hellman Foundation Fellowship, the Lionel Cantú Graduate Award at UC Santa Cruz, the UC MEXUS Dissertation Research Grant, and the National Science Foundation Fellowship. This work is an imperfect offering, and I am grateful to the reader for their graciousness and engagement.

Gracias infinitas to all the ancestors who guide, *a los guardianes de la tierra y las cuatro direciones. Tlazohcamati Nana Meztli por tu guía profunda y a Tata Tonatiuh por tu luz cada dia. Gracias Yemayá por estar presente. Tlazohcamati madre Tonantzin Coatlicue por tu abundancia y enseñanzas. Tu hija*, Susy Tonalmetl.

Tlazohcamati. Aho. Ometéotl.

A NOTE TO THE READER

As you read this book, you will come across words in Spanish and Náhuatl. I don't do this to exclude anyone—instead, I found in the course of writing that the Spanish and Náhuatl words illuminate the deeper, more complex meanings of the dimensions of my writing. Using the word in the language that fits is part of a larger intentional political project that acknowledges the incommensurability of words, language, and culture. This perspective is rooted in understanding what is at stake in the languages we utilize. When language is colonial, in this case English and Spanish, the words you choose have a signification.

In the text, where a direct translation is possible, it is typically offered at the first appearance. You will also encounter words that are not translatable and therefore aren't translated into English. A list of words and their translations follows here to support your reading of this book.

aires	winds of emotion
altares	altars
amoxtli	this Náhuatl word is more accurate than the Spanish *codices*
antepasados	ancestors
baño de temascal	ceremonial steam bath
camino	pathway
Centroamericana	Central American

ceremonias	ceremonies
conciencia ancestral	ancestral consciousness
conocimiento	consciousness
curandera	practitioner of traditional healing
curanderismo	healing tradition
danza	dance
danzante	dancer
enseñanzas	teachings
excavando	tracing, digging, or unearthing
familias	families
gente	a people
herramientas	tools
historias	stories, histories
Indígena	Indigenous
limpia	energetic cleansing; letting go of old wounds
lesbiana	lesbian
madre tierra	Mother Earth
maestra	teacher of spirit work
mujeres	women; mujeres is a racialized and gendered formation
mujeres Indígenas	Indigenous women
ofrenda	offering
palabra	sacred word
partera	midwife
permiso	permission
pláticas	talking circles
pueblo originiarios	original peoples
rezos	prayers
sabiduría Indígena	Indigenous wisdom
sanación	healing
sanadora	a person who guides spiritual healing
susto	fear or fright; shock; trauma, soul loss
susto profundo	profound fear or shock
temascal; temazcalli	Mesoamerican form of ceremonial steam bath
testimonio	testimony
tlalli	Náhuatl for Earth
tlazohcamati	Náhuatl for thank you
Tonanztin Coatlicue	Náhuatl for Mother Earth
trabajo	spiritual work
tristeza	sadness
vergüenza	shame

QUEERING MESOAMERICAN DIASPORAS

INTRODUCTION

Tracing Queer Mesoamerican Diasporas

At its core, this book is a historical and contemporary remembering, a genealogy of select queer Indígena (Indigenous) cultural and knowledge producers that examines the layers and tensions of race, class, gender, sexuality, nation, and dislocation. Remembering is a decolonizing methodology particularly for Indigenous peoples who have been forcibly dislocated from their culture, knowledge, and land.[1] Working at the intersections of transdisciplinary forms of scholarship on feminisms of color, queer of color critique, and studies of race, Indigeneity, and decolonization, this book highlights the often overlooked yet intertwined legacies of Chicana feminisms and queer decolonial theory through the work of lesbians of color and queer women of color feminist formations. I trace the ancestries and silences of non-heteronormative (e.g., gender nonconforming, gender queer) people of color to address colonial forms of epistemic violence and methodologies of transformation (e.g., spirit research). Drawing on oral history interviews with Xicana/x and Latina/x diaspora cultural producers, building with gathered archival materials, raised ceremonial altars, and analysis of decolonial artwork, I argue that the matriarchal roots of Xicana/x and Latina/x feminisms are forms of diasporic knowledge that can be remembered through Indigenous-centered visual narratives, cultural wisdom, and spirit practices. I work to trace and remember hidden histories and silences of queer Mesoamerican Indigenous ancestries and medicinal practices in order to locate ceremony and remembering as forms of activism that utilize the knowledge production of women of color feminists, including their decolonizing methodologies and representations of cultural memory.

Queering Mesoamerican Diasporas consciously brings together academic knowledges with spirit praxis for the sake of reimagining the root work, dis/connection to land, and the political decolonization of Xicana/x as hemispheric peoples. Emphasizing creativity as spirit work, I place meditation, *rezos* (prayer), ancient wisdom, ceremony, and spirit research in dialogue with the field of Chicanx studies and other related fields of inquiry such as feminist studies, Latinx and Latin American studies, queer studies, Chicana/x cultural studies, and Indigenous studies. The book focuses on queer Indígenas, primarily Xicana Indigenous-identified *mujeres* (women) who were largely born in the United States yet trace their roots across the hemisphere. Some mujeres are not of Mexican roots, which exemplifies how Chicana as a signifier is not limited by blood or colonial demarcations of territory. Instead, this work illuminates vibrant political forms of consciousness connected to Chicana/o/x. These cultural producers, organic theorists, philosophers, practitioners, and writers are knowledge holders of grounded politics and hemispheric consciousness in their visions of bringing justice to the Earth and communities worldwide. They are reflections of their communities, who are deemed unworthy or second-class because they are the third world within the first world. Their formation as mujeres Indígenas is a political naming that previous generations have fought for through deep remembering of complex histories. There is much continued debate over the intertwined histories of Indigenous peoples in what is colonized as the Americas, where Indigenous North America is often referred to as Turtle Island. Mujeres Indígenas is also a complex identity formation that generates tension in terms of the dispute over Chicanx peoples identifying as Indigenous, a long-standing debate over identification often pitted in the contradistinction of tribal Indians or ethnic Indians.[2] This is a central problematic that this work seeks to unravel to create a clearer interconnected pathway toward decolonization that remains aware of colonial logics, including the structures of "settler" colonialism and violence of racist logics.

Chicana historian and elder Yolanda Chávez Leyva ends her short essay in *La Voz de Esperanza* by wisely articulating that "Chicana/o historians have taken the first crucial steps of uncovering, recovering, and documenting our histories. Those histories have provided the basis for political organizing, cultural revitalization, and community building. It is time for Chicana/o scholars to go beyond writing and teaching Chicana/o history. It is time for us to confront the profound consequences of that history in the lives of our students and our communities and to find the ways to heal that pain."[3] Almost twenty years later,

Leyva's title that cites Ines Hernández Ávila's words feel more urgent than ever, particularly her directive of the need for "una gran limpia," a major energetic cleansing, to heal the traumas, pain, grief, *susto* (soul loss) found or invisiblized in Chicanx historical accounts.[4] It is vital to learn the threads of complex histories of colonization, forced migration and removal from land, de-Indigenization, hierarchies of race, gender, class, and sexuality, for example. Yet, it is simultaneously significant to activate the praxis of utilizing tools to heal from those ancestral wounds and historical traumas that have been passed on, particularly in thinking about next generations. As a Xicana Indígena scholar and a student practitioner of traditional Indigenous medicine, I feel the need to create spaces that can hold tensions, conflicting feelings, disillusionments while simultaneously creating an environment for truth telling, connection to ancestors, and sacred tools for healing.

It is important to make a distinction and to allow for multiplicities among detribalized Chicanx who have "Indian ancestry," yet whose families and ancestors have experienced forms of de-Indianization (a Mexican state project of the elimination of the Indian) and de-Indigenization as a people. There are Chicanx people who know they are Indigenous to the continent yet cannot fully trace their lineages. There is also a spectrum of original peoples of Mexico and larger Mesoamerica, or Anahuac, the Náhuatl-centered concept, who have maintained their way of life despite colonization as Indígenas in consciousness and practice including speaking Indigenous languages of this continent (e.g., Náhuatl, Zapotec), holding ceremony for rites of passage, wearing traditional clothing, healing traumas with plant medicine, and cultivating and eating traditional Earth-centered foods. I aim to honor and argue for the various pathways to *sabiduría Indígena* (Indígena wisdom) and *conciencia ancestral* (ancestral consciousness), from *abuelas* (grandmothers), *abuelos* (grandfathers), abuelxs, even when we are met with trickster energies on the *camino* (pathway), a way to re-member, as in bring all of our fragments back together, that were disrupted due to colonization. In "Speaking across the Divide," cultural theorist Gloria Anzaldúa emphasizes the pain of detribalization, responding to the question "What does it mean to you to have Indian ancestry?" Her response: "To have Indian ancestry means that mi cuerpo (my body), soul, and spirit have raices (roots) in this continent. El árbol de mi vida has indigenous roots."[5] She affirms that, as a seventh-generation Chicana born in Texas, she has Indigenous ancestors who are connected to this hemisphere, even as her exact lineages remain unknown. Anzaldúa continues:

> To have an Indian ancestry means to fear that la india in me that has been killed for centuries continues being killed. It means to suffer psychic fragmentation.

> It means to mourn the losses—loss of land, loss of language, loss of heritage, loss of trust that all indigenous people in this country, in Mexico, in the entire planet suffer on a daily basis. La gente [people] indigena suffer a loss that's cumulative and unrecognized by the masses in this country, a loss generations old, centuries old. To have Indian ancestry means to bear a relentless grief. To have indigenous ancestry also means to bear the promise of psychic integration. As broken and shattered people we are driven to re-gather our spirits and energies, to reorganize ourselves . . . to have entry into new imaginings.[6]

Anzaldúa's formulation of "la gente [people] indigena" opens up possibilities for bridging Native and Chicanx communities, which is a political project she contributed to greatly in her scholarship. In an e-mail interview-dialogue curated by Inés Hernández-Ávila and Domino Perez, Anzaldúa offered a much-needed vulnerability and open-hearted language for the struggle of being an "india" while holding open a space for mestizaje, which arguably leads to disconnection from Indigenous and African lineages and practices. In response to accusations of appropriation, Anzaldúa wrote as part of this e-mail exchange:

> I've always claimed indigenous ancestry and connections, but I've never claimed a North American Indian identity. I claim a mestizaje (mixed-blood, mixed culture) identity. In participating in this dialogue, I fear violating Indian cultural boundaries. I'm afraid that what I say may unwittingly contribute to the misappropriation of Native cultures, that I (and other Chicanas) will inadvertently contribute to the cultural erasure, silencing, invisibility, racial stereotyping, and disenfranchisement of people who live in real Indian bodies. I'm afraid that Chicanas may unknowingly help the dominant culture remove Indians from their specific tribal identities and histories. Tengo miedo que [I'm afraid that], in pushing for mestizaje and a new tribalism, I will "detribalize" them. Yet I also feel it's imperative we participate in this dialogue no matter how risky.[7]

There is fear or perhaps a deeper susto indicated by her words "tengo miedo" and by an intense, arguably painful, disidentification with "real Indian bodies" due to the trauma of detribalization and de-Indigenization. Anzaldúa's words illustrate a deep paralysis that Chicanx peoples at times experience due to the external questioning of their belonging and claiming of Indigeneity. Building from the *enseñanzas*, or teachings, of this fear articulated by Anzaldúa offers the desire to move toward collective liberation, I ask: how do Xicana/x do the work to carve an autonomous pathway toward re-Indigenization in solidarity with Native American, Indian, Indigenous, and original peoples across the hemisphere and beyond? One immediate and powerful step here is to meditate with the seismic genocide endured by Native American peoples who reside in the colonial United States. For many detribalized Chicanx peoples and Indigenous migrants this can be especially disconcerting yet aligning to see the interconnections within the state violence to eliminate Indian and Indigenous peoples in Mexico, Mesoamerica, Anahuac, Central America, and beyond.

For Anzaldúa, as a Chicana mixed-blood mestiza-identified writer, she theorizes the fear of not being Indigenous enough, which makes it difficult for her to root herself as Indígena. Yet her courage is present. Anzaldúa's hesitancy reveals a complex awareness that the formulations of "mestizaje" and a "new tribalism" are not generative of interconnections that honor the current existence and continued struggles for sovereignty, autonomy, and recognition among Native and Indigenous communities. Both concepts can disappear Indigenous past, present, and future. Anzaldúa's impulse to theorize a "new tribalism" can appear as an uprooted concept that does not fully acknowledge the specificities and lineages of Indigenous past, present, and future, particularly as she laments that the "original tribes are all but gone."[8] Yet, as Hernández-Ávila interjects, "here is the crux of the matter: the original tribes are not all but gone."[9] Anzaldúa's vulnerable contributions and engagement are significant because they have opened "Indigenous intersections."[10] Her determination to keep her "india" consciousness and practice present in her expressions of Xicana Indigeneity made significant foundational inroads in bridging Native and Chicanx communities and building a decolonial dialogue, even if tense, across communities and intellectual formations with Indigenous roots in this continent. Anzaldúa is often regarded as a scholar who is central to shaping decolonial thought on this hemisphere.[11] Her writing, use of concepts, and theorizations shifted over time, and opened many doors around spirit work and Xicana Indígena decolonial ways, particularly because she is rooted in women of color feminisms that are anticolonial, antiracist, and anti-imperial.

Because forms of colonization differ based on regions, geopolitics, and colonizing forces—*distinct* histories of loss, uprootedness, and disconnection emerged within the same hemisphere. Therefore, complicating relations and igniting conflict based on racial and gender hierarchies. In a significant communication between AnaLouise Keating, coeditor of the anthology *This Bridge We Call Home*, and Ohlone-Costanoan Esselen writer and poet Deborah Miranda, Keating poignantly asks about "the place of chicanas (especially those . . . who work hard to claim their indigenous ancestry & connections)" in Miranda's formulation of "native women & others."[12] This opens a generative exchange about "Chicana indigenism," where Miranda articulates how "we essentialize because U.S. and Mexican national mythologies have been constructed around the same issues—colonization of indigenous people—in two very different ways."[13] Miranda suggests that in the United States "the idea of a Manifest Destiny" is central and "demands the colonization of the land and destruction of any "primitive" inhabitants."[14] Colonization in Mexico was "not just about the taking of land but of souls" through state investment in the existence and reproduction of the "mestiza offspring."[15]

Within these distinct and extremely complex colonial historical contexts, the land that became known as Mexico was conquered primarily by the Spanish Crown, while the tribes and land colonized by the United States experienced the colonial forces and legacies of the English, French, Russian, and Spanish.[16] Another major distinction in the colonialisms that targeted Native and Chicanx communities relates to cultural claims and cultural erasures. Simon Ortiz interestingly views Chicanos as claiming the colonial Spanish force as their culture, which relied on a dominant form of whiteness that aimed to erase the Indigenous roots of the people, la gente Indígena.[17] This is reminiscent of the state-imposed categorization of "Hispanic," which "whitens" and homogenizes Black and Indigenous populations. In many ways, mestizaje can be seen as akin to Hispanic. The term *Latina/o/x* has also been understood as a term that does not acknowledge the specificity of Indigenous lineages or roots. The Chicano movement, although complicated in its early efforts, aimed to do the work to re-root *la cultura* in Indigenous forms of self-determination to counter colonization. Although at times the Aztec and Mayan were not seen through their depths—their medicines, songs, ceremonies, philosophies, and worldviews—there was a direction of aiming to reclaim Indigeneity. In the U.S. context, Miranda describes significant differences in lived experience due to the government's violent implementation of reservations on stolen land, as well as boarding schools and the mission system.[18] Ultimately, "Native and Indigenous" people on either side of the Mexico–United States border are rooted in distinct and multiple experiences that must remain complicated in order to resist homogenization of Indigenous formations across the hemisphere. This structure of competing colonialisms creates distinctions in regional locations, identification, practices, languages, spiritual philosophies, and forms of political status (e.g., autonomous, sovereign nations, or those who remain unrecognized). Against this backdrop, Miranda writes that "there are good reasons to include Chicanas as indigenous women, and complex reasons for my hesitation to commit what many Indians would call the heresy of inclusion."[19]

This book builds a decolonizing approach to ancestry and re-Indigenizing, "no matter how risky." To do the *trabajo*, or work, to unravel what it means for Chicanx people to have "Indian ancestry," or even more provocatively, to name themselves as Indigenous or Indígena—this requires the acknowledgment of these layers of truths and the multiplicities involved. The search involves the tracing or weaving of ancestors and their respective homelands, languages, lineages, spiritual practices, and the connected sacred elements that reflect cultural and ancestral traditions. There is a responsibility that comes with understanding the wisdom of walking a path of prayer, guided by ancestors; the trabajo of re-membering emphasizes honesty and truth telling, as well as vulnerable openheartedness and a commitment to reciprocity. Therefore, the possibility of stepping out of a hybrid or uprooted identity formation that is, the state imposed mestiza/o/x and moving into a rooted sense of self allows for a distinct awareness to heal the traumas and wounds of the colonization that cause fragmentation, and cure the anxious feeling of not belonging to the land, a disconnection from the mother.

Through a *curandera*—healer—perspective, Elena Avila writes of the race mixing due to the Spanish Conquest:

> The first mestizos, those born from the intermixing of the Spaniards and the Indians, were homeless and had no definite place in society. Many of these children were rejected and discarded when the Spaniards returned to their families in Spanish, or found Spanish wives in the New World. Mestizos were agonizing reminders to Indians of the Conquest and the defeat of their culture, religion, and souls. When African slaves were later brought to the New World, they experienced the same suffering and oppression. But somehow we descendants of those outcasts of mixed blood have survived, which is a reflection of how strong our spirits are. We have shared our medicines with one another, as well as our diseases and pain. Curanderismo is a gift that our ancestors left us. African and indigenous Americans have not healed completely, and we will suffer from the effects of detribalization, soul loss, and envy, but in curanderismo the secrets of our ancient folklore and healing have been preserved and continue to grow.[20]

The heart of this book is focused on the detribalization, de-Indianization and de-Indigenization of Xicana/x and Latina/x peoples and the planting of seeds for cultivating paths of healing through remembering, where the growth is guided by inner wisdom, and aligned connection to ancestors and elders. Detribalization signals the process of Indigenous peoples' loss of identification with their lineages, spiritual practices, and land-based connection and culture due to the harm of colonization, namely, forced migration and removal from land for resource extraction, and the logics of racialization that aim to eliminate the Indian. As Luna, in her discussion of the politics and knowledge systems that inform Chicana/o stated, "it has been crucial for Xicana/os to claim and assert their indigeneity."[21] She continues by offering that while claiming indigeneity it is important for the mujeres, the women, the femmes to have a space to imagine and build. Luna proposes a vision of the signifier Xicana that would be inclusive of all genders. Luna wrote that, "rather than fear the feminine, it is my hope and foresight that it will be embraced, not only on paper, but in the lived ways we honor, treat, and respect women, women power, and feminine energy. It is my hope that the collective community will come to view itself through the lens and ideology of 'Xicana'; a more complete view that carries memory and a call for action.[22]

As a person on a healing path, I acknowledge that we need records and reminders—embodied and cosmic pathways reopened and reconnected to facilitate remembering—especially when susto or soul loss has been a central part of intergenerational existence—traumas passed on generations to generation who have experienced various forms of displacement, disconnection, and loss.[23] The curandera work of examining susto is illuminating that this soul loss is connected to memory. It is said that these traumas take form in cellular memory, in DNA. Maestra de los aires de emociones (teacher of the sacred winds of emotion) Estela Román, like other healers, discusses in her *pláticas* that migrants who have crossed the imposed territorial border in some way, shape, or form likely have susto. Kickapoo, Comanche, and Nahua scholar and author of *Red Medicine* Patrisia Gonzales writes in the article "Calling Our Spirits Back": "While they [Indigenous midwives] do not use the term disassociation, many of the curanderas and midwives speak of susto inhabiting Mexican migrants, with their being split. As the midwife Doña Enriqueta Contreras instructs: Their bodies are North of the border, while their spirits remain South of the United States."[24] Illuminating forms and causes of lingering susto or trauma in the body. The depth of this truth is rooted further when we think of Indigenous, undocumented, and documented migrants who on crossing the United States–Mexico border are forced into new identities that depend on racist social and political contexts, customs, languages, and ways of being that enforce disconnection—from shifts in food, and diet, to living conditions that may limit access to plant life, ceremony, and community, moving people even further from the traditional Indigenous medicine that contains the cures for susto, and perhaps more importantly, that sustains life.[25]

The vision of this book is to offer a weaving of cultural producers, storytellers, artwork, ceremony, and narratives that intentionally work to unravel dominant narratives and interject alignment into disjointed understandings of traditional ancestral narratives, movements, peoples, and *historias* (histories). As Castañeda suggests, "Historians have come to focus on the historiography of Chicanas (and Chicanos) as a battle of exclusion versus inclusion. Since the 1970s, Chicana and other women historians of color, have been arguing that the issue is not simply one of exclusion versus inclusion, but rather one of construction. Ours is a conceptual and historiographic struggle."[26] In terms of reimagining historical narratives, some questions for consideration for de-tribalized Chicana/x and Latinx people arise: How does one do the work to re-root or re-ground oneself when displaced from land, culture, knowledge, and spirituality without reproducing forms of colonialism? What are the politics and pathways of claiming Indigenous ancestry when it is difficult to trace one's lineage due to dominant forms of colonial erasure? The identity formations of Xicana Indígena and queer Indígena are simultaneously political projects that articulate a remembering of ancestry and spiritual practices while intrinsically holding space for contemporary methodologies and practices that work to address injustices, traumas, and healing.[27] I work to unravel historical threads of inconsistency and harm that can homogenize Xicana/x and Latina/x peoples in terms of de-Indigenization, normative gender and sexuality, and forms of racialization.

So far, I have articulated a nonlinear interweaving of Xicana, Xicanx, Chicana, Chicana/o/x, and brought in Latina and Latina/x. These are all multidimensional social formations and signifiers with particular histories and narratives.[28] My intentional, complicated, and interchanging use of this language speaks to the tensions, and particularities, when possible. Chicano as a signifier in and of itself has a dynamic and contested community history that over time has manifested into political, social, and community movements, as well as a basis for knowledge formations in the academic, cultural, and artistic production realms.

While Xicana, Xicano, Xicanx roots the re-Indigenization of Chicanx peoples, with the "X" at the forefront reflecting the unraveling of a history, present, and future that is grounded in Indigenous knowledge and practices prior to colonization, and the "x" at the end signals a consciousness of gender queer, nonbinary, and gender nonconforming peoples. The emergence of the "a" to replace the "o" at the end of "Chicano," for example, written as Chicana, Xicana, and Latina, reflects hard-fought feminist interventions to reposition and make visible matriarchy, women and the feminine, lineages of mujeres, and non-visible elder lesbians as part of the movements, and contributors to philosophical social thought and political praxis.[29] Similarly, I utilize the word "mujeres" instead of "women" to emphasize and remember *la lucha de la mujer* (the struggle of women) to have a rightful place in the unraveling of patriarchal logics. Using "mujeres" is a signifier to illuminate the strength of feminist (often queer) women of color raising their voices while raising our families and communities with political consciousness at the center.

I use Latina, Latina/o/x, and Latinx cautiously and intentionally. Since Latinx is quite controversial due to its potential homogenization and erasure of

Indigenous and African peoples and lineages due to its colonial roots, I activate it for quite the opposite purpose. My larger project is reflective of mujeres from geopolitical locations and racialization beyond what is known as the territory of Mexico, particularly of Central America. Latina/x proves useful in certain context because it facilitates a critical discussion of peoples in diaspora of Mesoamerica and beyond what is known as the nation-state of Mexico, as well as it allows for conversations of solidarity and connection across the hemisphere.[30] Similarly, Indígena and Indigenous are two critical signifiers in this text. Both are gender inclusive and informed by region.

Tracing Ancestry and Spirit Research

When I think about my ancestors, I wonder how "the queer" expressed themselves—the two-spirit, the trans, the girl-boys, the he-shes, *las otras* (the Others), *las raras* (the rare ones), the nonbinary. I do not question whether they existed, but wonder how they negotiated their existence.[31] Were their methods similar to our current strategies of survival and identification? Did they pray with their ancestors, past and future? What roles did they play in their communities? What impact did colonization have on their realities? We will never know the exact answers. The work of tracing, however, makes it possible to piece together expressions of historical memory that have endured or that have been reimagined by succeeding generations through cultural production. I navigate tracing as a queer nonlinear hxstorical methodology that allows us to re-root ourselves in the past in order to imagine reflections of ourselves and open possibilities for transformation in our present and future.[32] At the center of this tracing are the voices, narratives, alignments, and energies that are silenced due to the disciplinary ruptures their existence necessitates.

The methodology of tracing or *excavando* (digging) with a good heart is productive for unearthing knowledge of historical and ancestral truths, particularly because many of the pre-Cuauhtémoc stories and practices have been violently destroyed, nearly eliminated, or necessarily hidden due to colonization, imposition of the dominant structures of faith, and forms of genocide. I use pre-Cuauhtémoc, instead of pre-Colombian or pre-Hispanic, as others do, to disrupt the colonial terminology.[33] I also want to note that I use purposefully use the word "excavando" to reflect the necessary literal digging, putting our hands into the earth to find fragments of ancestral stories, to remember the narratives of Mesoamerica prior to colonization, including, the archaeological uncovering of the massive Coyolxauhqui stone in 1978 opens a pathway to remember origin stories.

Prior to significant interventions by scholars in lesbian, feminist, Xicana, transgender, queer of color critique, and Latinx studies, the complexities of silence, erasure, and exclusion would best describe the written and visible histories of queer Chicana/x and Latina/x communities in diasporas.[34] Leyva posits a methodological framework for studying Latina/Chicana history—one that redefines the analytic of silence by exploring its complexities, arguing that silence for Latina/Chicana lesbians is "a paradox—both protecting and harming us."[35] This framework allows one to trace or queer the stories, by excavating the silences of earlier generations through a revised perspective. Tracing the silences of "deviant" communities in resistance disrupts colonial forms of epistemic violence and erasure.[36] Silence is connected not only to erased discourses but also to social and political exclusions or suppression of marginal or "othered" peoples and voices due to the threat of violence. My tracing of these historical narratives primarily takes the form of archival research and analysis, participant observation, formal and informal interviews conducted in California (primarily 2009–18) with queer Xicana/x Indígena and diasporic Latina/x Indigenous artists, special archives librarians, and key social actors in queer trans people of color communities. Threaded together, these weaved stories collectively comprise a transformative and visual historiography that centers the radical efforts of lesbians of color, Latina *lesbianas*, queer Indigenous women, Xicana Indígenas, and "third-world women" to construct another world. I use "Latina lesbianas" instead of "Latina lesbians" as a way to reflect the context and emergence of this complex identity formation and community, which I detail in chapter 4. In many ways, the backbone of these efforts are groundbreaking women of color feminist anthologies.[37] My use of the term "radical" is informed by an urgency found in early women of color feminisms in texts such as Cherríe Moraga and Gloria Anzaldúa's *This Bridge Called My Back: Writings by Radical Women of Color*, which illuminates the necessity of seeing the interconnections among forms of harm, violence, and toxic energies by examining the root cause, trauma, or susto, to become aware, cleanse and heal, in order to disrupt destructive cycles.

My goal in articulating "queering Mesoamerican diasporas" is to intentionally unravel and complicate the tensions of nation-state demarcations to show the interconnections and interrelationality that are often hidden when people exist in contrived and often limited categories of Hispanic, Mexican, mestizo, lesbian, etc. This work is in dialogue with several scholars who articulate the formulations of Mesoamerica in their analysis to meditate with and unravel the separations that political nation-state borders demarcate for the purpose of dislocating peoples and imposing colonial borders.[38] Within these articulations of Mesoamerica there is an emphasis on healing traditions such as *curanderismo*, the presence of *parteras* (Indigenous midwives), the *baño de temascal y la temazcalera* (ceremonial steam bath and guide), and working with herbs and plants as relatives and remedies.[39] Chicana historian Emma Pérez's methodological tools call for the unraveling of historical constructs that present themselves as dominant truths by positing the "queer of color gaze."[40] Pérez builds on Anzaldúa's formulation to make the methodological point that a distinct search is necessary when constructing histories of "queer" or "deviant" sexualities of Chicanas and Latinas or the multiple structures which render them invisible or an anomaly. Through Pérez's conceptual lens of "queering the borderlands," it is plausible to ask: how can we (as a people) move beyond what has been introduced to us as truth—dominant narratives that have become our habitual way of being?[41] How do we remember the time before nation-state borders, territorial and state ownership of land, and imposed modes of illegality?

In the landscape and political history of Mesoamerica or Anahuac, which geographically refers to Mexico and Central America, the rigid domination of the Spanish Crown outlawed traditional Indigenous spirit practices—violent methods were instituted in an attempt to disrupt a collective consciousness and ceremonial praxis. This knowledge fuels another layer of the significance of this book, which serves to illuminate how queer Indígena writers, artists, cultural workers, and ceremonial practitioners actively bring us back to life through their creative work and ceremony by "calling our spirits back" with intrinsically collaborative intergenerational art that offers a pathway to ancestral remembering and praxis in the present moment—creativity as spirit work.[42] I define ceremony as an internal prayer of transformation that often occurs in community and is guided by ancestors, elders, and lineages, often based on traditional Indigenous praxis with the intention to restore alignment with spirit or re-root connection to the Earth. I have no intention of revealing any rigid prescriptions, remedies, rituals and/or ceremonial protocols. I fully respect the sacredness of ancestral teachings and refrain from detailing intricacies in print.

Women of Color Feminisms: Theorizing Is Sacred

Women of color feminisms, as a site of knowledge production, demonstrate that theorizing is sacred. Feminist of color scholars provide a pathway to think seemingly disparate institutions and forms of power together, through a radical root centered analysis that unravels heteropatriarchy, the state, logics of colonization, and racial hierarchies.[43] Women of color feminisms intervene in this disconnection by configuring a critical intellectual site in academia that outwardly connects politics with ancestry. To imagine a separation of a political vision of justice from ancestors is a forgetting that upholds colonization, a forced and unbalanced fragmentation—a re-colonizing of self through the separation of mind and heart. Women of color feminist frameworks open up healing, *sanación* (healing), and a way of resisting western secular spaces through forms of remembering, by creating spaces of ceremony, including reciprocity and respectful relations.[44] Although the avenue of prayer or rezos is distinct and varies from community to community, lineage to lineage, tradition to tradition, there is a connecting line and vision when the practice is decolonial—disconnected from dominant religious institutions aimed to convert and sever relationships from ancestors.

Women of color feminisms disrupt the logics of the western academic world and the larger political systems that (1) silence spirit practices and discredit Indigenous practitioners and scholars for their interconnected belief systems (until they are proven by science); (2) locate spirit praxis in the personal realm only; and (3) inevitably disconnect the spiritual from the political work of seeking justice and freedom. Alexander's writings on "the Sacred" in her "Remembering *This Bridge Called My Back*, Remembering Ourselves" and "Pedagogies of the Sacred: Making the Invisible Tangible" are important pathways to mapping third world feminisms, feminists of color, and queer trans two-spirit legacies of spiritual methodologies.[45] It is this *presence of spirit* or the sacred that is often rejected or rendered unimportant in academic spaces.[46]

As visionary intellectual sites of knowledge production, women of color feminisms more generally tend to be trivialized in academic debates because of the unrecognizable or unwelcomed commitment to creativity, collaboration, and collectivity. What is often incited within this site of knowledge are layered, complex, and at times seemingly unresolvable interventions to current power structures, for example the abolition of prison systems, militarized borders, and nation-states. Feminist and queer of color theorists Alexander and Mohanty, E. Pérez, L. Smith, and Cruz-Malavé and Manalansan build their own decolonial analysis and methodologies to argue that colonial legacies represent forms of modernity that seep into current knowledge formations, such as Chicana/o/x studies and queer studies and reproduce violence in the form of misrepresentation and erasure.[47] Hidden histories and narratives that need to be uncovered for the purpose of social transformation include unraveling silences that exist around the complexities of nonbinary gender, queerness, sexuality in connection with creativity, and erasure of Indigeneity and Blackness. In *Decolonizing Methodologies*, Linda Tuhiwai Smith illuminates these colonial legacies by showing the connection and distinction between imperialism and colonialism. The most striking part of Smith's delineation of imperialism is her assessment that imperialism needs to be seen as a layering within oppressive structures, as does colonialism. There are structural conditions of inequality, which allow these legacies to continue to exist in the modern or contemporary moment, where the imperialist, racist, and colonial influences are almost unseen due to being normalized.[48]

The formulation of "queering Mesoamerican diasporas" is my effort to create a generative dialogical space among Xicana/x Studies, queer Latinx studies, queer of color critique, and race and decolonization studies. A useful framework is found within Juana María Rodríguez's *Queer Latinidad*, where she productively complicates Latinidad and race geographically. Rodríguez writes that "latinidad is about the 'dimensions' or 'the directions in motion' of history and culture and geography and language and self-named identities. Even if individual narratives used to chart these discourses contradict or exclude one another, the site of rupture will itself serve as a new site of knowledge production."[49] Rodríguez's formulation of the "site of rupture" is noteworthy because it seeks to work across multiple fields of knowledge or rupture, including studies of race and decolonization, women of color feminisms, Indigenous studies, and queer of color history.[50] These sites of knowledge are not congruent. Rather, they are themselves ruptures in the sense that these fields of study emerged through oppositional forms of thought and resistance-based critiques of systems of domination. Their emergence allows for reimagined possibilities that build on the past yet have their own structures and imaginaries.

In arguing that Chicana feminisms exist in diaspora, this book traces the forms and histories of the cosmic and queer "borderlands" and highlights the forced migrations and colonization of Xicana/x, Latinx, and Latin American communities, a tracing that simultaneously challenges the notion that queer or nonnormative sexual identity formation is U.S.-centric.[51] It is therefore necessary to trace ancestries, histories, and diasporas through a queer Xicana Indígena focus or center that reflects the legacy of Chicana feminisms that in many ways formed through iterations of lesbians of color and women of color feminist formations. Sandoval and her analysis of U.S. third-world feminism illuminates social actors in struggle and movements that construct forms of knowledge through a worldview of decolonization.[52] Building on Sandoval's theory of "oppositional consciousness," my work moves toward articulating another layer of this knowledge formation, spirit consciousness or spirit praxis, that I argue is implicitly part of women of color feminist frameworks. It is the space of "spirit praxis" that is of central importance for my larger arguments. Familial lineages and integrations of ancestral wisdom (sabiduría ancestral) within women of color feminisms increasingly reveal deep roots in U.S. third-world feminism.[53] Women of color feminisms are a central site of knowledge that conceptualizes against and beyond the nation-state in a critical form. Many who align with this site of knowledge do the root work to connect with their homelands and peoples through their sites of praxis, protest, and creative works, whether through visual forms, oral storytelling, or practices of ceremony.

Women of color feminists or feminists of color consciously exist within hierarchical systems—simultaneously working to disrupt it, to bring social transformation, and to expose epistemic violence and forms of harm.[54] *Queering Mesoamerican Diasporas: Remembering Xicana Indígena Ancestries* is invested in exposing the tensions of imposed militarized borders that divide and conquer land, resources, and peoples into nation-states, and signaling the need to continuously unravel and question how our communities are separated and divided by war, debt, extraction, and dominant ideologies. Of particular importance here are those relatives who are disconnected from their own spiritual roots, ancestors, and traditions that hold memory of who they are and/or a pathway for reconnection. The challenge is to open intellectual discourses in order to see the academic richness and methodological dimensions of women of color feminisms, specifically the Indígena spirit work necessary for healing and decolonization. This is especially significant for peoples who are detribalized and whose relatives have experienced de-Indigenization and as a result have inherited traumas, susto, that cause misremembering or forgetting.

The critical task that emerges from the intersections of these sites of knowledges is a decolonization of societal categorical framing and growth of consciousness by unearthing, queering, and disrupting hidden histories, thus creating space for rooted, ancestral, or radical praxis. The frameworks or methodological tools of this book necessarily address the tensions among diasporic, hemispheric, transnational communities rooted in so-called Latin America and the United States. Anibal Quijano's conceptualization of a "colonial structure of power" provides an analytic framework from which to map the complexities of histories, memories, and silences.[55] This is part of a colonial legacy that is addressed by the truth-telling writings of women of color feminisms or U.S. third-world feminisms. By demonstrating that there is a "third-world" within U.S. borders that is characterized by poverty, terror, and disease is a direct critique and intervention in dominant understandings of nation state ideologies and structures. An important component of women of color feminisms has been its long-standing critique against U.S. imperialism, war, colonialism, genocide, slavery, and their legacies that continue to exist in our unjust modern capitalist world.[56]

Women of color feminisms, particularly radical women of color feminist epistemologies, are not trying to figure out whether their work is political.[57]

Their "political projects" call for rigorous methodological designs that are attentive to interdisciplinarity, their own geopolitical location, and complex analyses of difference, the everyday, and the structural. There is a vision of interconnectedness in many women of color feminist frameworks, including explicit linkages to peoples and lands. Many times, in our global world the connections are shaped by hierarchical formations of capitalism, colonialism, imperialism, law, labor, the nation-state, policy, and logics of racism, which are usually narrated as unrelated. Yet the interconnectedness is made increasingly visible through theory and praxis that is rooted in a holistic interdependent vision. A major methodological intervention of the women of color feminist epistemological tradition is the project of remapping dominant historiographies to make visible and graspable the intersecting tensions of race, class, gender and sexualities.

The community of scholars outlined here provides tools and insights to search for what is hidden, contested, or not easily seen because, as these authors argue in varying degrees, what is not easily traced holds truth in ways that could disrupt a colonial social order or structure. Particularly important are the interventions that hold the tensions of race and gender alongside class and sexuality. Collectively, they make space for sacred sexualities, re-memberings and re-rootings through cultural production, and create communal or community spaces of healing through cultural memory. The methodological work of queering archives and histories in the growing field of Latinx sexuality studies is also significant to the work of *Queering Mesoamerican Diasporas*.[58] Queer of color scholars have done the work to build this knowledge by undertaking alternative and creative ways of building, redefining archives, and queering archives. Horacio Roque Ramírez's "A Living Archive of Desire: Teresita la Campesina and the Embodiment of Queer Latino Community Histories" is an important articulation that maps tensions, dialogues, and stories within historically diasporic and transnational communities. As Ramírez argues, "storytelling, autobiography, and the *testimonio* tradition have a central place in history and theory."[59] He centers his essay on the "life and memory" of Teresita la Campesina (1940–2002), a Latina male-to-female transgender performance artist who impersonated Lola Beltrán and was living with AIDS. Ramírez argues, "her life history frames a living archive of evidence that responds to both the whiteness of queer archiving practices and the heteronormativity of Latino historiography."[60] To declare Teresita a living archive is to revere her as a carrier of historical, ancestral, and cultural knowledge, where the evidence is her lived expression of walking her own path regardless of the categories imposed on her, and in this way creating new possibilities. Ramírez's approach to studying queer of color history is particularly influential in framing my inquiries in chapters 3 and 4.

Remembering: "Detribalization," Memory, and Decolonization

The positioning of a violent narrative as ideology that requires the absence of spirit praxis is a symptom of colonization. Bonfil Batalla's discussion of Mesoamerica in *Mexico Profundo* is an important intervention that illustrates how this iteration of colonization is built on the layered interconnection between Christianity, genocide, conquest, and de-Indianization of Indigenous peoples in the land demarcated as Mexico.[61] To fully participate in decolonization of Xicana/x requires a deep look at a peoples' spiritual beliefs, cosmic understandings or worldviews, languages known and spoken, cultural practices, food, clothing, relationship with the elements, and the ideologies or philosophies held as truth.[62] In a 1991 interview with Inés Hernández-Ávila, Chicana lesbian philosopher Gloria Anzaldúa suggested that "we have to listen to the indigenous part of ourselves."[63] What does it mean to critically remember the relationship between Anzaldúa's concept of *conocimiento* (knowledge) and "the indigenous part" of Chicanas/os/xs? Or Xicana Indígena? Or the larger Mesoamerican or Anahuacan diaspora?

It is a colonial legacy to forget, and it is a response to trauma to have gaps in memory; conversely, it is a practice of decolonization and healing to remember. This is not an easy or linear path to walk. Remembering through storytelling is particularly important in discussions of Xicana/x and Latinx migrant, Indigenous, and diasporic communities who have, to differing degrees, been displaced, "detribalized," and "de-Indianized."[64] Colonization was a source of harmful fragmentation for most peoples in Mesoamerica and beyond, it continues up to the present day through colonial legacies of forgetting or misremembering. Cherríe Moraga and Celia Herrera Rodríguez suggest that it is important for Xicanas and Xicanos to "re-member" the histories that have been erased due to colonization in order to recover the connections among ancient cultures, stories, art, architectures, languages, spiritualities, and diverse and distinct sexualities. The "re-member" they articulate has within it the mending needed to stitch together fragmented memories. Diane Taylor sheds light on this debate by speaking of "the colonizing project" and directly addresses the intentional destruction of ancestral cultures and memories. As Taylor argues, "part of the colonizing project throughout the Americas consisted in discrediting autochthonous ways of preserving and communicating historical understanding. As a result, the very existence/presence of these populations has come under question. Aztec and Mayan codices, or painted books, were destroyed as idolatrous, bad objects. But the colonizers also tried to destroy embodied memory systems, by stamping them out and discrediting them."[65] What continues to exist despite this violence is the ancestral knowledge that lives within the people—a spirit of resistance and resilience in *la palabra*, or the word. These cultural memories manifest through visual imaginings and representations, such as sculptures, altars, paintings, photographs, and films.[66] The artists featured in this book embody that spirit and offer paths to decolonization through forms of cultural memory.

Memories are complicated because they are not exact evidence of something; instead, memories are held in narratives that are collective re-memberings or imaginings. As Marita Sturken suggests, "memory is a narrative rather than a replica of an experience that can be retrieved or relived."[67] She continues: "All memories are 'created' in tandem with forgetting. . . . Forgetting is a necessary component in the construction of memory. Yet the forgetting of the past in a culture is often highly organized and strategic."[68] Sturken offers a vital piece of knowledge in this formulation that is needed for remembering, since the forgetting is not accidental. There are significant reasons for the forgetting, including historical and sexual traumas. As Andrea Smith argues, sexual violence is a central component of colonization.[69] The effects of colonial legacies are still being felt at epidemic levels in Native, Black, Indigenous, and people of color communities today through incest, sexual violence, and other forms of harm, such as domestic violence. There is a need for intentional remembering for the purpose of transformation or healing.[70] I am suggesting that re-membering, becoming aware of or clarifying a memory, can assist in the process of healing historical and/or sexual intergenerational traumas that have been inherited and maintained due to heteropatriarchal structures.

This book is concerned with how generations re-member or what many elders articulate how we re-remember, particularly when records and memories have been destroyed or mutilated due to forced dislocation and spirits and bodies have been harmed.[71] As transnational feminist scholar M. Jacqui Alexander asks, "How, why and under what conditions do a people remember? Do spiritual practices atrophy? Or do they move underground, assuming a different form? What is the threat that certain memory poses?"[72] Her theorizations of memory and the sacred prove to be extremely useful for the visioning within this book. Alexander continues: "How does one know the stories and histories of one's people? Where does one learn them?" Later she states that "we had forgotten that we had forgotten. Missing memory. . . . How will I come to know the stories and histories of *my* people?"[73] In the wake of colonial violence, visual representations that evoke cultural memory in ceremonies can become guides to re-root practices and memories that have been displaced over generations. Macarena Gómez-Barris suggests that visual art "has the capacity to speak to, contest, elaborate upon, and produce collective experiences that escape the domain of 'politics as usual.' . . . Visual art carves out new modes of representation that escape the binary logic of history and memory whose reductionist outcome expresses itself as erasure of the experience of violence."[74] The very experience of remembering creates meaning through a particular context of time and space, while bringing life to a specific praxis, genealogy, or legacy.

I work through a queer Xicana Indígena methodology, root work, of remembering that purposefully generates a productive tension between colonial and non-colonial frameworks that signify the entangled complexities of historical narratives and cultural memories. While the term "queer" on its own is often understood as a western hegemonic or umbrella term that erases women of color, trans people of color, and others.[75] The writing of the phrase "queer Xicana Indígena" signals a disruption or queering of colonial legacies that impose norms of gender, race, sexuality, ceremony, and spirituality—actively creating space for decolonized alterities.[76] Similarly, the use of the "X" in the term "Xicana," as previously discussed, signals a conscious politicized identity that insists on intentionally remembering Indigenous ancestors, cultures, languages, roots, and hidden histories of Mesoamerica or Anahuac. Within this framework, the concept or energy of Ometéotl signals duality, often thought of as balance between two, as between feminine and masculine energies. Not as in opposing or static, but in fluid complement to each other. In this way, Ometéotl can be likened to the representation of two-spirit that is significant among Native American and Indigenous communities.[77] Because forgetting is a colonial legacy, this queer Xicana Indígena methodology makes it possible not only to support interjections or reimaginings that disrupt and counter dominant narratives, but also to trace a pathway to remember ancestors and traditions through re-Indigenization, such as remembering our two-spirit elders and ancestors through Anahuacan cosmology. Living in duality, in balance is key. Colonization intentionally sought to break our spirits and sacredness by disrupting our balance; this is why offering prayer of the four directions is so significant. Through this honoring of los cuatro rumbos, los cosmos, and the Earth, the circle of relations is remembered. The balancing of the four directions illuminates rooted worldviews that reflect philosophies of interconnectedness.[78] That reconnection, that call, grounds you back to your root.

Decolonized Sites of Knowledge Formations

I build on several contested sites of knowledge formation, ruptures, and praxis to trace, weave, or illuminate links, interconnections, and interrelationality for the purpose of mapping complex alternative genealogies and histories that connect queer diasporic Mesoamerican and Xicana/x and Latina/x Indígena subjugated knowledges, histories, and cultural productions. It is important to critically interrogate U.S., transnational, and hemispheric paradigms, historiographies, dominant narratives, and politics by showing interconnectivity in what otherwise appear as singular histories, disconnected groups or peoples, and the viewing and treatment of land, Mother Earth—*madre tierra*—and the environment as ownable property, as an unlimited resource for the entitled, for capital, for profit. At times, disciplinarity or adhering to canons of knowledge can reduce an engagement with the intellectual sites or critical formations of women of color feminisms, queer of color critiques, and Indigenous paradigms. Therefore, I argue for more direct intentional engagements with decolonized sites of knowledge formations in order to illuminate grounded frameworks or pathways to examine tensions and contradictions that may arise.[79] I trace hidden interconnected or transcommunal histories, traumas, and gaps in memory through visual storytelling and creative knowledge formations.[80]

This book is a provocation that illuminates remembering and generational memory, how stories or histories are passed from one generation to another, particularly for people in diaspora whose lineages, histories, and knowledges have been interrupted, destroyed, colonized, or co-opted. Each chapter addresses the intersections of these themes. Chapter 1, "Decolonizing 1848: Unraveling Conflicting Colonial Histories of Land and Race to Trace Queer Ancestry," is a historiographical re-narration of moments in history that need complicating in order to honor the current historical moment. I argue that the logic of mestizaje implemented by the Mexican nation state has led to widespread de-Indigenization of Chicana/x peoples in diaspora. Building with Anzaldúa's bold analysis in which she suggests that "the border fence that divides the Mexican people was born on February 2, 1848 with the signing of the Treaty of Guadalupe-Hidalgo," I complicate the Chicano nationalist imaginary of Aztlán.[81] I argue that Chicano/o studies is built from a foundation of constricted historical narratives that must be decolonized. I ask: what would a limpia, a deep letting-go of old wounds, look like for the field of Chicanx studies? The queer Xicana Indígena root work I propose here signals a consciousness of Xicana/x as peoples in diaspora, as detribalized migrants searching for and re-rooting themselves in Indigenous languages, lineages, tribal names, and traditional ways. The United States–Mexico War had imperialist motivations, and therefore an analysis of key texts provides clarification that at minimum the land now known as the U.S. Southwest was shared among various Indigenous peoples. The unequal relations within and between Mexico and the United States overshadows historical ancestral truths of connection across imposed militarized borders. These historical connections across pre-national borders create space to reimagine queer Mesoamerican historical narratives. Chicana lesbian writers, theorists, and poets have historically worked to decolonize Chicano studies intellectual spaces by complicating its foundational tenets.

Chapter 2, "Enseñanzas con la maestra Gloria, In Ceremony with Anzaldúa: Altars, Archives, and Aligning with the Cosmic Borderlands," focuses on Anzaldúa's work as an artist and visionary, and includes an analysis of her classic text, *Borderlands/La Frontera*. As part of my spirit research, I meditate with Anzaldúa's sacred altars and archives to argue that the ancestral knowledge of creating altars is foundational to Anzaldúa's visionary work as a methodological pathway to remembering. Anzaldúa offers these materials as examples of creative forms of knowledge that contribute to building language and methodologies that illuminate visual narratives. Through an Anzaldúan framework, I maintain the possibility of Coyolxauhqui as a matriarchal ancestor of decolonization. In conjunction with Anzaldúa's remembering, I conceptualize this sacred energy as an ancestor of decolonization and as the praxis at the heart of this chapter, which spends time unraveling Anzaldúa's curandera knowledge. These designations of Coyolxauhqui and Anzaldúa are in alignment with la Gloria's writing and build on my own queer Xicana Indígena root work, which requires me to experience "archival research," including my viewing of Anzaldúa's altar collection, as ceremony and a queer decolonial archive. Anzaldúa breathes life into Coyolxauhqui through her interdimensional writing, which illuminates Anzaldúa's curandera offerings. The altar becomes a methodological pathway to remembering what was central to her curandera spirit practice rooted in her grandmother's Mamagrande Ramona's traditions. Like other early women of color feminists, Anzaldúa did the pathbreaking work to build language around emerging identity formations and political projects. In many ways, Anzaldúa's visionary work opened a path—a methodological meditation grounded in spirit, intuition, and creativity.

"Queer Indígena Art: Visual Prayers for Remembering Grandmother Earth through Oral and Visual Storytelling," chapter 3, centers on the organic and intergenerational efforts of queer Indígenas to construct their own narratives and histories through visual representations as a practice of decolonizing knowledge and regaining cultural memory. I argue that the artists featured in this chapter evoke spirit and healing as they create, visualize, and interconnect the past, present, and future through their narrative representations—they are hxstorians of the contemporary world and the storytellers of ancestors. As visual storytellers who allow spirit to enter their creative work, these artists work in the cosmic realm to offer their sculptures, paintings, and installations as medicine through a soul experience. An intervention I make in chapter 3 is focused on how the visual prayers of queer Indígena artists allow us to think through the relationship between oral and visual storytelling, particularly when searching for the unseen when we are trained in dominant paradigms. The work of remembering makes it possible to piece together expressions, theories, and stories that have endured and been reimagined by succeeding generations via alternative (creative) methodologies, representations that engage the complexities of difference and the interconnections of local and global relations of power, and forms of cultural production that retell history through a subaltern historical lens that creates spaces of transformation and healing. Central to chapter 3 are queer Indígena artists who create sacred space with their respective artworks. In their art, there is a visible constant connection with Indigenous practices and traditions; spirituality, prayer, and ceremony are central elements of their art and existence.

Chapter 4, "Tracing Latina Lesbiana Historias of Resistance, Solidarity, and Visibility: Genealogical Archives of a Generation of Gatherers and Guardians of Knowledge," centers the work of archivists, scholar-activists, and photographers to create a trajectory of Latina lesbiana histories that counteract the detrimental and heteropatriarchal ideas and sites of knowledge that do not give lesbians of color ample space to exist. This chapter argues that the international politics of solidarity formed during the late 1970s and 1980s as a response to patriarchy and militarized rule directly challenged remnants of various forms of colonization and colonial rule by building networks, collectives, and collaborations of solidarity. This chapter maps a shift in the historical terrain that renders queer Latinx visible and significant to historical analysis by focusing on a generation of Latina lesbiana gatherers and guardians of knowledge. Through their respective efforts to manifest anthologies, establish political formations, reconstitute library databases, and create photographic documentation of Latina lesbians, I argue that there has been a collective establishment of creative and historical archives that focus on Chicana and Latina lesbiana historias and feminist perspectives. I examine these critical interrogations as queering Mesoamerican diasporas to show how women of color and lesbians of color emerged as a force to map history, culture, and knowledge. Chapter 4 addresses the central question of how Latina lesbianas do the work of tracing and archiving knowledges. I aim to show that women of color and Latina lesbiana thinkers, artists, and visionaries make integral contributions to formulations of hemispheric, cross-border, and intercontinental feminisms and practices of solidarity through visual and textual representations.

Although the analysis in this book builds with the intersections of various fields, reflective in many ways of my own expanding worldview, including Xicana/x studies, Indigenous studies, and feminist studies, at the root are meditations on de-Indigenization and decolonization. The decolonizing of a space is a form of clearing energy to see truth, where renewed and restored energy can lead to transformation. The decolonization of land is the return of the land to the original peoples, or *pueblos originarios,* depending on the geographic region—that is, in the United States, in Mexico, in Guatemala, or another location. This praxis of returning, redesignating, re-Indigenizing land can heal the disconnection and shift relations toward balance.[82] The thread of decolonization at focus for queer Xicana Indígenas and their peoples is one that considers stories that have been fragmented due to forced displacement and migration, as well as the interconnections of racial hierarchies that have material social political implications, establishment of nation states, homophobia, transphobia and heteropatriarchy, and other systems of inequality.[83] The traditional Indigenous medicine of the Mesoamerican/Anahuacan cosmologies and lineages open pathways to re-member for detribalized Xicana/x peoples.

To decolonize is also to have a heightened consciousness of self, community, social location and interaction so as to not perpetuate and reinforce structures of domination: "Decolonization involves thinking oneself out of the spaces of domination, but always *within* the context of a collective or communal process. . . . This thinking 'out of' colonization happens only though action and reflection, through praxis."[84] Decolonization is directly linked to the way peoples relate to one another and how they experience land-based geopolitical traumas.[85] The work is constant, when aspiring to be clear and accountable. An important starting point for Xicana/x history that seeks to uproot settler colonial tendencies is to critique the emergence of the United States as a nation-state with political borders that divide relations by upholding the discourse of "manifest destiny," which was responsible for not only a loss of land and forced removal—a displacement and genocide of Native and Indigenous peoples—but also an attempted destruction of various cultures, languages, and spiritual traditions.

Like Manifest Destiny, larger structures of colonization have affected cultural memory, in particular the assault, cooptation, and simultaneous disappearance of Indigenous languages.[86] Miller says of "tribal languages" that "the loss of language is the loss of a unique worldview that cannot be transferred to English or any other language."[87] What is lost from the primary use of English in the United States and the Spanish language in Mexico? A major decolonial act is the continuance of people speaking, learning, teaching the Indigenous language of Náhuatl and the connected philosophies and cosmovisions, for example. Both Anzaldúa and Bonfil Batalla show in their work the importance of this language for this field of study.[88] From a similar perspective, Ngũgĩ wa Thiong'o starts *Decolonising the Mind: The Politics of Language in African Literature* by stating that this will be his last book in English. Recommitting to writing in his "mother tongue" of Gĩkũyũ, Thiong'o offers an important reflection on his "colonial school" in Kenya and shows the shift in his educational experience when the "harmony" of language and community "was broken."[89] Because of the imbedded connection between colonialism and language, de-coloniality offers important contributions to naming the power structures of coloniality with the purpose of mapping alternative histories.[90] Decolonial scholars like Mignolo build on Quijano's (2000) "coloniality of power" to offer theorizations of "de-coloniality."[91] Interestingly, Mignolo builds a hemispheric interdisciplinary site of knowledge with W. E. B. Du Bois and Gloria Anzaldúa as scholars from the United States that are part of this "genealogy" of thought.[92] In this site of knowledge, feminist philosopher Maria Lugones critiques Quijano for his "too narrow" understanding "of the oppressive modern/colonial constructions" of gender.[93] As Lugones suggests, "Quijano's lenses also assume patriarchal and heterosexual understandings of the disputes over control of sex, its resources, and products."[94] Lugones opens decolonized sacred space for two-spirit, transgender, and gender nonconforming peoples through her formulation of "modern/colonial gender system" and close reading of feminist literature.[95] Linking the intellectual genealogies of women of color feminisms, Chicanx studies, Indigenous studies, and decoloniality opens space for histories and forms of knowledge of queer Mesoamerican diasporas that are otherwise obscured due to colonial legacies.

I build with the legacy of the work of Chicana feminists to shift the exclusionary nature of the scholarly discourses through the introduction of a new language that reflects Xicana Indígena feminist politics. In her now-classic essay about "sitios y lenguas" (sites and discourses), Pérez discusses the need for Chicana lesbians to project new sources of language in order to better articulate their own realities and histories.[96] Feminist of color historian Maylei Blackwell reminds us that "historiography is a political practice" and is therefore created with intention and foresight, echoing Castañeda's insights.[97] Often, Chicano movement narratives focus on racial injustice and internalized colonialism with a blind spot to the colonial legacies they were employing through heteropatriarchy and sexism. Blackwell's and other early Chicana feminist interventions in the history of male Chicano politics are significant and create a path for continued interventions into accepted Chicano historical narratives through the introduction and engagement of queer Mesoamerican and Xicana Indigena histories.[98]

To queer Chicanx history requires a revamping of its foundational tenets, not only for the purpose of inclusion but also for the reigniting of ancestral memories and practices of ceremony that are matriarchal and honor the multiplicities of embodied gender formations. The concept of "queering" or disrupting the norm, barriers, and borders is central to the arguments of this book. Warner suggests that "queer" should be thought beyond its connection as an umbrella term to lesbian, gay, bisexual, transgender, two-spirit, queer, and questioning communities, and instead as a disruption of the norm—a queering of the heteronormative.[99] Because norms are mechanisms of regulation—often of the criminal, deviant, or queer—they enforce a particular regulatory form of the dominant, usually an illusion of whiteness in the United States—an "American" whiteness that demands assimilation and a rejection of one's true self including lineages and ancestry. Queering also aims to dislodge the static colonial concept and implementation of the gender binary by facilitating a space of visibility and existence, putting a spectrum of possibility where genderqueer, third gender, fourth gender, nonbinary, two-spirit, transgender people are at the forefront. Queering as such can call for a societal shift, or a reimagining of how we envision beyond genders and sexualities in the collective and throughout time.

In these terms, queering can help shift and decolonize the terrain of Chicanx studies because it asks the discipline to reexamine its roots, reflect on shortcomings, and expand boundaries and possibilities through language and action.[100] While the now-classic *This Bridge Called My Back: Writings by Radical Women of Color* holds stories of homophobia and colonialism, as well as fierce cultural critiques of established societal norms such as the tenets of racism, classism, and heterosexism, its theoretical, political, and spiritual intervention is still in need of deeper attention.[101] I aim to address the way Chicanx studies tenuously hold queer and trans peoples, so that the field is not transformed at the root by queer of color or feminist of color intellectual interventions; instead, it is a sympathetic incorporation with no desire to uproot the systems or ideologies that created the inequalities.[102]

The archive for this project is consistently under erasure. To manifest this work, I set myself the task of building an archive of decolonization by digging for it, excavando, asking critical questions of the emerging archives, including reimagining the trace and existence of a queer Mesoamerican or Anahuacan diaspora that was outside histories and narratives we have inherited. Setting out to map a social and political network of lesbians of color in its 1970 formation to locate interventions in the archives by Chicana lesbians was a barren path. My focus had to re-shift to what existed as a living archive so that I could recraft my vision to be able to see a deeper story. Oral histories with queer Xicana and Latinx activists, artists, writers, and scholars became central to the writing of this; whether I cite the particular oral history or not, the stories offered became critical texts, and revealed the existence of an archive.[103] In 2005, the UCLA Chicano Studies Research Center was my first archival visit to meet with Dr. Yolanda Retter because of her publications, including her 1999 dissertation on lesbian activism in Los Angeles from 1970 to 1990. I asked her, a practitioner of oral history and an archivist, for guidance on my research. Retter encouraged me to see the oral histories as a conversation, a dialogue.

Also central to the unfolding of this text and a bit unexpected was the Gloria Anzaldúa Altares Collection held in Special Collections and Archives at UC Santa Cruz. In connection with the Altares collection, McHenry Library named a room after Anzaldúa and placed a few items of her archives and library on permanent display. The establishment of this room when I was graduate student and the invitation from Irene Reti to speak alongside Bettina Aptheker at the opening were also key to my integration and spirit research into what Anzaldúa's home altars provided as a critical text and site of knowledge. I spent time with the Gloria Evangelina Anzaldúa Papers in the Nettie Lee Benson Latin American Collection at the University of Texas, Austin. My archival research on lesbians of color also took me to the USC ONE National Gay and Lesbian Archives at the University of Southern California and Special Collections at the UC Berkeley Ethnic Studies Library, where I interviewed Lillian Castillo-Speed. Finally, I circled back to UCLA Chicano Studies Research Center with a focus on the Laura Aguilar Papers.

Archival searches in personal collections especially allowed for a rare opportunity to imagine creative processes and see documentation that reflects their visions.[104] Many of these documents are one-page flyers, newsletters, photographs, and booklets—sources that are not academic or scholarly but remain significant because of the specific content and context they represent. I searched for or traced the social movements associated with both visible and silenced political formations of lesbians of color and radical women of color. I consistently found that the spaces of resistance created by networks of queer Latinx artists and writers held a critique of colonialism, colonization, and capitalism. I attempt to shed light on a specific concern in the case of queer Indígenas, Latina lesbianas, lesbians of color, and women of color.[105] The significance of queering representations, practices, and theories of Mesoamerican diasporas lies not only in locating or documenting hidden histories and realities, but also in exploring the structures and historiographies that cause the invisibility, particularly because we know that sexuality and especially queer sexuality often exists as a discourse of *known* silence—a space that is characterized by colonial violence. By racing the "queer" and queering and re-Indigenizing the "Xicanx" and "Latinx," *Queering Mesoamerican Diasporas: Remembering Xicana Indígena Ancestries* traces the tensions and dialogues manifested in these historically diasporic and hemispheric communities. I trace layers of colonization and silence, and this excavando unmasks epistemic violence that fails to see women of color or lesbian of color feminist knowledge formations as anchoring feminist theory and practice.

CHAPTER 1

DECOLONIZING 1848

Unraveling Conflicting Colonial Histories of Land and Race to Trace Queer Ancestry

Aztlán—as a territory, imaginary, homeland, and concept of belonging—is understood from multiple, often contradictory and conflictual, perspectives. Here I articulate meditations as queer Xicana Indígena root work with a focus on land and race to illuminate the possibilities of healing susto, defined as intergenerational trauma that can be traced to colonization. This is possible through trabajo that aims to unsettle Aztlán's settler colonial tendencies and to trace queer ancestry. I argue the knowledge formation that emerged as Chicano studies in the late 1960s and that has outgrown its patriarchal male signification and exclusionary mode of resistance. Some of the seeds of this necessary shift came from early urgings of Chicana feminisms, Chicanx Indigenism, and Xicana Indígena philosophy and practice. This queer Xicana Indígena root work is part of articulating an emerging dialogue around a vision of Xicana/x Indigenous studies that is grounded and aware of itself and consistently reflective in praxis.

I argue that the early insistence on the notion of a U.S. Southwest land-based heteropatriarchal Aztlán posits a surface-level understanding of the Aztec peoples as the dominant culture with a patriarchal emphasis, and in so doing has led to forms of soul loss or susto in the field of Chicanx studies and in Xicanx communities outside of academic institutions.[1] This, along with "de-indigenization" and the imposed racial hierarchy of mestizaje that aims to erase or dilute specific Indigenous and African lineages, reinforces the logics of whiteness and colonial nation-state borders. Together these structures have intentionally, and in some cases unintentionally, created distance from knowing and working with spiritual ancestral lineages, traditions of *canto* (song), danza, and ceremony, complex historical narratives, and Mesoamerican healing modalities that open pathways toward healing from colonial forms of harm. The consequences of a settler colonial notion of Aztlán, along with the philosophy of mestizaje, can create the illusion of disconnection with ones' ancestors, particularly Indigenous and/or African familial lineages, and disruptions in the knowledge and practices of traditional medicine, through disassociation from Indigenous languages, philosophies, sexualities, and food from the Earth, all of which can sever connection to cosmological worldviews.

In a grounded manner, this work meditates on the concept of *susto profundo* as a pathway to healing intergenerational trauma with the tools and philosophies offered by traditional medicine as a system of root knowledge.[2] In part, I am arguing for a recognition of spirit praxis—a pathway of doing spiritual trabajo to remember ancestral knowledge and sabiduría Indígena that was left out of early Chicano studies or spoken of as folklore that was not rigorous or intellectual. Spirit praxis is a life force that brings enseñanzas and sanación from ancestors, in ceremonies with plants, movement, food, and the honoring of Tonantzin Tlalli Coatlicue, guardians of the sacred directions, and the sacred elements, including water, air, earth, and fire. Part of the work of spirit praxis is remembering to honor the four directions (east, west, north, south)—seven directions (cosmos, earth, heart), while looking backward to remember our future that is being created as we walk. There is also a necessary expansive consciousness created in spirit praxis where one is rooted in the present aware of the vastness of the past and at peace with the uncertainty of the future.

Indigenous, Native, and Chicana/o/x scholars have worked to establish the tenets and central critiques in this field of study relevant for detribalized Xicana/x peoples, including Jack Forbes, Cherríe Moraga, Patrisia Gonzales, Jennie Luna, Roberto Hernández, Roberto Cintli Rodríguez, Lourdes Alberto, Irene Lara and Elisa Facio, Estela Román, and Lara Medina and Martha Gonzales.[3] Many of them have done this through their own spirit-based writing and praxis. Collectively these scholars and practitioners demonstrate through various forms of "theory in the flesh" that writing is an act of sitting in a circle with grandmothers, grandfathers, abuelitxs (grandparents of all genders), and elders, to trace and respect spiritual lineages while being accountable to their walks of life, prayers, and guidance.[4]

In cultivating this body of knowledge, these scholars have provided a solid foundation from which to ask complex questions, as well show vibrant pathways that are guided by a consciousness that centers ceremony, spirit work, and remembering as methodologies of decolonization. How does one do the work to re-root, or to re-ground oneself when displaced from land, culture, knowledge, and spirituality without reproducing forms of settler colonialism, internal colonialism, or colonization?[5] What narratives and origin stories are important to remember and re-center? How does one respectfully walk a path of remembering and reclaiming Indigenous ancestry when it is difficult to trace one's familial lineage? The vision of this queer Xicana Indígena root work is to contribute to an explicit site of analysis and praxis to connect the vision of Xicana/x studies again to spiritual roots, traditional medicine, and ceremony.

The queer Xicana Indígena root work I propose here signals a consciousness of Chicana/o/x peoples in diaspora, many as detribalized migrants, consciously reconnecting with their Indigenous roots, languages, lineages, tribal names, and traditional ways that have been subjected to imposed forgetting. In many ways, the Chicano movement of the 1960s sprouted the roots of remembering by centering Indigenous elements of *los Aztecas* as part of its ideologies; the Mexica philosophies and use of the Náhuatl language was a central offering of this movement, yet many times the roots were not excavated fully nor understood as living entities, a living people, and one people of many peoples. Moraga writes: "I am not Mexica, but that herencia was gifted to me through the Chicano movement."[6] While this heritage (herencia) is extremely significant, dominant representations of "the Mexica" maintain a particular idea of Aztec peoples and generally known ideologies as the center of the Chicano movement and of Chicano people that often do not reflect the deeper teachings found in the *amoxtli* (codices), cantos, and oral stories. There is almost a palpable colonial block cloaked in assimilation and whiteness that aims to impede a deeper knowing of ancestral traditions, culture, discipline, and the decolonial pathway of spirit. As Pulido offers, "Chicana/os' legal whiteness and the various attempts to erase their indigeneity illustrate the power of the state in shaping racial and political subjectivity."[7] To *sanar el susto* (heal the fright or soul loss) and address the colonial legacies that have been inherited, requires the unraveling of many intertwined *aires* (emotions) based in intergenerational traumas. As a result of this disconnection or susto, critical analysis or deep incorporation of the Mexicayotl tradition, and other Native and Indigenous traditions and African based spiritual traditions as sites of knowledge has been limited in the field of Chicana/o/x studies.

This is an important acknowledgment, a humble step toward a conscious examination within the field of how the colonial trauma or legacy of susto can impel Xicana/x scholars in diaspora to unintentionally support knowledge formations that can in fact inflict harm through erasure. Feminist scholar Aimee

Rowe argues for "theorizing the relationship among Chicana identity, indigeneity, and land as incommensurate."[8] Rowe demonstrates that an examination of "settler logics" is needed in our family histories to understand our complex and at times harmful relationships with the original peoples of the land of California, for example.[9] Similarly, Pulido's call for an analysis of "settler colonialism" in the field of Chicana/x studies opens the possibility to see the decolonial offerings of Aztlán and the potential shortcomings in particular when conceptualizing the 1848 Treaty of Guadalupe Hidalgo.[10] Does the land-centered narrative of Aztlán within early formations of Chicano nationalism contribute to the structure of settler colonialism?[11]

Although this analysis centers the field of Chicana/o/x studies, the content is especially relevant for detribalized Chicana/x peoples who have experienced "de-Indigenization." As Patrisia Gonzales extends her work in *Red Medicine* and theorizes de-Indigenization, she offers this: "I think what is important to remember about all of this is that as Mexican people become de-indigenized, some of that knowledge stays, but they may not know from what tribe it is, because it has been an ongoing process of de-indigenization."[12] Roberto Hernández discusses the difficulties in tracing Indigenous blood and knowledge pathways, while others have experienced "family genealogies indicating their indigenous lines." He writes, "Historically speaking, however, many Chicana/os have not always known their own lineage and have had to search through family albums and converse with relatives not always willing to acknowledge their own Indian blood."[13] To remedy this forgetting, Gonzales suggests an in-depth "looking back" or remembering of peoples' stories, pathways of connecting with the Earth: "as descendants of the original peoples of this continent, Chicanos and Xicanas have body memory of ancestral knowledge."[14]

This proposed recognition of spirit praxis can lead to a "path of *conocimiento* [knowledge]," in Gloria Anzaldúa's words, and the *sanación* or healing of intergenerational traumas for Chicanx detribalized peoples, without re-creating forms of violence or the fear of appropriation.[15] This trabajo requires that one walk aligned with ancestors, even when it is not an easy journey. In "Indígena as Scribe" Moraga writes, "I am afraid of this way of seeing, of recognizing my own proximity to my ancestors, that collective source of knowing that comes from el otro lado [the other side]."[16] Moraga's vulnerable yet instructive offerings shed light on what the path can look and feel like. This knowing includes walking in a way that is respectful of original peoples and of the landscapes we walk on this hemisphere and beyond. The root work of tracing or excavando is further complicated when one is perceived as an "Indigenous imposter" due to nation-state formations, logics of de-Indigenization, and imposed racial categories and hierarchies (especially caste systems) that uproot pueblo origins and set in motion de-Indianized potentially homogenizing racialized categories such as Hispanic, Mexican, Mexican American, and mestizo.

It is evident that the Chicano studies field holds susto, tied to the traumatic disconnection of detribalized and de-Indigenized *familias* from ancestral ways, along with the racist violence experienced in white supremacist institutions such as the academy and beyond. This susto has everything to do with traumatic histories connected to the Spanish conquest and militarized imperialist wars. Chicanx and Latinx peoples have increasingly become disconnected from their specificity through state-imposed assimilative categories (e.g., Hispanic) and Eurocentric requirements that normalize the western standard, including the use of the English language. I argue with compassion that many of us have forgotten how to honor our traditions, ourselves, our relations, and our complex stories, and at times, each other due to intergenerational trauma. Building on Leyva's argument of the need for "una gran limpia,"[17] I ask: How would the field of Chicana/x studies shift if community healing, and remembering our sacred selves and our ancestors/relations (human and nonhuman), were at the center of our intellectual work?

What becomes clear on the path of tracing ancestral lineages is the importance of intergenerational sharing of wisdom from elders, including acts of remembering through visual guidance, and the need to unravel and unhook from the colonial logics that propel the structures that de-Indigenize. Queer ancestors and elders planted seeds that illuminate a path of coming to consciousness, and they offer guidance to find the tools with which to examine traumas and harm to our spiritual and sexual whole selves through a political and structural analysis. From their survival of battles for balance comes wisdom that has taught next generations to unravel and disrupt violent cycles. In this way, we are a threat to normative structures that uphold racial and gendered forms of harm and exclusion. Many times, these structures are ideological so the cultivation and regeneration of ancestral ideas that support matriarchal formations is needed. In particular, Cherríe Moraga's storytelling in *Xicana Codex of Changing Consciousness*, accompanied by a series of line drawings by Celia Herrera Rodríguez, serve as elder intellectual and visual guidance for this root work. Moraga writes that "story makes medicine. I am in daily search of these acts of remembering of who we once were, because I believe they will save our pueblos from extinction."[18] In particular, Moraga's essay, "Indígena as Scribe," Rodríguez's visual representation of la "Nepantlera," and the essay "Sola, Pero Bien Acompañada" in Moraga's *Xicana Codex* offer ancestral guidance and Indigenous wisdom (*sabiduría Indígena*) for the arguments toward re-rooting as

Xicana/x peoples.[19] The "Nepantlera" drawing by Rodríguez, in honor of Gloria Anzaldúa's theorizing, puts Coyolxauhqui back together, yet still visible are her fragmented limbs, while she is in ceremony, in motion, looking to the cosmos, offering her *danza*.

A central thread of this queer Xicana Indígena root work is the trababjo with la madre tierra, Tonanztin Tlalli Coatlicue, Mother Earth making offerings, and especially walking with reverence among plants and herbs, in relation to what Patrisia Gonzales calls an "Indigenous healing system."[20] As Gonzales (2014) notes in her discussion of plant teachers, what some call plantcestors, the significance of holding a mutually respectful relationship with plants and their medicinal properties is embedded in the wisdom passed down from generations.[21] This allows for healing in direct relation and necessary connection with la madre tierra, to cure unbalances such as susto and most other ailments that the body mind spirit suffers. Gonzales conceptualizes susto as a "Mesoamerican framework of soul sickness." She writes that, "while the literal translation of *susto* means fright, the term refers to a variety of responses that reflect the experience of soul displacement, a strongly experienced event that stirs emotional or mental distress, and trauma."[22] Gonzales advocates for the coming home of the spirit to the body, for calling the spirit home through a return to our first mother, the Earth, and giver of life, creation—including the practices of putting one's hands, blood, sweat, and energy back into the Earth through various forms of ceremony and offerings such as gardening, writing, or *un baño de temascal* (a ceremonial steam bath).[23] On the path of re-membering we learn to heal from this susto profundo and understand how to sharpen our tools for this sanación.

Re-membering: Working through Intergenerational Trauma

Re-membering *con toda conciencia* (with full consciousness) unravels a discourse of forgetting in the context of colonial histories and violences that erase and attempt to disrupt ancestral land connections and Indigenous practices. To start to unravel the questions posed early on, I rearticulate how ceremony and re-membering are methodologies of decolonization. Patrisia Gonzales intentionally opened the need to engage "the implications of *susto profundo*" that build on Bonfil Batalla's *México Profundo*. Gonzales argues for the need to begin to heal from intergenerational trauma, including, "processes of genocide, de-Indigenization, gender oppression, poverty and the loss of land, culture and identity."[24] It becomes clearer that *la limpia* and traditional Indigenous medicine are central to Xicana/x Indígena decolonization, which in part has its roots in women of color feminisms and third-world decolonial feminist consciousness.

For many, the disconnection from their ancestral homeland, teachings of the old ways, immense culture of Mesoamerica, tribal lineages, language, and ancestral traditions have led to a disruption of prayer and ceremony and understandings and practices of interconnectedness. How do we heal from this susto profundo? How does one remember the sacred enseñanzas that the Earth offers through the elements (fire, water, land, air) we need to live, heal, and thrive? What are the tools necessary and available for sanación? How do we integrate healing methodologies in the field of Chicana/x studies that honor multiple peoples' ancestral lineages, living Indigenous traditions, and peoples of the hemisphere? How can Chicana/x studies, as a field, respectfully build with Native American and Indigenous studies, Central American, and hemispheric scholars with regard to honoring sacred relations? How does Chicana/x studies need to shift and grow? What would an energetic cleansing, a deep letting-go of old wounds, look like for the field of Xicana/x studies?

A question to unearth toxic logics of domination is: what are the heteropatriarchal and racist logics that embed colonial logics, homophobia, transphobia, anti-Blackness, Mexican nationalism, and de-Indigenization? The key, as we learn from the Combahee River Collective is that the systems of oppression are "interlocking." A deep understanding that the racist, imperialist, colonialist, patriarchal logics are intertwined and employ each other to cause disruption, discrimination, and destruction. Andrea Smith provides a powerful analysis of the logics at work in the United States, therefore they will not pertain directly to international and transnational contexts, however there is insight in how she views the forms of racialization and the structures of domination.[25] Smith articulates the three intertwined logics as "slavery/capitalism," "genocide/colonialism," and "Orientalism/war." She argues that "heteropatriarchy is the building block of US empire," suggesting that "colonizers must first naturalize hierarchy through instituting patriarchy. In turn, patriarchy rests on a gender binary system in which only two genders exist, one dominating the other."[26] Therefore, key to disrupting domination, including white supremacy, is the unraveling of structures of gender and sexuality, where balance and *not* hierarchy, based in whiteness or maleness, are central in relations.

The provocative dialogue about Chicanx people as tribal peoples is not new.[27] My inquiry stems from generations of serious debate, and much blood, sweat, and tears. I work to offer a historiographical re-narration of moments in history that need complicating in order to honor the current historical moment. Indigenous studies scholar Ines Hernández-Ávila, in a 1991 interview with Chicana philosopher Gloria Anzaldúa articulates, "I see the term 'Chicanos' itself as almost synonymous with Pan-Indian or intertribal, because we're not all Aztec.

Certainly many of us are." Hernández-Ávila continues: "We need to go beyond surface allusions because it's not about romanticizing an Indian past, either. It's about really coming into touch with what that Indian past means and what it means to have raíces in this continent, in this hemisphere. Because we were interrupted in our relationship with the land, there are many people who don't know what it feels like to be connected to a land base."[28] When people are forcibly removed from their land or flee, in migration for survival, the enseñanzas or teachings they receive from ceremonies and growth in connection with the land are interrupted, yet can continue in other formations.

Hernández-Ávila called for "a revindication of each person's lineage" opening up and insisting that Chicana/x do the work to trace who their ancestors are and not rely on surface level understandings of their ancestors that may include the Aztec, Mexica, Maya, Olmec, and Toltec.[29] Instead, this interjection calls for doing the work, the spiritual trabajo, to regionally and geographically trace one's ancestors, since many, if not most, traditional Indigenous practices are directly connected to enseñanzas of living and connecting with the spirit of the landscape. It is significant to know or understand the elements that surrounded our ancestors in their childhoods, such as river, mountains, and ocean. This spirit work unravels a discourse of forgetting of colonial histories and the erasing from historical Chicanx memory of ancestral locations such as Teotihuacán, la Plaza de Tres Culturas, el Templo Mayor, Tenochtitlán, and Xochitlcalco (the place of flowers), for example, all located near and around what became Mexico City and can provide a pathway to remembering one's layered connections to ancestors. The Aztecs (Mexica) are one of many ancestral tribal peoples from what is now designated as Mexico, not to mention Indigenous communities that continue to thrive, for example, Zapotec, Mixtec, Maya, Yaqui, Rarámuri, Otomi, Purépecha. However, the Mexicayotl tradition is not always honored in its depth and complexity for various reasons, yet within Xicanx communities who walk the red road there is a distinct and palpable reverence to these ancestors, often through danza, the study and practice of the Náhuatl language, and the decolonial reading of codices, amoxtlis.[30] These are practices of reconnection that Chicanx, Latinx, detribalized peoples, and people who know their lineages, are actively engaging more intensively and outwardly in the last fifty years. Not to mention, collaborations with the American Indian movement, and in particular the Lakota people, that have provided a compassionate pathway to remembering for Xicana/o peoples. Important urban manifestations of remembering and decolonization include growing Native and Indigenous foods, relearning languages, and practicing curanderismo and other forms of traditional medicine, including ceremonies with plants.

In the interview mentioned earlier, Anzaldúa says to Hernández-Ávila, "we cannot undo the encounter, the contact, because you and I would disappear as mestizas." Hernández-Ávila responds: "But we would still be here as Native women."[31] The echo of this provocation of Xicanas as Native women and a move away from mestiza, in dialogue, affirms and sheds light on the camino of being Indigenous to the hemisphere as well as the intense inner work, shadow battles, Xicana/xs experience due to the uprooted sting of colonization and existing colonial logics that provoke susto. This echoes Reid Gómez's complication of conquest, which worked "not to deny the violation of Spanish Colonization, but to note that these violations are not our points of origin."[32] This is a critical point of departure that invites further meditation for Chicana/x studies scholars and beyond, particularly in the absorption of mestizaje and its necessary uprooting to dislodge colonial racist logics that hold Spanish blood as pure and Black and Indigenous blood as impure, stained.[33] In tracing our lineages, how do we create spaces that are accountable and do not reproduce or enact colonial logics against ourselves and our ancestors? I argue for the importance of creating spaces for detribalized and de-Indigenized Xicana/x and Latinx peoples to experience their worth in tracing their ancestral lineages, even when not fully knowable.

Disconnection with madre tierra and Earth-centered methods of healing due to colonization, genocide, forced migration and relocation, imposed borders, enslavement, and global structures that are intertwined with capitalism, imperialism, and destructive corporate wealth have led to various forms of intergenerational trauma that have manifested in our DNA. Familial lineages that have been "whitened" can also hold susto that manifests in a silencing of traditional medicinal practices and their multigenerational relationship to the land. When we analyze the vitality of community and familial genealogical structures, we need to incorporate discussions of susto and ceremony for body mind spirit healing. Gonzales states that "*susto* can help conceptualize how even recent trauma, reinforced by the inter-generational traumas experienced by Indigenous peoples, impacts them in individual and collective ways, including their ecologies."[34]

Unsettling the Logic of the Mestiza and Mestizaje: Reimagining Aztlán in Chicana/x Studies

The task of unsettling the logic of the mestiza/o and the larger nationalist colonial project of mestizaje in the field of Chicana/x studies is a generative project that can be furthered by bridging intentions and intellectual trajectories with Native American, Indigenous, and critical ethnic and race studies scholars—critical interjections that need to be taken seriously in ethnic studies fields that desire to move towards decolonization, Indigenous solidarity and sovereignty, and the abolition of militarized nation state borders. The colonial logic of mestizaje implemented by the Mexican nation state led to widespread intergenerational de-Indigenization of Chicana/x peoples in diasporas. At times, the emergence of mestizaje is understood as the start of a mixed blood people, that can dilute traces of Indigenous and African ancestors. Gómez articulates: "A mestizo origin is in part a mistaken emergence, a misplaced origin. It accepts, in some way, the initial and continual erasure of tribal peoples and tribal memories."[35] If possible, it is a significant journey for detribalized Xicana/x people to trace their own complex peoples and lineages, to remember ancestors who are Indigenous to this hemisphere, to learn the histories of the geopolitical lands of their antepasados (ancestors), and to ask: how long did my ancestors reside in their original lands, what were the reasons for migration, what were land-based practices, and what are their origin stories? Rodríguez articulates: "This disruptive de-Indigenization process has convinced Indigenous peoples that they have had no history or narrative of worth prior to the arrival of Europeans." His work, focused on "maíz narratives," "challenges the practice of assigning 'narrative' status to Western master narratives of dominant narratives while assigning counternarrative status to all others."[36]

Here I illuminate an analysis that is often obscured due to racist state logics and legacies of colonization, that many have internalized due to disconnection. The intention of this queer Xicanx Indígena root work is to clear a path to hidden hxstories, traumas, and ceremonies that open possibilities for remembering and re-creating interconnected "missing memory" or creation stories, ancestral knowledges and reviving connections to land that have been forgotten due to colonial impositions and the internalization of dominant racist narratives, including the caste system, which consistently favored the racially white, light skinned and European blood/ancestors and severely scrutinized those with Black blood.[37]

I engage and critique Anzaldúa's formative work in *Borderlands/La Frontera: The New Mestiza*, particularly her first chapter, "The Homeland/Aztlán/El otro México." I argue that in spite of the critiques Anzaldúa's work has received and the necessary unraveling of Anzaldúa's work that I attempt here, her ceremony-centered writing has contributed to laying the groundwork for Chicanx Indigenous studies by opening a conversation with Indigenous studies scholars and communities, among other Chicanas who did this early work.[38] In her earlier work, Chicana lesbian philosopher Gloria Anzaldúa, in her imaginative and frequently cited *Borderlands/La Frontera*, theorizes the birth of the first Mexican

American.[39] In fact, she points to the birth of a *raza* (a people) as occurring at the time of the Conquest. Anzaldúa writes about these processes of racialization at the time of Spanish Conquest: "En 1521 nació una nueva raza, el mestizo, el mexicano (people of mixed Indian and Spanish blood), a race that had never existed before. Chicanos, Mexican-Americans, are the offspring of those first matings."[40] It is this trajectory and naming that many Chicanx peoples who are on their journey of searching for a sacred path tend to gravitate toward in their conceptualization of ancestry. It is precisely because of the innovative interventions that Anzaldúa's *Borderlands* offers, as well as her larger body of scholarship, that we must unhook and critique some of the colonial threads and unfinished stories she built with to create and inform her analysis. Sheila Marie Contreras criticizes Anzaldúa's sources and argues how the emphasis and ancestral line drawn to the Aztecs was somewhat motivated by a Chicano nationalist impulse and therefore needs to be complicated and unraveled.[41] In "Letter to Gloria Anzaldúa," Emma Pérez laments the critiques of Anzaldúa's "mistake of using Vasconcelos" in *Borderlands*, suggesting that critics naming her "anti-Indigenous and anti-Black" is an extreme measure for her (mis)use of "la raza cósmica," Vasconcelos's articulation.[42] Therefore, a compassionate yet critical rereading or unraveling of concepts, ideas, philosophies, and ideologies is a necessary and healing pathway, and praxis of liberation.

In this spirit, Chicana cultural theorists Rosa Linda Fregoso and Angie Chabram question how Chicano studies can proclaim an agenda of "community empowerment" based on "the notion of a singular Chicano cultural identity."[43] They argue in their provocative article that "Chicano identity was framed in Aztlán. And, Aztlán provided a basis for a return to the roots, for a return to an identity before domination and subjugation—a voyage back to pre-Columbian times."[44] They continue: "Chicanos emphasized native as opposed to European origins," however, the Native roots they focused on were primarily identified with Aztlán, and limited to Aztec lineage. In their view, "Chicano identity was often a static, fixed, and one-dimensional formulation. It failed to acknowledge our historical differences in addition to the multiplicity of our social and cultural identities as a people."[45] It was formulated on the binary "Anglos vs. Chicanos," perhaps out of a sense of survival, but this dated limitation erased many complexities, including sexuality, gender, working-class "form[s] and practices," and Indigenous lineages.[46] Fregoso and Chabram poignantly argue that "the short-sightedness of Chicano studies intellectuals was that they assumed that the construction of their own self-representations as subjects was equivalent to that of the totality of the Chicana/o experience, and that this shared representation could always be generalized in the interests of the entire group. This myopia did not permit them to see that this new representation would be alien to other Chicanas/os who had their own self-representations."[47] This analysis, although powerful in terms of challenging the Chicano nationalism of Aztlán, simultaneously can be understood as negating the notion that Chicanx peoples are Indigenous to this continent, whether or not they identify spiritually or politically with their lineage or ancestral practices. It is significant then to examine the historical context of the imposed border that Anzaldúa theorized so profoundly through a decolonial lens to unravel how the imposed categories of identities from the state have colonized peoples understanding of themselves and their relatives.

This is a critical point of departure that invites further meditation for Xicana/x studies scholars and beyond, particularly in the absorption of mestizaje and its necessary uprooting so that racist colonial logics are not allowed to linger. A major intervention is to create space for detribalized and de-Indigenized Xicana/x people to experience their worth as part of their reconnection with Indigenous relatives and spiritual legacies, and not be accused of reproducing or enacting colonial logics because they are reclaiming and remembering their path as Indigenous.

Histories of Ancestors: Racialization and "De-Indianization"

Mexican Anthropologist Bonfil Batalla (1996) argues that while warring and domination were already in motion before the Conquest in Mesoamerican civilizations, the ideologies of whiteness and Christianity that accompanied the Spanish crown were not yet in place. Anzaldúa writes about these processes of racialization at the time of the Conquest, which did not yet have a name when the Spanish arrived in the early 1500s.[48] During these colonial times, in what became New Spain or colonial Mexico, the mixed-blood mestizo had more authority than the Indigenous (pure blood), simply because mestizos possessed Spanish blood. Historian Maria Elena Martínez names this "*Limpeza de sangre*," which translates into the purity of blood. In the Americas, "the colonial discourse of purity of blood was . . . initially propelled by the Christianization project and by Spanish distrust of the religious loyalties of Jewish converts—by religious utopias and anticonverso sentiment." As she argues, "Spanish notions of purity and impurity of blood were fictions, ideological constructs based on religious and genealogical understandings of difference that despite their invented nature were no less effective at shaping social practices, categories of identity, and self-perceptions."[49]

Martínez's analysis is particularly insightful because she names this system of "purity and impurity" as a fiction, illuminating how racialization itself is based in the fictions of created stories of eugenics, white superiority, and logics of domination.[50] Within this spectrum of blood characterization, Indigenous people were deemed to have "stained ancestry." One of the biggest fears the Spanish held was that converted people, even those who accepted baptism, would not let go of their ancestral beliefs. As a result of this fear based on the fictions Martínez describes, Indigenous rulers and Spanish nobles who encouraged the Indigenous people to "reject Catholicism and retain ancestral beliefs" were often tried and found guilty of being idolaters. According to Martínez, it was clear that "indigenous people were going to be policed and punished" for religious "transgression."[51] In a similar form to the way racialization was linked to punishment, sexuality was colonized and surveilled. The consequences were severe and could even be deadly for those outside of normative categories of gender and sexuality, in particular for LGBTQ2S people, demonstrating how competing forms of colonialisms have direct consequences on knowledge formations.[52] The site of Chicano studies inherited the colonial binary notions of gender that insisted on the rigid demarcations of male/female and heteronormative forms of sexuality and family that viewed queer, trans, and gender nonconforming people as deviant.[53] As Moraga writes, "when *El Plan Espiritual de Aztlán* was conceived a generation ago, lesbians and gay men were not envisioned as members of the 'house,' we were not recognized as the sister planting the seeds, the brother gathering the crops. We were not counted as members of the 'bronze continent.'"[54]

Decolonizing Conflicting Histories

This historiography places in tension the intertwined legacies of the field of Chicano studies and the traumas of the Treaty of Guadalupe Hidalgo next to Gloria Anzaldúa's legacies and theories of *Borderlands*.[55] With deeper focus revealing the complex histories of colonization and racialization that have shaped the realities of "Mexican American" people or Chicanas and Chicanos, "people of the Sun," on both sides of the United States–Mexico border. I argue that a series of interconnected constructed legal borders, colonial violences, and racial divisions work to separate people, their histories, and their ancestry. The unraveling or decolonizing of conflicting histories opens possibilities for mapping and seeing interconnected historical formations and community praxis. I frame my work using the theoretical concepts of "the decolonial imaginary" and "decolonization," which are helpful for unraveling historical silences in Chicano historiographies.[56] By centering decolonization, this analysis disrupts accepted imaginaries and opens up a feminist of color consciousness of the borderlands and an analysis of the settler colonial tendencies of Aztlán.[57]

Building on this broader context of a decolonized Chicana/o/x studies, I place in tension three interconnected legacies or constricted imaginaries: the heteronormative settler colonial formation of Chicano studies and its reliance on the construction of the Aztlán in the U.S. Southwest, the U.S. colonial history of the Treaty of Guadalupe Hidalgo and the complicated and violent formation of the United States–Mexico borderlands, and the conquest of central México and the process of "de-Indianization" in Mexico and larger Mesoamerica. Chicana feminist analyses, including the concept of "*mita y mita*" from Anzaldúa's *Borderlands/La Frontera*, are critical in queering these historic temporalities and imaginings that are often too narrow and that disregard the "female," matriarchal, and queer ancestors and legacies.[58] There is a push from Chicana feminists, women of color feminisms, and third-world feminist consciousness for Chicano studies to be increasingly expansive and work from a decolonial space of connectivity instead of loss, fear, susto, and scarcity.

The intention of this chapter is not to revisit moments of the past to reconstruct them or assert a romanticized, easy harmony. Instead, the purpose is to see how colonial legacies have limited our perception of the geopolitical locations known as México, Aztlán, the U.S. Southwest, and *las Ámericas*. I am interested in exploring precolonial and pre-national racial and gender formations that existed on these lands in contrast to those that were constructed after conquest and the formation of the nation-state on both sides of the United States–Mexico border. Constructed borders constrict imaginings and produce dominant, heteronormative, or hyphenated namings of a community or a people. Some central questions are: How and why did Aztlán emerge as a central "sacred" site for the Chicano movement? In what ways did the Chicano movement build itself on limited notions of gender and sexuality, spirituality, and land? How do these legacies influence the knowledge formation of Chicano studies? What does a focus on the "loss of land" due to the Treaty of Guadalupe Hidalgo in 1848 obscure in terms of ancestry and land in larger Mexico and Mesoamerica, Anahuac, and the shared histories with Native peoples?

An historical inquiry into Aztlán is important to the project of recovering silences about queer Chicana sexualities because it proposes a decolonizing of the central tenants of Chicano studies—a field of study, that particularly in its earlier formations, tended to tokenize and exclude based on gender and sexuality. In the field's attempt to know itself and bring an important analysis of race and colonization, a comprehensive feminist analysis is starkly missing—particularly in terms of revised understandings and unravelings of the gender binary, and the more expansive and intertwined relations between femininity and masculinity, transgender identities, duality, and nonbinary genders.[59] Further unraveling of

Aztlán will facilitate a tracing of queer ancestry that is not easily visible in colonial and nation-based legacies of history. Narrow and regional understandings of land and race are significant components of early conceptions of Aztlán that formed what Pérez describes as the Chicano historical imaginary. Castañeda questions the narrative structure of that history in reenvisioning the border.[60] Critical understandings of Aztlán by Chicana feminists and Xicana/x Indígena scholars disrupt this nationalist Chicano imaginary that contains a colonial impulse and build toward (1) unraveling unseen histories of queer–nonbinary, and transgender ancestry and (2) redefining complex understandings of geography, land, and race, respectively.[61] One notable organic intellectual who has lived a legacy of media making that uplifts matriarchy and decolonial forms of gender, sexuality, and familia is queer Chicana filmmaker Osa Hidalgo de la Riva, who made *Two-Spirit* about Native and Chicana/o gay and lesbian communities in the United States. The time frame and context of de la Riva's film are connected to the foundational Native American literature on two-spirit formations, which is generative in the process of remembering Indigenous forms of sexualities in Mesoamerica, so-called Latin America, and across the hemisphere that were interrupted by colonial forms of gender and sexuality.[62]

In *Borderlands/La Frontera*, particularly in the chapter "The Homeland/Aztlán/El otro México," Anzaldúa reenvisioned the United States–Mexico borderlands, specifically the U.S. Southwest:

> This land was Mexican once,
>   was Indian always
>   and is.
>   And   will be again.[63]

In this short poetic interlude, the word "again" brings us back to the future and the imagined past of the Southwest. This land was claimed as a territory of Mexico when it became a nation in 1821.[64] Before this, the U.S. Southwest fell under the colonial rule of New Spain as a result of the Spanish Conquest in the sixteenth century. After the United States–Mexico War (1846–48) and the implementation of the resulting Treaty of Guadalupe Hidalgo in 1848, the Southwest became a territory of the United States. The history of this land therefore shows various forms of militarized occupation and competing colonialisms over the course of hundreds of years.

In the above-cited passage, Anzaldúa acknowledges what increasingly Chicanxs, especially Xicana/x, are practicing in their ceremonias—the land known as the U.S. Southwest is Indigenous Native land, within what is known by some as tierra Anahuac and by others as Turtle Island. This land existed as the Estados Unidos Mexicanos from 1821 to 1848—twenty-seven militarized years. Although it is known that Chicano or "Mexican" ancestors inhabited and migrated within this land for generations, it was consistently shared with other Indigenous peoples, a fact that at times feels elided in the forms of implied ownership contained within settler colonial understandings of Aztlán. Here is where Tuck and Yang's provocation that "settler colonialism and its decolonization implicates and unsettles everyone" is generative.[65] This important rethinking of Aztlán goes hand and hand with the re-Indigenization of "detribalized" and de-territorialized Xicana/x peoples. This is the critical work that must occur across communities, families, peoples: the need to revisit their familial lineages and their relationship with the land they currently live with, on, and/or occupy. It is important to remember that it was in the context of de-Indigenization and deterritorialization that Mexican Americans, migrants, and Chicanos were racially read as foreign, "illegal" invaders; it is also important to remember that this trauma was brought on by U.S. colonial forces, including manifest destiny, and it birthed a solution that was reactive and exclusive out of a form of survival and therefore must be decolonized. As the next generations of Chicana, Xicana/x, and Chicanx peoples emerged, we see the unearthing of the dominant narratives that are not representative of true forms of liberation, including how naming the state of California as Califaztlan can erase the history of California Native tribes. The narrative of the seven tribes of Aztlán is one to be honored and remembered, yet it is also important to complicate how the land known as the U.S. Southwest is shared by other tribes, original peoples. Part of the decolonization process is to ask and connect to the local Indigenous people, plants, ways of being, and learn the languages or names used by the first nations Native people of that land to name the region.[66] When Anzaldúa says the land has always been, is, and will be Indian again, she is doing the work to unravel the narratives that have interrupted this awareness and knowledge of the stolen Indian homelands. The interconnected vision and work of Indigenous sociologist John Brown Childs on "transcommunality" alert us to a framework that opens the possibility of exploring shared histories of distinct peoples to fully understand the implications of the structures of racism and colonization, including forms of epistemic violence that may led to disconnection with an interrelated history.[67]

My interdisciplinary analysis, which builds with Indigenous studies, feminist of color and queer studies, and Chicana/x studies, and critical Latin American and Latino studies challenges outdated, dominant notions of Aztlán that get taken up as a form of nostalgic memory, yet acknowledges the decolonial work that occurs within the signifier Aztlán.[68] This work seeks to build interconnections among distinct histories and aims to offer a queer feminist Indígena critique of Chicano studies, the Chicano movement, and other representations of heteronormative centered Chicanismo. I see this historical analysis as building from other forms of "Xicana root work" that emerged in the 1960s and 1970s. My use of the term "root work" evokes the Xicana feminist trace of ancestral memories through present-day representations or stories that disrupt dominant nationalist or male-centered narratives of history. The conceptual frame of Chicana with an "X"—Xicana—is borrowed and grown from a generation of writers, artists, and scholars who mapped out a feminist critique of Chicanismo and emphasized Indigenous roots, practices, and matriarchal forms of *la mujer* within this identity formation. The work of this generation includes Ana Castillo's *Massacre of the Dreamers: Essays on Xicanisma*, Moraga and Rodríguez's "Mission Statement" for La Red Xicana Indígena, and Ester Hernández's artwork that uses the "X" in its title, *La Virgen de Guadalupe Defendiendo los Derechos de los Xicanos*.[69] Artist and scholar Amalia Mesa-Bains argues that Hernandez's artwork "breaks the traditional role of the Virgin de Guadalupe as icon and repositions her as a feminist assertion" and that her "Guadalupe Karate Fighter" is one of two "signature pieces of her generation."[70] This vision of Xicana feminists or queer Xicanas assists in rethinking the histories of land, race, gender, and sexuality.

The nation-centered heteronormative Chicano movement built itself on limited notions of gender and sexuality, spirituality, and land; these legacies plague recent knowledge formations of Chicano studies. Chicana lesbian scholar Yvonne Yarbro-Bejarano poses a significant challenge to the field of Chicanx studies by suggesting that Chicano studies is a site that can potentially do the work of reconfiguring its central tenets and incorporating a meaningful analysis of sexuality instead of the typical "add-on" technique or additive model. She argues that this reconfiguration would require a thorough examination of nationalism. As part of her recommendation to the intellectual field of Chicana/o studies, Yarbro-Bejarano encourages Chicanas and Chicanos "to retain the contestatory critique of U.S. state domination, while exercising increased vigilance over the ways our own narratives can dominate and exclude."[71] In particular, she is concerned with challenging what is considered "normative" in terms of race, class, and sexuality. Although she does not directly discuss colonial relations, Yarbro-Bejarano questions the central historical tenants on which the field and related fields of study were formed. She asserts that "the stakes in the theoretical expansion of Chicana/o studies as an academic discipline are particularly high for lesbians and gays of colour, given the exclusionary politics of domination that have characterized the histories of both women's studies and American ethnic studies."[72] In signaling the possibilities of this field, Yarbro-Bejarano writes that "Chicana/o studies can be an ideal site for contesting rather than reproducing hegemonic scripts such as male or white supremacy, upper-class superiority or compulsory heterosexuality."[73] Here, Yarbro-Bejarano articulates a central tenant of women of color feminisms—the constant analysis of the intertwined hegemonies of race, class, gender, and sexuality in order to reconfigure power relations that tend to favor the nationalist, male-centered, heteropatriarchal subject in historical narratives.

My research process of digging (excavando) and unearthing historical narratives has revealed stories, myths, and provocations that at times contradict one another, and in other instances erase one other. How does one reconcile these tensions and honor contradictory representations to illuminate the complexity of history? Seeing the layers of dominant legacies or colonial imaginaries allow for the unraveling of rigid boundaries within Chicano historical narratives to be seen and cleansed. These narratives adhere to a heteronormative conception of the Chicano family and community that tends to tokenize Chicana and Latina women, rather than see them as artists, leaders, and visionaries. Because imaginaries of racialization and "loss of land" were constructed by colonial impulses within the Chicano movement, impulses that close off connections to matriarchal and otherwise (non-patriarchal) histories. I argue that the focus on the legacies of the United States–Mexico War is limited, as is focusing only on the Spanish Conquest in central Mexico. Critically revisiting the seven-thousand-year history of Mesoamerica, particularly from a feminist perspective, makes Indigenous and queer ancestry become increasingly central to the erasures within the story of the so-called Mexican American.

While the field of Chicano studies emerged from social movement struggles against racism and through narratives of liberation, its early roots remain dominated by colonial legacies of war and limited understandings of race, gender, sexuality, spirituality, and history. The way the Chicano movement of the 1960s and 1970s conceptualized the Treaty of Guadalupe Hidalgo of 1848, the resulting "loss of land," and the dominant construction of the mythical land base of Aztlán, are key imaginaries in the knowledge formation of Chicano studies that require a shift. As I argue here, the way Aztlán was defined within the early Chicano nationalist movement must be considered part of a colonial legacy. I seek to uproot or complicate that narrative.

Decolonial Readings of 1848

The Chicano nationalist imaginary suggests that the signing of the Treaty of Guadalupe Hidalgo that ended the United States–Mexico War of 1846–48 marked a moment of historical colonization of Chicanos by the United States, when Mexican land was stolen. The Treaty of Guadalupe Hidalgo officially ended the war, which began due to an invasion of the Mexican state by the U.S. imperialist nation that was fueled by philosophies and practices of manifest destiny and the colonial mentality that sanctified the takeover of land for economic profit and the growth of imperialism. Griswold del Castillo writes about the start of the war: "He [Polk] ordered General Zachary Taylor to advance to the Rio Grande to 'possess' the territory for the United States. It was not long before Mexican and U.S. troops exchanged shots and joined in battle, thereby giving President Polk his rationale for a declaration of war. Judging from the votes in the U.S. Congress, there was little disagreement over the correctness of the Texas boundaries: the House of Representatives voted 174 to 14 in favor, the Senate 40 to 2."[74]

Land was forcefully taken, and racial hierarchies were established through the divisive language of the treaty of 1848. This treaty caused a significant shift in political and national boundaries, forming the United States–Mexico borderlands and recolonizing the land. Due to the imperialist praxis of the United States, Mexico lost about one-fourth of its territory. The entirety of what are today the states of California, Arizona, New Mexico, Texas, and parts of Colorado, Nevada, and Utah were excised from Mexico. The treaty sanctified this loss through shattered promises of citizenship and continued access to territory. The treaty is therefore part of a larger U.S. colonial project that creates divisions and invisibilities.

The United States–Mexico War had imperialist motivations and was guided by a vision of manifest destiny that plagued the birth and expansion of the United States. The U.S. failure to honor its treaty with the Mexican people is evidence of the racist logic that drives the United States, a nation-state that repeatedly does not honor treaties over land and territory, particularly with Native peoples. So while it is important to remember this trauma or susto in Chicano history, it is equally as important to heal from it in a complicated form, so the grieving can be generative. How do legacies of war create and shape limited imaginings of history? Building a movement within this colonial imaginary is limiting possibilities for the Chicana/o community, culture, movement, and the knowledge formation of Chicano studies, now ascending to Xicana/x studies. The implications of the legacies of war are detrimental, especially when not acknowledged in their full complexity, as in the present case of the Chicano movement.

Building on legacies of war shapes social and political imaginaries and allows these colonial violences to structure present discourses of history, memory, and forgetting. Renya Ramirez argues that "by claiming their Indian roots through a mythic story of an Aztec Aztlán, this early work of Chicano nationalists leaves out the historical presence of Indian tribes in the Southwest area," not to mention Mesoamerican ancestors.[75] The Chicano nationalist movement elides the existence of Native peoples on the land identified by the United States as the Southwest, as well as the multiplicity of tribes and homelands, for example Mexico. Similarly, Daniel Alarcón argues that *el plan espiritual de Aztlán*, put forward in 1969 as part of the Chicano movement, "justifies its goals on the basis of European and Anglo American colonization and oppression, yet does not grapple with mestizo colonization and appropriation of Native American lands in the Southwest during the Spanish colonial period. The colonization is instead transformed into a legitimization of Chicano territorial rights based on Chicanos' roles as 'civilizers of the Northern land of Aztlán.' To date, competing claims to the region by Native Americans, Asian Americans, African Americans, and the *mestizaje* of these different cultures have yet to be addressed in most discussions of Aztlán."[76] Complicating the shortsighted historical narratives proposed by earlier generations of Chicanos assists in seeing how the land known as the Southwest is home to many other people. A closer examination of Native history shows that the land known as the U.S. Southwest is in fact Indigenous land that has been colonized by various forces and empires. The Hopi, Navajo/Diné, Comanches, and Pueblo peoples are some of the tribes Indigenous to this land.[77] It also releases Chicano imaginaries from the fiction that the Southwest is the only homeland for people who identify with the politics of Chicanismo. Simultaneously, this reformulation and decolonial lens opens the possibility of connection to ancestors in the nation-state known as Mexico and the larger region of Mesoamerica, for example, where astronomically aligned ancient structures have increasingly been uncovered over centuries to demonstrate intellectual capacity and deep interconnectedness with the earth and the cosmos.[78]

These legacies of war have shaped our imaginaries and relations due to colonial notions of land and race. Decentering war makes space for harmony and a revised way of envisioning a relation to land and people that is not focused on property and ownership, or racialized notions of superiority and inferiority. In *Borderlands/La Frontera*, Anzaldúa parenthetically notes that "the Treaty of Guadalupe Hidalgo created the Mexican-American in 1848."[79] It is to a discussion of the hyphenated identity formation of the "Mexican-American" in relation to laws, regulations, and hierarchies of racialization that once considered Mexicans "white" that I now turn in exploring further the complicated history of the Treaty of Guadalupe Hidalgo.

Mexican Americans, Law, and Race

The legal struggle for land through the 1848 Treaty of Guadalupe Hidalgo is an important case to unravel for Chicano and Native interrelated history. Based on Chicano historian Richard Griswold del Castillo's analysis of the treaty, it is evident that the legal and political discourse of the treaty shows a compelling connection between Chicana/os and Native peoples in their respective struggles for land, citizenship, and overall recognition by the U.S. government.[80] The Southwest was officially part of Mexico only from 1821 until 1848.[81]

The longer and misleading official title of the 1848 treaty is the Treaty of Peace, Friendship, Limits and Settlement between the United States of American and the United Mexican States. This treaty was arguably a form of militarized occupation. Its racist divisive demarcations denied the use of Spanish language in the United States, did not allow Mexicans who had territories adequate time to claim their property, and brought about a denigration of the Mexican culture. One of the most upsetting moments of the implementation was the striking from the final treaty of article 10, which marked a significant shift by the U.S. Senate. This article protected "Mexican land grants." As Griswold del Castillo explains,

> this article struck to the heart of a question that would be the basis for hundreds of lawsuits and many instances of injustice against the former Mexican land holders. The treaty makers knew well that most of the Mexican citizens occupying land grants in the ceded territories did not have perfect titles to their lands and that the majority were in process of fulfilling the requirements of Mexican law. Frequent changes in political administrations, the notorious slowness of the Mexican bureaucracy, and many individual circumstances had made it difficult for Mexican landholders to obtain clear title in an expedient way. Article X would have allowed them to complete the process under an American administration. The article specifically recognized the unique condition of the Mexican land-grant claimants in Texas, most of whom had been dispossessed of their lands by Anglo Texans following Texas Independence. The article would allow them to resurrect their claims and fulfill the conditions of Mexican law.[82]

In short, this article would have protected the rights to land for "Mexican" people; this was a major disappointment for many who were displaced as a result.

At the same time, article 8 shifted the citizenship rights for "California Indians." According to Griswold del Castillo,

> the fate of the California Indians is further evidence of the violation of the spirit of the treaty. Under the Mexican Constitution of 1824, Indians were considered full Mexican citizens. Upon the transfer of territory to the U.S. government, however,

> the Indians received neither U.S. citizenship nor the protections of the treaty as specified in Article VIII. The California state constitutional convention recoiled from the idea of granting Indians full citizenship. In violation of the treaty, the California Indian tribes were deprived of the protections specified in the treaty. Consequently they became the victims of murder, slavery, land theft, and starvation. The Indian population within the state declined by more than 100,000 in two decades. Whites overran tribal lands and people were exterminated.[83]

Griswold del Castillo suggests that, in terms of the fate of California Indians, "genocide is not too strong a word to use in describing what happened to the California Indians during that period."[84] Clearly, the treaty not only did the work to redesignate (colonize) land, but it also redefined the boundaries, histories, and destinies of people. As Anzaldúa states, "the border fence that divides the Mexican people was born on February 2, 1848 with the signing of the Treaty of Guadalupe-Hidalgo."[85] Her articulations are reminiscent of the experience of people who had familial roots and land on both sides of the imposed border, including the Tohono O'odham and Kickapoo nations whose lands are divided by the border.

The language of the treaty enforced these hierarchal relations in the language of occupation and statehood. Sociologist Laura E. Gómez shows another layer of the racism at work in the geographic area of New Mexico: "During this period, the majority of Mexican American men, who had received *federal* citizenship under the peace treaty of 1848, held a kind of second-class citizenship in which their rights were limited because Congress refused to admit New Mexico as a state due to its majority Mexican and Indian population."[86] On the one hand, there are property-owning "Mexicans" and on the other there are "savage tribes" who *occupy* the land. Griswold del Castillo shows the conflicts around land and the divisive tactics of the United States and the treaty when he argues that, "under Article XI of the Treaty of Guadalupe Hidalgo, the United States was bound to prevent Indian raids into Mexico from the U.S. side of the border."[87] This turned out to be very expensive. The U.S. government stationed eight thousand troops along the border, an initiative that cost more than the original treaty.

This racialized history that functions through the legality of the treaty is directly connected to forms of hierarchy or colonial legacies in California, such as white supremacy. Building on George Fredrickson's work,[88] Tomas Almaguer is quite correct in stating that "the attempt to make race or color a basis for group position within the United States was defined initially during the colonial period when notions of 'civility' and 'savagery,' as well as clear distinctions between 'Christians' and 'heathen,' were used to inscribe racial difference and divide humankind into distinct categories of people."[89] This designation as "Mexican-American" emphasizes a hybrid or mixed-blood, mestizo identity, usually as a "hybrid of Anglo, Indian, Spanish and African Blood."[90]

According to Carrigan and Webb, "the majority of Mexicans occupied a liminal position within the racial hierarchy of the southwestern states. The law classified them as white," unless of course one was of a lower class, which then required that mixed-blood people with impure status were "pushed to the margins of whiteness."[91] The language of the treaty puts these groups into competition and conflict with each other, and a hierarchal relationship is established that inevitably supports and enforces white supremacy.[92]

These historical narratives reveal the multiple and complicated layers to colonization, particularly in the way that racialization is connected to these hierarchies, such as ownership of property. For example, in the nineteenth century, Native tribes were outside the legal bounds of ownership, whereas Mexican rancheros were allowed to own property and were classified as "white." This shows the conflation of race and economic status that established an unjustified hierarchy of racialization and ownership. An important loss of self occurs when Mexican people are considered white, an argument that extends and yet compliments Bonfil Batalla's arguments about de-Indianization in Mexico.[93]

The treaty also established colonial legacies that elide Native people's history and misrepresent Mexican American history. Historian David J. Weber writes: "From 1540, when intensive exploration north from Mexico got under way, until 1821, when Mexico became independent of Spain, today's Southwestern states of California, Arizona, New Mexico, Texas, Nevada, Utah, and much of Colorado formed part of the wealthy Spanish colony of New Spain, as Mexico was then called. Spain had only a nominal hold over this vast territory; permanent colonies were established in coastal California, southern Arizona, the Rio Grande Valley of New Mexico, and in Texas. Yet, the years of Spanish control over the Southwest left remnants of Spanish culture firmly stamped on the area."[94] Weber continues: "What is most often forgotten is that this colonial period in today's Southwest belonged as much to Mexico and Mexicans as it did to Spain and Spaniards. Although the leaders of Spain's exploring and colonizing expeditions were usually persons born in Spain of pure Spanish blood, the rank and file of those groups consisted of persons born in Mexico, usually of mixed blood, whose culture combined Indian and Spanish elements. These 'Spanish' pioneers were neither Indian nor Spanish, but Mexican."[95] Weber's analysis of the Southwest and the positioning of white "Mexicans" as being the owners of the land as much as the Spanish colonizers were simultaneously erases the Indigenous peoples native to the land and places Mexicans in the position of colonizer instead of pointing to a potential tribal relation or connection between the "mixed blood" people who had "Indian and Spanish elements." In many ways, he minimizes the Spanish colonization of these lands that are now separated by a United States–Mexico border. This is not to say that Mexicans, especially Mexican rancheros, did not claim ownership of colonized land, but it is necessary to complicate this narrative and show that there are multiple and complicated layers to colonization and that racialization is connected to these hierarchies of ownership. The claim that the land "belonged to Mexico and Mexicans as it did to Spain and Spaniards" gives Chicanos or Mexican Americans the space and reign to claim that their land was stolen through the Treaty of Guadalupe Hidalgo in 1848 as a result of the United States–Mexico War; it enables a conceptualization of Aztlán as this "lost land," and position people like the Hopi, Dine/Navajo, Miwok, Ohlone, Chumash, Tongva, Hoopa, Kumeyaay, and Pueblo Indians as outside trespassers of their own ancestral lands.

Another example of this colonial legacy emerges from General Stephan Watts Kearny's speech in New Mexico in 1846, at the start of the war, in which he maintained that "I have come amongst you by the orders of my government, to take possession of your country, and extend over it the laws of the United States. We consider it, and have done so for some time, a part of the territory of the United States. We come amongst you as friends—not as enemies; as protectors—not as conquerors. We come among you for your benefit—not your injury."[96] He was insistent in his racist and divisive speech: "From the Mexican government you have never received protection. The Apaches and the Navajoes [*sic*] come down from the mountains and carry off your sheep, and even your women, whenever they please. My government will correct all of this. I will keep off the Indians, protect you in your persons and property; and I repeat again, will protect your religion. I know you are all great Catholics.[97] In this example, the U.S. conquest imposes a protection based on colonial religion through military occupation in the disguised form of a friendly gesture and positions Native people as trespassers.

These ideas about occupation and trespass also speak to the boundaries and legalities of "whiteness" for Mexican Americans. Gómez presents an insightful history of this process.[98] She argues that "Mexican Americans became a wedge racial group between whites and blacks. While Mexican Americans were relegated to second-class citizenship in virtually are all areas, they had access to legal whiteness under a kind of reverse one-drop rule: one drop of Spanish blood allowed them to claim whiteness under certain circumstances."[99] Gómez shows yet another layer of division that supports white supremacy when she argues that "the separate racial ideologies that developed with respect to Mexican Americans and African Americans highlight the complexity and contradictions within white supremacy."[100] In their discussion of the "lynching of persons of

Mexican origin" after the 1848 treaty, Carrigan and Webb point out that, due to legal and racial classifications that positioned Mexicans as white, it is impossible to know how many Mexicans were lynched unless one does archival work case by case (between 1848 and 1928, mobs lynched at least 597 Mexicans).[101] The authors make the point, however, that the numbers of lynched Blacks or African Americans are always significantly higher (between 1882 and 1930, it is commonly noted that at least 3,386 African American died at the hands of lynch mobs).

Almaguer breaks away from "the shadow of the black/white encounter" and maps white supremacist legacies in California.[102] In his formulation of the "racialization process" he argues for "'elective affinity' between material interests of whites at different class levels and the racial ideologies that simultaneously structured the new Anglo-dominated society in California."[103] Although Almaguer does the work of complicating the idea that there was no "simple binary" or "one principle fault," his approach to the racial "groups" maintains unnecessary divisions among histories that actually converge in many forms, particularly through their various histories of presence on the land now named California.

Here the scholarship of Brown Childs and his concept of "transcommunality" is critical. He suggests that our analysis of structures such as racism in the United States can become more complicated if we consider overlapping histories among populations, for example, Native and Black.[104] He argues that through this frame of shared histories we can map "centuries of genocide, forced removals, slavery, segregation, lynching, and resistance" and ultimately unravel complex histories.[105] For example, a closer analysis of the historical moment of 1848 when the United States took over land that previously was claimed by the nation of Mexico would reveal that slavery was a motivating factor to gain more territory for the United States. When the Republic of Texas joined the Union, it did so as a slave-holding state. Mexico had abolished slavery in 1828, before the Republic of Texas formed in 1836.[106] This layered interconnected research would therefore ask: What are some of the interrelated or "transcommunal" hidden histories of Chicanas/os/xs, Native Americans, and Indigenous Mexicanos/as? I now turn to a larger discussion of the queer histories of ancestors that are often too narrow or nonexistent in Chicano movement discourse.

Complicating Chicanx Histories: Unraveling Homophobia

Historian Deena González offers a testimony of homophobia that offers compelling evidence of the need to reform Chicano studies. In 1991, González reported that her comments at the National Association of Chicano Studies (NACS) were a "strategic intervention" in the organization due to its "deeply rooted" homophobia, an ideology that is "so pervasive," González argues, "that the needs, desires, ideas, and skills of gay and lesbian Chicanas/os are systematically overlooked, denied, and trivialized."[107] González illuminates her arguments by relaying the story of a Chicana lesbian administrator who was not publicly out due to a "horrible attack on her presumed sexuality" in the 1950s. González explains:

> This woman had never revealed to anyone, except her lovers, that she was a lesbian. She said she had never even imagined doing that because in the late '50s she had been silenced, labeled, and harassed by two Chicano colleagues who had written a memo suggesting that her vote on their search committee was founded on her problematic identity as a lesbian. How they knew of her sexual preference, or as she called it, her private life, was unclear, but the fear engendered by the accusation, and her closeted life thereafter, she believed, were the choices she had available, the only choices.[108]

This narrative demonstrates the years of silence around queer sexuality in the academy, particularly when an environment is characterized by "patriarchy and misogyny" and "is supplemented in steady doses" by "heterosexism—that hegemonic ideology that says all people are heterosexual."[109] Although Chicano/a studies in general and the NACCS organization are now in a different moment than the grim situation González addressed in 1991, her provocative questions remain unanswered.[110] She asks: "Can you imagine a NACS conference whose topic is queer theory and its impact on the discipline? Where would Chicana literature be without lesbian writers, poetry without Chicana lesbian poets?"[111] González's final question points directly to one of the arguments of this book: the importance of acknowledging that foundational Chicana writers and poets are queer, and that their lesbianism directly sharpens and grounds their critiques of patriarchy and misogyny, which they work to dispel. Chicana lesbian writers, theorists, and poets have historically worked to decolonize Chicano studies intellectual spaces by complicating its foundational tenets.

Chicano studies, which was highly influenced by the emerging Chicano movement, centers Aztlán and the Aztecs as foundational narratives.[112] Leading Chicano literary scholar Rudolfo Anaya wrote in "Aztlán: A Homeland without Boundaries" about the importance of naming Aztlán as a "homeland" for the Chicano movement in "the late 1960s."[113] He comments that it "was a spontaneous act which took place throughout the Southwest, and the feat was given authenticity in a meeting that was held in Denver in 1969 to draft *El Plan Espiritual de Aztlán*."[114] Anaya explains the implications of naming the Chicano movement: "The naming ceremony creates a real sense of nation, for it fuses the spiritual and political aspirations of a group and provides a vision of the group's role in history. These aspirations are voiced by the artists who recreate the language and symbols which are used in the naming ceremony. The politicians of the group may describe political relationships and symbols, but it is the artist who gives deeper and long-lasting expression to a people's sense of nation and destiny."[115] While this book builds from the idea that artists play a key role in defining community and establishing cultural memory and visual storytelling, what Anaya does not address is the conflict, silence, and disconnection that arise when the artists and politics highlighted in the nation support a male heterosexual homogenized settler colonial formation as the norm for the Chicano community.

Chicana cultural feminists have argued against the inconsistencies and legacies of this logic within Chicano nationalist framings.[116] Catherine Ramírez offers an important and useful critique of Aztlán through her discussion of Norma Alarcon's *Third Woman*: "The concept of Aztlán gained currency among a number of Chicana and Chicano writers, artists, and activists during the late 1960s and 1970s and was championed in 'El Plan Espiritual de Aztlán,' a manifesto produced at the Chicano Youth Liberation Conference in Denver in March 1969."[117] Ramírez's analysis of the publication *Third Woman* exposes "the constructedness of Aztlán (i.e., it shows that Aztlán, like the nation-state, is neither natural nor a given, but created)."[118] Ramírez continues: "It reveals that there is no such thing as a singular Chicano or Chicana homeland, history, or experience."[119] Ramírez's work directly challenges the "carnalismo" or "community of men" that makes up this "Aztlán," and offers a revised Chicana feminist or women of color feminist perspective that challenges the male-centered nation.[120]

As historian of Mexican American religions Davíd Carrasco emphasizes the limitations of geographic land claims that were put forward by the Chicano movement leaders: "In the early days of the Chicano movement that articulated its plans through the *Plan Espiritual de Aztlán*, most if not all commentators on the Aztlán traditions ignored one major aspect—namely the central role of the sacred mother. . . . As more and more women, especially female artists, have expressed their visions of Chicano history, religion, soul, and existence, the theme of the sacred mother in Aztlán has become a major expression."[121] Carrasco simultaneously points to the shortsighted engagement with Mesoamerican ancestry, and to the gender-imbalanced heteronormative practices of the movement where the male figure was dominant. The violence experienced in the United States–Mexico War and the resulting Treaty of Guadalupe Hidalgo in 1848 clearly left significant scars on the memories and experiences of Chicanos. Yet an embrace of Aztlán as homeland and the myth of the Aztecs were starting points that need to be unraveled, particularly when the "homeland" and movement were exclusive, and when ancestry in Mesoamerica and the land known as Mexico was not fully explored. What was the population of gente Indígena in the United States when the naming of Chicano occurred? What was the relationship to Native people and their homelands? How were Native American and Chicanx people already sharing ceremonial space as the Chicano movement was emerging? How does ceremony open another site of interconnected relations across the continent?

Norma Alarcón also suggested a similar move away from identity politics by pointing to the complexity and fluidity of identity formations: "The quest for a true self and identity which was the initial desire of many writers involved in the Chicano movement of the late 1960s and early 1970s has given way to the realization that there is no fixed identity."[122] The works of Chicana cultural feminists invite important critiques of the Chicano movement, Aztlán, and a nationalism that depended on heteronormative forms of family, community, and spirituality. These scholars move us toward a Chicana feminist critique of nationalism that opens up possibilities for various imaginations of the politics that shape Chicano identities, visual culture (representations), and ideologies that allow for the complication of the dominant narrative of Aztlán that shapes the field of Chicano studies.

Chicana feminist legacies therefore bring attention to the way a field of knowledge that represents marginal social actors can still erase or undermine communities of other social positions. Pérez's *The Decolonial Imaginary* (1999) is an exemplary text in Chicana studies, which does the work of mapping out new terrains in the field of Chicana/o history. She moves outside of the Chicano canon of knowledge to map alternative or subaltern forms of knowledge.

Pérez writes about the treacherous waters of this methodology: "Breaking out of the borders is like choosing to go outside, into the margins, to argue or expose that which no one will risk. Going outside the accredited realm of historiography means daring to be dubbed a-historical. It means traversing new territories and disciplines, mapping fresh terrains such as cultural studies, women's studies, ethnic studies, and of course, Chicana/o studies."[123] Her research and theorizations interrupt dominant historical narratives and open space for methodological possibilities that work to decolonize Chicano studies. Pérez writes: "Chicana/o historiography has been circumscribed by the traditional historical imagination. That means that even the most radical Chicano/a historiographies are influenced by the very colonial imaginary against which they rebel. The colonial imaginary still determines many of our efforts to write history in the United States."[124] Pérez's work moves toward a radical transformation of patriarchal knowledge formations, including Chicano studies.

My goal is not to blame or bring shame but instead to shed light on the uprootedness many people experience in the context of Chicanx studies, a contested ethnic studies field that can never be taken for granted. I argue that this disjuncture has a lot to do with the attempt to root oneself in a field of study that builds itself on a movement in which the idea of Aztlán was foundational, but whose limitations do not allow for a path of deep connection for most. The settler colonial impulse to claim the U.S. Southwest as solely Mexican land, next to surface-level understandings of Aztec traditions and philosophies, supports the logic of heteropatriarchal nationalism, an intensely masculine brotherhood centered energy that does not allow for a balance with the Earth and people of all genders and all relations. This is a tension that needs to be continuously unraveled and reflected upon as part of a decolonizing project.

Daniel Alarcón asserts with certainty that "the concept of Aztlán, as formulated by Chicano nationalism and Chicano scholarship since 1969, presents an overwhelming number of apparent contradictions."[125] Alarcón suggests that when Aztlán is understood as a palimpsest it is no longer "ahistorical and instead insists on an examination of the Mesoamerican narratives from which it was drawn."[126] Similarly, Marez's research and critique calls for the necessity to introduce "other histories of conflict" to understandings of "Chicana/o popular performance," instead of relying on the usual historical narrative, that is: the Spanish Conquest leads to the fall of the Aztec Empire and becomes the basis for the Chicano movement and Chicano studies.[127] It is only with these revised perspectives on decolonizing and queering the study of history and of Aztlán that this analysis can move to the complex implications and heal the wounds of the Treaty of Guadalupe Hidalgo.

This question arises: How to open up dialogue for decolonizing Aztlán by uprooting the myth or idea by asking: how does Chicanx studies make room for tribal affiliations, original pueblos, familial lineages while still holding honorable space for the Mexica/Azteca? How can we insist on theories and practices, as well as research and curriculum that supports, acknowledges, and respects Native, Indigenous, and Indígena identified students, while also making a space for "detribalized" or "de-Indianized" students who are actively tracing their Indigenous lineages, traditions, and sacred ways? Recognizing the connections between displacement, forced migration, and colonization.

Part of this work requires destabilizing the idea of a singular homeland that elides Indigenous histories. Roberto Cintli Rodríguez offers an important intervention in understanding a Chicano homeland: "This question formed part of my original research and is relevant not because the maps locate the, or an, actual homeland but rather because this nationalized migration narrative has been permanently etched into the Chicano psyche, so much so that it comes close to eclipsing the much older maíz narratives."[128]

Critique of Anzaldúa's *Borderlands* and Mestizaje as a Central Concept of the Field

In connection with my larger arguments, the danger of Chicanx studies centralizing *Borderlands* as a vital text in the field, without incorporating Anzaldúa's later works, is that the mestiza, in-between, mixed, hybrid space without the larger spiritually rooted vision can lead to an erasure or continue the disregard of traditional Indigenous medicine as well as Native, Indigenous, and African survivance across the hemisphere. Simultaneously, it can disrupt rooted guidance of detribalized Xicanx who are tracing their tribal lineages or even an acknowledgment of self as Indigenous because of the focus on a politics of in-betweenness without a root. Similarly, it can be misleading when people interpret Anzaldúa's work as staying in the state of *nepantla*, "a Náhuatl word meaning tierra entre medio," literally in-between land. Anzaldúa further described nepantla as "living in a liminal zone," which "means being in a constant state of displacement—an uncomfortable, even alarming feeling. Most of us dwell in nepantla so much of the time it's become a sort of 'home.'"[129] Arguably, Anzaldúa articulated nepantla as part of the journey, not the entire journey. This is reflected in her essay, "Now Let Us Shift," where nepantla is one of the seven stages of conocimiento.[130] Staying in the liminal without a grounded connection to ancestors, traditional practices, or knowledge of one's familial story can be disconcerting. There are spirit scholars who are doing the critical work of being *nepantleras* yet rooting themselves in the work of Indigenous ancestors.[131] I believe this pathway is closer to what Anzaldúa intended in her formulation of nepantla. Rodríguez takes this further by identifying a "backward-looking frame" through which "Chicanas/Chicanos (as well as Mexicans and Central Americans) are perceived as the descendants of Mesoamericans, not as part of live and dynamic Indigenous or maíz-based cultures."[132] He continues: "Chicanas/Chicanos became the inheritors of this timeline/framework and narrative. They were not contextualized as Indigenous peoples but rather as 'descendants of' Indigenous peoples. Even when they were conceived of as mestizos, the Indigenous part of the equations was relegated to the past."[133]

Similarly, Smith, in her critique of Anzaldúa, argues that "in queer of color critique in particular, mestizaje and queerness often intersect to disappear indigeneity through the figure of the diasporic or hybrid queer subject. The consequence is that queer of color critique, while making critical interventions into both critical race and queer studies, generally lacks an analysis of settler colonialism and genocide."[134] In this case, Anzaldúa's early work, and some core tenants of early Chicano studies, fall within these logics and need to be unraveled to move toward a process of decolonization. However, it is fair to say that Anzaldúa's work, as a whole, does acknowledge genocide and forms of settler colonial structures.

Reid Gómez knowingly asks, "what does the concept of Mestizaje do to the notion of Indian?"[135] Gómez suggests that a mestizo origin "speaks of a refusal of responsibility, to listen to, be informed and restored by land. . . . It gags the mouths of the ancestors, and the descendants of the ancestors."[136] Sandy Grande also argues for the need to move outside of western logics in her formulation of Red Pedagogy, and she engages Anzaldúa's "critical notion of mestizaje" as a "transgressive subjectivity."[137] She cautions, however, that mestizaje "both furthers and impedes indigenous imperatives of self-determination and sovereignty."[138] She later suggests that while mestizaje contains "anti-colonial aspects," Indigenous communities "require a construct that is also geographically rooted and historically placed."[139] She ultimately posits that "the transgressive mestizaje functions as a potentially homogenizing force that presumes the continued exile of tribal peoples and their enduring absorption into the American 'democratic' Whitestream."[140] Alberto is likewise critical of the "second major wave" of "Chicano indigenism" and the "feminist revisions and practices whose hallmarks were theories of mestizaje that echoed Chicano indigenisms, but with significant revisions and critiques."[141] She argues that the *indigenismo* central in Chicano indigenisms are colonial legacies "largely responsible for dismantling indigenous culture and society through its assimilationist policies throughout the Americas."[142] In Mexico, "mestizaje" needs to be similarly unraveled as it limits the way back home.

Jack Forbes, who Anzaldúa cites early on in *Borderlands*, was also critical of the logic of mestizo. He poignantly asks, "is the mestization of the Mexican-Chicano people a concrete social reality or is it primarily the European's imposition of alien descriptive categories upon the Mexican-Chicano masses?"[143] According to Bonfil Batalla, the process of forced Christianization can be conceptualized as the de-Indianization of a population.[144] A central project of the Mexican nation was to de-Indianize the people, so that Indigenous and ancestral roots, including spiritual practices, were not the center of identity formations or understandings of self. Instead, a mixed-blood or mestizo race took form that was legitimated because of its malleability within the imperial world; most importantly, for the purposes of colonial strategy, it eliminated the "Indian." As Indigenous scholar Renya Ramirez argues, "the dominant discourse says that Indian identity must remain silent and hidden" and "in both Mexico and the United States, the Indian is supposed to disappear."[145] Ramirez further argues that "if a criterion utilized in the United States to determine Indian identity were employed in Mexico, almost ninety percent of Mexican population has enough Indian blood to be considered Indigenous, if Mexicans knew their tribal ancestry. These figures demonstrate how the Mexican Nationalist narrative [of] mestizaje has decreased the power of the numerically strong Indian population in Mexico."[146] This knowledge of ancestry is particularly significant in that, as Ramirez notes, "if mestizos in Mexico decided to identify as Indians, it could transform the political and ethnic composition in Mexico dramatically."[147]

De-Indianization is a state project that encourages people towards a mestizo way of being that in some ways relies on traditional practices, but it simultaneously erases the ancestral languages, clothes, and relationships with the land, la tierra, sacred tlalli that teach philosophies of interconnectedness. As Bonfil Batalla states,

> De-Indianization is a historical process through which populations that originally possessed a particular and distinctive identity, based upon their own culture, are forced to renounce that identity, with all the consequent changes in their social organization and culture. De-Indianization is not the result of biological mixture, but of the pressure of ethnocide that ultimately blocks the historical continuity of a people as a culturally differentiated group. Many cultural traits may continue to be present in a de-Indianized collectivity. In fact, if one looks in detail at the cultural repertoire, the way of life, of a traditional agricultural mestizo community and compares it with what happens in an Indian community, it is easy to see that the similarities are greater than the differences. Similiarities are obvious in housing, foodways, *milpa* agriculture, medical practices, and many other aspects of social life. Even in language one can find the mark of the Indian past, since the local Spanish of a "mestizo" community frequently includes a great number of words from the original Mesoamerican language.[148]

This is definitely true of Indigenous Náhuatl words found within the colonial Spanish language.

Bonfil Batalla further argues for the recognition of the Mesoamerican civilization, the Indigenous peoples of Mexico that have survived over five hundred years of colonial domination. He discusses the sense of "schizophrenia" within Mexican society, the sense of being caught between two distinct cultures that he characterizes as *México profundo*, or the Indigenous and Western civilization, which entered through conquest.[149] Bonfil Batalla follows Ramirez's critique of mestizo in suggesting that "mestizaje" erases the Indian, disrupts the Indigenous ancestry of a people, and shifts the relation to the land. He offers a revised "reflection" on the practice of reading history, one that "help[s] us to better understand how we came to be where we are today," and one that traces ancestry, instead of conforming to the nation-centered politics of Mexico.[150] The reading practice that Bonfil Batalla proposes remembers the Indigenous, and particularly the ancestral practices and existences of what he continuously refers to as *México profundo*, literally translated as a "profound Mexico." I understand his formulation to mean the ancestral heart or roots of Mexico. As Bonfil Batalla states, "the viewpoint of the colonizer ignored the profound ancestral perspective of the Indian who saw and understood this land, in the same way that it ignored the Indian's experience and memory."[151]

Decolonizing Xicana/x Studies

Chicanos are a people in diaspora. The current historical memory in Chicana/o/x studies does not fully reflect a decolonized search for ancestries, ceremonies, or ways of harmonizing, and it leaves very little room for the possibility of queer ancestors. The critical discussions of "half and half," "two-spirit," "muxes" and critiques the berdache, as named by anthologists, opens historical space for further exploration. Through an interrogation of the formation of Aztlán in the U.S. Southwest, a reimagination of ancestry, and a discussion of the Treaty of Guadalupe Hidalgo of 1848 and its complex creation of the U.S.-Mexican borderlands, I argue that seemingly distinct moments in history must be thought together in order to map complicated layers of interconnected violence and possibility. The purpose has been to propose a transformation of the central tenets and historiography of Chicana/o studies that allows for the existence of a queer history of ancestors.

Archeology has not been fully considered in Chicana/o or Xicano/a history for purposes of tracing nondominant narratives.[152] Physical artifacts or ancient structures, as well as amoxtli (codices) and the study of the Náhuatl language tell stories of sacred lands that held space for exchange and ceremony. While stories of ancient structures have been imagined, the question that consistently needs to be asked is by whom and through what lens? How do we learn a different history when we enter with a queer Xicana/x Indígena decolonized vision?

This chapter is an intervention in the historical context of Chicano studies, which, since its emergence in the late 1960s, like the Chicano movement, has been a contested site of knowledge. Chicana feminists, and queer Latinx more generally, have challenged this field of study for its sexist and homophobic tenets that typically desexualize race and prioritize nation. This chapter extends these critiques by asking questions of land, ancestry, and the historical formation and racialization of the Mexican American. When the settler border was constructed through the western concept of nation-states, in particular for Indigenous communities who migrated, traded, and traveled, it set up a separation from practices of connection with the land, themselves, and other Indigenous relatives. The capitalist colonization of the land, including forced removals and detachments of spirit, is an ungrounded way of living that is contested and complicated in the next chapter.

Estela Román, a philosopher who was my first maestra de los aires (teacher of the winds), including susto and medicine for the soul, would emphasize giving *ofrendas* (offerings) to the earth and land we were currently residing on, sitting on, or praying with. She wanted us to remember that we are visitors and have no right to own la *tierra sagrada*, tlalli, sacred land. In fact, we are her children. These seeds of consciousness shape my understandings of forced migration, colonization, and settler colonialism. These enseñanzas assist tremendously in sharpening the *herramientas*, tools, to heal from the traumas of de-Indigenization that have caused disconnection for generations of Xicana/x peoples.

CHAPTER 2

ENSEÑANZAS CON LA MAESTRA GLORIA, IN CEREMONY WITH ANZALDÚA

Altars, Archives, and Aligning with the Cosmic Borderlands

To be healed we must be dismembered, pulled apart.
—Gloria Anzaldúa, *Borderlands/La Frontera*

This chapter intentionally bridges intellectual academic work with spirit work to deepen understandings of Anzaldúa's contribution to conocimiento or cosmic consciousness and to build on the framework of decolonization. In order to do the work of healing from intergenerational traumas of susto (soul loss) that have been internalized over generations due to colonial state logics of racism and projects of de-Indigenization, a focus on creating spaces of ceremony are necessary. The image of the altar in this chapter honors the four directions, four sacred elements, and remembers that the original peoples on the land it was created on, namely the Patwin people (fig. 1). As the facilitator of the "Self Limpia Workshop" organized for Sexual Assault Awareness Month on the University of California, Davis campus, I asked the students who participated to sit around the altar with me as we had a plática (talking circle) before we did the work of cleansing body-mind-spirit with herbs and sacred smoke. As a maestra, Anzaldúa guides through her teachings when I offer spirit work. In particular, as a queer detribalized Xicana Indígena, I learned early on that my deep silence and inability to feel my own worth came from a long line of sexual violence and domestic violence in both my maternal and paternal lineages. Therefore, to remedy the colonial, is not only to engage the wounds that have been caused by legal systems, nation-states, and the impositions of borders. Instead to move

Figure 1. Community altar honoring four directions for "Self Limpia Workshop" organized for sexual assault awareness month, held at the University of California, Davis (Patwin Land), April 11, 2016. Workshop led and altar raised by author. Altar is highly influenced by Anzaldúa. Photo by author.

toward decolonization, it is important to see the interconnected heteropatriarchal violence and harm that has impacted our bodies, land, and spirits from surviving as peoples who have been disconnected from our sacredness.

Anzaldúa, a decolonial feminist of color scholar, opened a pathway for Chicana/o, Xicana/o, and Xicanx peoples to remember Indigenous identity formations and spirit-centered practices including curanderismo. I consider Anzaldúa's visionary work in her classic text, *Borderlands/La Frontera*, and her posthumously published *Light in the Dark/Luz en lo Oscuro* as central parts of Anzaldúa's archive of the cosmic borderlands.[1] To root this analysis, I meditate with Anzaldúa's sacred altars and archives to argue that the ancestral knowledge of creating altars is foundational to Anzaldúa's visionary work as a methodological pathway to remembering.[2] As part of my spirit research, I've set intentions to unravel and shed light on the influence of Anzaldúa's writings and sacred works on traces of ancestry, ceremony, and spirit work across generations of Xicana Latinx Indígena scholars, writers, and artists that have succeeded her through their own tracings and feminist rethinkings of ancient energies or ancestors.

There is a deep connection and sacred relation between Anzaldúa and Coyolxauhqui as a matriarchal ancestor of decolonization. Anzaldúa gives attention to Coyolxauhqui in *Borderlands*, so much that in the introduction to the third edition, Clair Joysmith names Anzaldúa a "Coyolxauhqui visionary."[3] This ancestor of decolonization and guiding force is also present in her *Light/Luz*, which at its core positions the wisdom Anzaldúa gained walking with Coyolxauhqui as central to her work. Anzaldúa evokes Coyolxauhqui and works with her energy, as well as enseñanzas of fragmentation and wholeness, in every essay of her book.[4] In the final essay of *Light/Luz*, Anzaldúa tells the story of her encounter with the ancient Coyolxauhqui stone at Templo Mayor in Tenochtitlán. This moment echoes cosmically coming home for many detribalized, re-Indigenizing, Xicana/x Indigenous peoples, among others, like Mexica descendants themselves: "In 1992 you first saw the huge round stone of the dismembered moon goddess Coyolxauhqui in Mexico City. She's lived in your imaginal life since then, and this arrebato embeds her and her story deeper in your flesh. . . . . Coyolxauhqui is your symbol for both the process of emotional psychical dismemberment, splitting body/mind/spirit/soul, and the creative work of putting all the pieces together in a new form, a partially unconscious work done in the night by the light of the moon, a labor of revisioning and re-membering."[5] Through an Anzaldúan framework, I uplift the possibility of Coyolxauhqui as a matriarchal ancestor of decolonization. In conjunction with Anzaldúa's "re-membering," I conceptualize this sacred energy as an ancestor of decolonization and as the praxis at the heart of this chapter, which spends time unraveling Anzaldúa's curandera knowledge. These designations of Coyolxauhqui and Anzaldúa are in alignment con la Gloria's writing, and are in alignment with my own queer Xicana Indígena root work, which requires me to experience "archival research," including my viewing of Anzaldúa's altar collection, as ceremony and a queer decolonial archive.

I aim to respect the many understandings, teachings, and methods of healing connected with Coyolxauhqui, as she is revered by many and in a multiplicity of ways.[6] I meditate primarily with the formulations of Anzaldúa as a wisdom seeker, cosmic curandera, philosopher, and elder who traced, found, and remembered herself through grandmother moon's existence and guidance. A main thread in Anzaldúa's undertaking is the constant association of Coyolxauhqui with sanación (healing), as a healer of colonization. Hartley names Anzaldúa as the "curandera of conquest."[7] I build from his notion of Anzaldúa as a *sanadora* and posit Coyolxauhqui as a major ancestral guide for Anzaldúa's cosmic vision in order to disrupt forms of patriarchy, including war and colonial violence before and after 1848. This grounded articulation has an intentional focus on healing the wholeness of the divine Self, re-rooting and reimagining nondominant dualities of feminine/masculine energies, nonbinary, gender nonconforming bodies, and creating a nourishing restorative pathway for alignment with all relations.

Often Coyolxauhqui's story is told where she is "murdered and dismembered by her brother Huitzilopotchli and banished into the darkness to become the moon."[8] Anzaldúa says, "Nuestra tarea [our task] is to envision Coyolxauhqui, not dead and decapitated, but with eyes wide open."[9] Early queer Chicana feminist writings guided a pathway to connect with Grandmother Moon, and to revere her as a matriarch; they gave permission to uphold the feminine as powerful and worthy. It is significant, in this contemporary moment, to shift out of or at minimum to complicate the dominant violent narrative told about the relation between Coalticue, Coyolxauhqui, and Huitzilopotchli to see the deeper enseñanzas of these ancestors connected to deeper philosophies. Scholars have planted seeds to reimagine these narratives through a decolonial lens, and these stories are held in images and songs. Given Emma Pérez's urgings of the necessity to unravel the "colonial mind-set" that exists through "normative language, race, culture, gender, class, and sexuality," it is important here to detach from the stories that do not resonate with our spirits. As we construct "decolonial history," Pérez reminds us that as soon as we begin to conceptualize categories and narratives, we are already leaving something out, leaving something unsaid: there are "silences and gaps that must be uncovered." Pérez asks "how . . . we contest the past to revise it in a manner that tells more of our stories."[10] One significant way is to reimagine the narratives we have been told about our peoples—doing the root work to complicate the layers of unearthed knowledge to consciously shift the narrative.

In the spirit of this decolonizing tradition, Coyolxauhqui continues to receive our prayers and guide nepantlera ways.[11] In this vein of thought, Luna and Galeana offer a productive intervention from an Indigenous partera (midwife) perspective. They see Coyolxauhqui's "story and representation as the moon" as part of a "metaphor for her role and relationship to birth and human reproductive life cycles."[12] Galeana writes that "this work revises the image of Coyolxauhqui by correlating it to the earth-moon-sun system, to women's menstrual cycle, and to the various phases of labor and delivery."[13] Building on decolonial scholars, and illuminating the limitations of western research methods and ideologies that cannot see the complexity of Indigenous knowledges, she argues that "the dehumanization of indigenous scientific theories originates from the fact that indigenous ideologies and cultural ideologies respect all forms of energies and life on earth," which is quite distinct from a colonial mode.[14] She is speaking here to a philosophy of interconnected sacredness—*In tloque nahauque*, where all is interrelated, including spirit, body, the Earth, the cosmos, and ancestral wisdom.[15] Galeana establishes Coyolxauhqui "as an example of a petroglyph technique that Indigenous societies used as a form of scientific writing."[16] Specifically, this work suggests that Coyolxauhqui's text facilitated the teaching of "anatomy and physiology of the female reproductive system."[17] Building on Anzures, she refers to Coyolxauhqui as the "cosmic grandmother," who has given birth before, as evidenced by the positioning of her four limbs, her "sacred center," and the shape of her breasts.[18]

Luna and Galeana build collaboratively on this argument about Coyolxauhqui as a birthing text or image, encouraging the reader to see her circular stone as a "living document" or "book of wisdom."[19] They put into perspective how Coyolxauhqui's 1978 excavation "led to the unearthing of an entire city, now known as el Templo Mayor, in the heart of Mexico-Tenochtitlan." They argue that her "emergence and revelation unearth[ed] a sacred, ceremonial center" as well as "gave birth to an entire re-imagining/re-imaging of Xicana feminist ideas and icons."[20] Critiquing early Xicana feminists, and rejecting anthropological readings, Luna and Galeana focus on Coyolxauhqui "as a diagram or guide for understanding life-giving force of women."[21] Through a "partera/midwifery lens," they draw out the significance of Coyolxauhqui being "in a danza position of reverence, looking upwards toward the universe," which is particularly significant for childbirth.[22] They suggest that "Coyolxauhqui and her story serve as a metaphor; the moon is whole and then eventually fragments into pieces. Her fragments or phases represent movement, the passage of time, and the regeneration of energy. Her body is not broken, but rather separated."[23] The wisdom of an Indigenous partera/midwife requires a deep knowledge of the ceremony and cycles of life and death, and being in tune with Coyolxauhqui and her purposes and phases. Luna and Galeana connect Coyolxauhqui to "women's menstrual cycles" and to the way the "bleeding cycle is governed by the movements of the Cosmic Mother Moon," explaining that the way "uterine blood lining dismembers itself and sheds" serves as evidence that dismemberment "is not violent, but ceremonial; it is more of a releasing," a cleansing.[24]

The knowledge and ceremonial opening generated by the 1978 reappearance and subsequent remembering of Coyolxauhqui by several generations provides the deep wisdom of a sacred alignment. This view of ceremony with Coyolxauhqui shifts the usual narrative of violence and dismemberment to "represent 're-integration' and the union of all cardinal directions and the cycles and rhythm of life."[25] In this context, women and people with wombs who bleed in a cyclical formation are intrinsically connected to the constant stages of transformation of this feminine ancestor of decolonization, and have the potential to birth life and cocreate in multiple forms, with their whole being. This analysis is presented in a similar formulation in In Lak Ech's "Coyolxauhqui Song," a prayer through drum, song, and danza, composed by Cristina Gorocica.[26] This "all-Xicana performance poetry group" honors Coyolxauhqui's spirit by making a connection to her being a cis-gender woman/ancestor who bleeds, gives life, and loves. The first verse, which is collectively sung to a singular traditional hand drum beat, sets up a transformation:

Coyolxauhqui,
tú eres mujer
en la Luna está tu imagen,
tú eres fuerte,
sangramos, damos vida,
damos leche y amor,
tú espíritu está conmigo,
soy fuerte, mujer.

Coyolxauhqui
You are woman,
within the Moon is your image,
you are strong,
we bleed, give life, give milk and love,
your spirit is with me,
I'm strong, woman."[27]

In the second half of this sacred song, we feel that transformation through a danza drum beat:

Coyo, Coyolxauhqui,
Coyo Coyolxauhqui,
danzante de noche,
brillando al cielo,
mandas energia,
para la vida.

Coyo, Coyolxauhqui,
Coyo Coyolxauhqui,
Dancer of the night,
shinning in the sky.
sending energy,
for life.[28]

In Lak Ech illuminates Coyolxauhqui as a danzante, a life-giving energy and spirit guide to connect and heal in ceremony. Luna and Galeana write that the "cascabeles/bells on her face and wrists rattle and make music as she dances through space." They point to her "ayoyotes used in Danza Mexica," her "dancer's *copilli* or headdress" to "confirm that Coyolxauhqui is indeed dancing" and depicting "poetry. . . . She emerges from the silence of the night with power and strength."[29]

Efforts to make visible representations of Coyolxauhqui's story by early Xicana feminist scholars opened a pathway for Indigenous midwives, Indígena artists, Xicanx feminists, and others to collectively and continually insist on a revision of this Mesoamerican ancestor in present-day praxis of Nahua cosmology. It is significant to find a cosmic reflection of a "fuerte" matriarch, a mother, abuela, grandmother, "Xicanawarrior,"[30] "Hija Rebelde" (Rebel Daughter),[31] neplantera mujer. This spirit work with Coyolxauhqui has been conscious and critical, necessarily complicating dominant narratives from fields including religious studies, anthropology, and archaeology. The readings of Coyolxauhqui discussed earlier offer Indígena feminist grounding, or ancestral narratives that offer connection across time and space. This is the way in which she appears in Anzaldúa's stories of her own writing journey. Anzaldúa breathes life into Coyolxauhqui through her interdimensional writing, which has supported the building of language and understanding. In her "Let Us Be the Healing of the Wound: the Coyolxauhqui Imperative—La sombra y el sueño," Anzaldúa shares her prayer for connection and for wisdom: "I stare up at the moon, Coyolxauhqui, and its light in the darkness. I seek a healing image, one that re-connects me to others. I seek the positive shadow that I've also inherited."[32] Anzaldúa's work signals a decolonial Xicana feminist reading of sacred Coyolxauhqui and the traditional Indigenous medicine of curanderismo, one in which dreams, images, feelings, and cosmic connections are experienced, seen, and manifested in transformative moments. As acts of remembering ancestors of decolonization, these moments give permission and open the pathway to be connected to ancestors in ceremony and prayer for the healing of Self, community, elders, future generations, and the Earth.

Spirit Research: Enseñanzas with Anzaldúa's Curandera Knowledge

> During my childhood, curanderismo and hechicerismo were an accepted yet disdained part of the Chicano community. Most Mexican Americans, having swallowed the whites' contempt for indigenous medicine, did not believe that curanderas could restore the soul and heal the body.
>
> —Gloria Anzaldúa, *Light in the Dark*

For Xicana/x Indigenous de-tribalized people the colonial seed of fear or susto is the uprooting of their connection to a healing path, ancestral wisdom, and balanced relations. Therefore, the struggle for traditional spirit formations, ceremonial knowledge ways, and Indigenous medicinal practices is a praxis of decolonization. It is the "accepted yet disdained" tension referred to in the above quote, that Anzaldúa perceived and articulated as traditional wisdom ways that are significant for la sanadora to observe, analyze, and shift. She internalizes the spirit battle—the existence, faith, and belief in the continual practice of curanderismo, next to nation-state colonial ideologies that aim to erase Indigeneity and uproot traditional medicinal practices connected to the land, including sacred food ways that honor the Earth. As Hartley argues, "Anzaldúa's decolonial project is in fact a form of curanderismo . . . she consciously applies the concepts and practices of the curandera to the social ills of colonialism that she hopes to heal."[33]

It is my aim to critically flesh out productive dialogues, enseñanzas (teachings), and illuminate practices within Anzaldúa's writings—her curandera offerings—that have birthed tensions, created methodologies, and guided pathways on a cosmically aligned level or spirit dimension that lead to healing and transformation. Emma Pérez (2005) assesses these theorizations of *Borderlands/La Frontera*: "Anzaldúa forged a new territory, a new intellectual locale, a new spiritual space, a new psychic and psychological terrain. She created fresh symbols, metaphors, and taxonomies to describe a material world where poverty, racism, homophobia are real problems and where a psychic, sacred inner world is as real as the material, tangible world. For her there were no boundaries. She leapt across borders between the real and imaginary because she knew that one could inhabit both at once."[34] Focusing in on the "spiritual space" she created, and emphasizing the "sacred inner world" and the inhabiting of multiple dimensions, is key to the analysis here. It is the cosmic borderlands, Anzaldúa's spirit work and "spiritual activism," as Keating discusses, that up until very recently were underexplored or under-analyzed in scholarly writing about Anzaldúa's work.[35] Keating details that in academic analysis of Anzaldúa's contributions to feminism and theorizations in *Borderlands/La Frontera*, "all too often . . . scholars avoid Anzaldúa's politics of spirit . . . they rarely examine the important roles Anzaldúa's spiritual activism plays in developing these theories and many others."[36] Poignantly, Keating faults western-centered forms of academic training that "rely almost exclusively on rational thought, anti-spiritual forms of logical reasoning, and empirical demonstrations"[37] for this lack of engagement. The silencing and attempted erasure of traditional Indigenous medicine and sacred Earth-centered wisdom ways uphold dominant forms of knowledge that need to be disrupted.

Anzaldúa's writing shifts the intellectual spirit terrain with her humble migrant working-class background that gives permission and allows her to recognize, see, speak, and work with other worldly ways with respect and honor.[38] Her "creativity as spirit work," along with other queer women of color feminists in *This Bridge Called My Back* and more intentionally with her altars as guides in *Borderlands/La Frontera* and beyond, allows us to move into the vision our ancestors had for us in the prayers they planted. Anzaldúa's curandera knowledge is rooted in the sabiduría of Indigenous grandmothers and ancestral traditions that intentionally work with matriarchal wisdom to find sacred balance, starting with embracing knowledge systems that arise from deep feelings and emotions. I emphasize the feminine, the matriarch, and womxn, yet our grandmothers/grandfathers, abuelitxs, elders are also two-spirit, transgender, queer, or in Anzaldúa's words "half and half," "mita y mita," so this sabiduría is inclusive of those who walk in balance, within, across and beyond the spectrums of femininities and masculinities, listening and in tune with their internal guidance.[39] In a 2001 interview with Irene Lara, titled "Daughter of Coatlicue," Anzaldúa says that she believes she acquired diabetes from the "exhaustion" of people often rejecting her contributions to incorporate a critical analysis of spirituality.[40] As Anzaldúa recounts, "the first conference where I really got panned for my spirituality was in '81—at the National Women's Studies Conference . . . when *Bridge* came out . . . about five or six of us were on stage telling people the situation with women of color and what changes we need. And here I go and speak about spirituality; everybody on stage and in the audience was horrified. Ever since then, I'd push at that issue."[41] It is from within a raw space of grief and gratitude that I do my spirit research trabajo (work), acknowledging that Anzaldúa spent her lifetime illuminating theories and opening pathways for decolonial knowledges that are based on "*bodymindspirit* balance needed to resist, survive, and transform," not just in her lifetimes but with a vision of transformation and wellness for future generations.[42]

The imprint of Anzaldúa's deep commitment to spirit work in her lifetime is reflected in the publication of *Fleshing the Spirit*, which is the "first anthology to entirely focus on Chicana, Latina, and Indigenous women's spiritualities."[43] Significantly, the editors and authors alike build with Anzaldúa's "spiritual activism" throughout their articulations.[44] As the editors state, "the essays are grounded in critical feminist thought with an emphasis on Anzalduan theory and methodology."[45] Notably, as a spirit work text, *Fleshing the Spirit* is organized thematically honoring the four directions—East, West, North, South—"drawing largely from the Mexica tradition."[46] Signaling to the collective intergenerational prayer, the editors share that it intentionally reflects Anzaldúa's "Now Let Us Shift," as it ends with a "ritual . . . prayer . . . blessing . . . for transformation" that honors the four directions as well as *el centro* (the center), underworld, and sky.[47] The honoring of the four directions are not identical in the two texts, yet both hold the invocation to intentionally initiate a ceremony through interdimensional space that reflects and builds with enseñanzas from elders. The respect of honoring the prayer of the four directions as part of the written text does the work to create spiritual connection with the reader, an openness that sets these texts apart, especially if read as a ceremony. *Fleshing the Spirit* provides a pathway filled with story, *testimonio*, ceremony, faith, and prayers, for present and future generations, of distinct walks of life, who are working to live a decolonized re-Indigenized spirit path. Arguably, this was a central goal of Anzaldúa's creative and theoretical work—to open up pathways of connection with spirit, ancestors, and the cosmos for all generations of displaced peoples.

This creativity of spirit took remarkable form in Anzaldúa's children's books as well. Hartley illuminates her curandera knowledge in a provocative read of her bilingual children's book, *Prietita and the Ghost Woman/Prietita y la Llorona*. He argues that "Anzaldúa shows in this *cuento* (story) that the turn to curanderismo itself is a decolonizing act, *and* that decolonization, by healing the wounds of conquest, is a form of curanderismo."[48] By discussing important elements of the tradition of curanderismo, illnesses/imbalances of the soul, and remedies/ceremonies such as limpias to cleanse and decolonize, he reflects Anzaldúa's sabiduría of this healing tradition that she explores in the narrative.[49] Hartley says that "the story thus becomes an illustration of the educating function of the curandera, of the necessary transmission of sacred knowledge from one generation to the next if there is to be health and cultural survival."[50] Indeed, in Anzaldúa's storyline, the known presence and trust of a curandera in Prietita's neighborhood that can offer remedies to cure her mom is an ancestral praxis that requires a remembering of sacred teachings and wisdom of plant life and old illnesses. Through the main character, Prietita is being sent into the woods, where "they shoot trespassers,"[51] by the curandera Doña Lola, to find the needed "planta curativa" (healing plant). Prietita builds courage on her journey while communicating with animals, the water, nature, the moon, and eventually, la Llorona, who guides her to the rue.[52] The story demonstrates a powerful journey of transformation for this young girl.[53] Working through her fears, with prayer and determination in her heart to contribute to her mother's healing, Prietita is given a "crucial experience that teaches her that her own development as a curandera requires fearless confrontation with colonialist violence."[54] This realization is a significant enseñanza in the praxis of decolonization.

Anzaldúa's intergenerational sanadora narrative articulates the importance of being in alignment with the sacred energies and elements around you, to be able to feel protected enough to trust in the journey, even when the path does not appear clearly before you.[55] Anzaldúa shows the reader that a central part of the curandera's spirit work, at any age, is listening with your heart, disrupting dominant narratives that fail to resonate with your experience, and finding the wisdom and sanación that Tonanztin Tlalli Coalticue (the Earth) offers. In conceptualizing the significance and praxis of Anzaldúa's curandera knowledge, Lara writes that "The bruja-curandera 'spiritual activist' is in the process of embodying and living this spiritual conocimiento, re-membering and creating powerful knowledges for personal and community healing."[56] Anzaldúa's *Prietita and the Ghost Woman* guides us through an intergenerational remembering of our connection with the Earth, and with the medicinal properties of plant life. At the beginning of the story, Prietita works the land in Doña Lola's garden, and the story concludes with this young girl placing a cutting of the rue (*ruda*) plant into the hands of the curandera. This powerful gesture full of courage and spirit wisdom signals to the ceremony one is living while experiencing life's joys, difficulties, and enseñanzas. As Castillo knowingly writes, "When we become knowledgeable about plants, we see proof that the traditional medicine of our ancestors indeed was curative. This knowledge . . . was taken from us . . . and is still kept from most of us who are integrated in Western society, replaced by synthetic treatments for illnesses through drugs and Western medical practices. My point here is not to make a blanket condemnation of modern medicine and medical technology, but to recognize that its basis lies in very ancient practices which are not necessarily inaccessible to us."[57] Is it with these insights of curandera knowledge that I continue to unravel Anzaldúa's offerings with a focus on her creativity as spirit work and enseñanzas with altars, an ancient practice that generations later, people of Mesoamerican/Anahuacan and Indigenous lineages continue to keep alive alongside other Indigenous Mexican traditions.

Spirit Work with Anzaldúa's Altares

The altar is a methodological pathway to remembering what was central to Anzaldúa's curandera knowledge. Here I consider the curandera spirit practice of building, creating, and raising altars as a method of setting intentions for transformation, connecting with self and the cosmos, and most importantly, being in community with all relations through intentional prayer. In particular, I trace Anzaldúa's spiritual trabajo with *altares* (altars) as a site of visual narratives/blessings de sanación (healing) and knowledge formation that were in direct dialogue with her writing. I build my argument primarily through a critical engagement with Anzaldúa's *Borderlands/La Frontera* and her 1982 unpublished essay, "On the Process of Feminist Image Making," as well as my reflections from visiting with her altares collection on Ohlone land.[58] Anzaldúa wrote in "Border Arte: Nepantla, *el Lugar de la Frontera*" that "the altars I make are not just representations of myself; they are representations of Chicana culture."[59] In many occurrences and some traditions, including the Mexicayotl tradition from which I write, prayers start with the praxis of creating a home, family, or community altar that is envisioned as the space and place to hold the sacred items for ceremony: it can include herramientas (tools), methodologies, and energies, usually with a tangible representation of the four sacred elements of air, water, land, and fire and set up in alignment with the four cardinal directions. For some, such as detribalized Xicanx Indigenous peoples, the altar can hold space for the shame, grief, *tristeza* (sadness), *vergüenza* (shame, imposed and internalized) of not knowing one's tribe, lineage, family members, traditions, foodways, language, yet simultaneously facilitate connection by creating a space for remembering and honoring through prayer, meditation, and intention. Important decolonial moments are, for example, learning origin stories, with guidance from elders and ancestors, that defy heteropatriarchal, colonial narratives and breathe forms of spirit and creation. I meditate with Anzaldúa's altares because this sacred practice is how I found my way home. The spiritual trabajo Anzaldúa did not all pertain to the Mexicayotl tradition or to Mexico, similar to the writing in *Fleshing the Spirit*, there are strong connections to Eastern spiritual traditions such as Buddhism, African diasporic spirit traditions such as Yoruba, and other influences from Indigenous peoples of the hemisphere are present in the raising of her altars. At some moments, Anzaldúa referred to this as "spiritual mestizaje," yet what I work to unravel here is her sense of self rooted in her own ancestors, and then resonance through awareness and respect of other cultural and spiritual practices with the vision of seeing commonalities to build and grow.[60] I trace her spirit work with her grandmother.

In her life trajectory, Anzaldúa was an ever-evolving philosopher and spirit-centered teacher, writer, and curandera, traveler, visionary artist. She wrote of the heart of her spirit work: "For many years what kept my spiritual flame lit was the memory of the picture of *la Virgencita de Guadalupe*, a Mexican manifestation of the Virgin Mary, that Mamagrande Ramona kept on her dresser-top altar alongside *las velas*, the votive candles, and snapshots of family members, *muertos y vivos*, the dead and the living. That memory led me to *el hecho de altares* (the making of altars), curanderismo (healing), *nagualismo* (shamanism), and other indigenous Mexican traditions."[61] Anzaldúa's remembering and storytelling is rooted in a visual memory of an altar that belonged to "her grandmother," Mamagrande Ramona.[62] Considering her classic text *Borderlands/La Frontera* and her subsequent writing, this memory gives space to conceptualize the roots of her curandera knowledge as part of "Indigenous Mexican traditions" or what Patrisia Gonzales names "Mexican traditional medicine (MTM)" or "traditional Indigenous medicine."[63]

Reti's book of photography, *House of Nepantla: Living with Gloria Anzaldúa*, shows bright, life-honoring reproduced images of Anzaldúa's living room altar, her computer altar, and her refrigerator altar, among others—the visuality and presence of sacred altars were an important part of Anzaldúa's daily life.[64] In "On the Process of Feminist Image Making," Anzaldúa articulates how altars were the sites of her prayers and of building connections, of thinking of writing as ceremony: "I use an altar as a source of inspiration and visualization."[65] Anzaldúa details that she did "most everything in sight of an altar" since she had altars in every room of her house, even the bathroom.[66] Her home in Santa Cruz, California, near the ocean, was a sacred sanctuary that held space for her creativity, vision, and journeying as a writer, artist, and curandera. Anzaldúa wrote: "On my bedroom wall I have a picture of my Nagual, a were-wolf-owl animal and a picture of Tlazoteotl, Coatlicue, and Xochitlquetzal. On the altar I have a woman's Eskimo knife called the ule, curved blade like the moon bound in leather string, a statue of an Earth goddess, vase with red roses, shell, rock, feathers, an Ojibwe drum to summon the spirits, my serpent staff, a crocheted bag filled with herbs and whatever object I'm trying to charge."[67] Her vision for transformation is reflected in what she held sacred, which included Mesoamerican sacred energies, natural earth materials, and Indigenous creations, some from distinct lineages, all that she honored, respected, and felt connected to.

My spirit research took flight when in 2010 I began to sit with Anzaldúa's sacred items, a collection of items from her home that belonged to her in the realm of the material world. In 2004, at the end of my first year as a graduate student at the University of California, Santa Cruz, I had my first and only chance to sit down con la Reina *y gran autora*—the vision of this meeting at Lulu Carpenter's Coffee Shop is still very clear in my third eye. At that moment, three weeks before she transitioned, I did not fully realize she was becoming my spirit maestra of curanderismo, as she is for so many. In sitting with her altares collection, I had a sense of entering into another world and of finding a path of knowledge that was grounded in the view of the world through a creative and visual lens. It was powerful and heartbreaking at once.[68] Being in ceremony by visually experiencing her altars and elements of Gloria Anzaldúa's spirit work, a maestra of Chicanx, queer, and feminist studies, philosopher of social theory, and key to Xicana Indigenous formations became a direct site of connection with her powerful Indígena Earth-centered vision.[69] Through pláticas that offered guidance with Irene Reti, oral historian, mentor, and Anzaldúa's writing *comadre* (companion), I started to rely on deep listening as a methodology of connecting with the sacred as part of my research. I had found this path to prayer earlier in life, and as a spirit-centered woman of color who needed grounding and re-rooting. The challenge I encountered for my research was allowing my heart-mind connection, in prayer, to lead my intellectual work, to give a conscious space for the role of the sacred in knowledge making. Previously, I had spent time with Anzaldúa through my reading and analysis of her writing, and I felt so many times that she was speaking to me directly even though it was clear she was writing to a larger collective of people, and at times very directly to queer women of color and/or Xicana/x people. I am intentionally naming the methodology "spirit research," which signals a complex form of communication with sacred energies that guide and communicate in modes that involve otherworldly ways. The practice of spirit research is different for everyone. For me, it often takes the form of ritual, sitting with a humble altar and offering sacred smoke with a *sahumadora* (clay vessel) and copal to open an intentional dialogue in the form of prayer, expression through words, song, movement, or simply listening with my heart. Often, I meditate on questions or set an intention beforehand; it is a continuous process and communication, and once it is opened in a good way, the heart starts to listen and becomes attuned and aligned.

My spirit research focused on the Gloria Evangelina Anzaldúa Altares Collection began by asking questions of the spiritual realm—of what is not easily explained in words but is experienced through feelings of connection and intentional effort to be in internal alignment with the energies of the cosmos and the Earth. This research asked me to turn inward to find resonances and answers instead of searching only outside of me, which is what is usually suggested in disciplinary spaces that seek rational logics in the research process. In my spirit research notes and writing, I meditated with questions like: How did you pray Gloria? What words, actions, or rituals did you use to deliver your sacred messages to *el Creador/la Creadora* (the Creator) or to the universe? What was your ceremony like? Gloria, how did you learn about Coatlicue, madre Tonantzin? When did her Náhuatl name enter your consciousness? In ceremony, reading a book, a song, during a visit to Tenochtitlán? What about Coyolxauhqui? Tlazoteotl? What was your dreamtime like? Did you travel frequently? Where did you acquire your copal? How did you learn to honor the four directions? What did Yemayá mean to you? These are not the usual questions a researcher ponders. However, after years of working to understand the potential of Anzaldúa's work, I realized that the strength, and perhaps the roots (heart) of her work, came from the intangible, what remained unseen by the reader, yet presented itself through phrases and images in her writing of sacred items reflected in her altars. Anzaldúa's literary, philosophical, and artistic work was a result of her meditative practice to build infinite connections with the universe through a body-mind-spirit alignment. She wrote that "when I'm writing I try to stay in a meditative state, a trance, that is, to stay in the 'other' world. . . . To be in a meditative state is to be "in touch" with higher self, my conscious self and my unconscious self."[70]

When I sat with the holdings of Anzaldúa's altares collection, which at that time consisted of thirteen full boxes, I immediately started to see evidence of her tracing of Mesoamerican peoples and Indigenous traditions, including Mayan and Mexica/Aztec figures, such as Coatlicue, in bright and bold turquoise green shades. I saw Anzaldúa's deep connections with sacred animals, *nahuales*, and spirit guides, including snakes, hummingbirds, owls, and jaguars.[71] There were medicine bags with copal, clear crystals of different shapes, rattles, masks, and fossils—sacred items that she used as part of her ceremony. Her connection to Yemayá (all-encompassing mother and ocean spirit) was also present through abalone shells and an iridescent sea otter.[72] I learned that some of her sacred items were gifts to her from various friends, and that the natural, Earth-based materials that were a part of her altares (like flowers, leaves, feathers, sage-and-cedar prayer sticks) could not be preserved in the library holdings due to the risks of infestation.[73]

It was in these instances of sitting with Anzaldúa's sacred items that I was able to connect her writing with visual images of her concepts and practices in relation to curandera knowledge. It was a clarifying moment of Anzaldúa's own practices of trabajo de limpeza (cleansing/curing work) to rid herself of aires (winds) when I saw the collection of her herramientas, sacred tools.[74] Anzaldúa made herself present as a sanadora (healer) in a manifested visual form at that moment. I realized her words and theoretical concepts were not only speaking to me, and to many others intellectually, but evoking a connection with the creative force, Great Spirit through the practice of building altars and prayer/meditation. Anzaldúa wrote that "the altar is the formal site of this connection with the cosmos."[75] A vision of social healing and transformation takes form in Anzaldúa's prayer for inner knowledge that is in communication with the spirit world or her creativity as spirit work. As Laura Pérez writes, "altar installation and related art forms have inspired Chicana artists" to "be more precisely connected to the search for, and expression of, alternative spiritualities and alternative art practices, particularly those that are visionary with respect to social justice and transformation."[76] To understand the complexities and layers of Anzaldúa's intellectual and philosophical contributions, it is generative to grasp the significance she placed on knowing through art, images, symbols—the visual.

In the Anzaldúa altares collection at the University of California, Santa Cruz, is a large wooden jaguar head that is featured on the cover of *The Gloria Anzaldúa Reader*.[77] This natural-color jaguar is almost life-size, with large fangs and a compassionate facial expression. In much of Anzaldúa writing, there is a signaling to the jaguar as a sacred nahual, or guiding animal spirit. It has a price tag that reads 90,000 pesos and gives the artist's name as "Franco"; it was most likely purchased in Mexico. Several of the sacred items in Anzaldúa's collection have their original handmade tag indicating their locality, where they originated from, and on some the artist or crafter's name remains. This is significant because it shows Anzaldúa's awareness of people's geopolitical locations and the interconnections with visual art. It is clear that she saw, in her own words, "the making of images as a way of healing."[78] Grounding her intentions in the visuality and placement of sacred items, Anzaldúa wrote that "the altar is a place for making connections for carrying on a dialogue—the images speak."[79] Anzaldúa and her spiritual work with altares teaches about the ancestral wisdom held within this sacred practice, and she offers her wisdom of the home altar: "These [sacred items] are residents in your home. They need to be cleaned, dusted, they need to be fed. I feed them thoughts (occasionally I put a fruit on their table, the altar) water is always there, in the vase a cauldron filled with dirt, fire-warmth (candles). I treat them as living entities. They sleep in my bedroom."[80] Anzaldúa's ritual with the altar is based on the belief that the stones, flowers, water, and additional items on the altar are life and have a deeper representation and connection with ancestors; if we are open, they have something to teach us about ourselves, our existence, interconnectedness, and cycles of life and death. In many ways, the altar can be a way to experience ancestral teachings of the sacred elements, synchronicity, reflection, respect, intergenerational inheritance, healing, balance, and love. Anzaldúa wrote, "the altar is a source of growth."[81]

The cosmological knowledge and practices that Anzaldúa was tracing are linked to Indigenous histories and the land that is now known as Mexico.[82] Mexico is a geographical place that experienced extreme violence due to colonization by the Spanish Crown and its heirs. Anzaldúa's work to re-member and recover cultural memory is a contribution to reestablishing Indigenous forms of ceremony, and it provides a pathway for acknowledging that Indigenous traditions, ceremony, and people are resilient and have always persisted. With her spiritual practice of altar and feminist image making, Anzaldúa directly challenged the imposed Christianity that came with colonization in her spirit research and in her theorizations in *Borderlands/La Frontera*. The dominant forms of Christian religion enforced by the Spanish Crown preached that "God" or "divine spirit" was outside of human beings, animals, and other creations of nature, exterior to the body or sources of life, including water, and land. In contrast, Anzaldúa, like other Indigenous peoples, communities, writers and artists, know spirit is held within each life form. To invoke the divine or seek connection was simply a process of going inward, and in some cases, being present or mindful of one's surroundings. Anzaldúa's details her own practice: "I look for omens everywhere, everywhere catch glimpses of the patterns and cycles of my life. . . . We're not supposed to remember such otherworldly events. We're supposed to ignore, forget, kill those fleeting images of the soul's presence and of the spirit's presence. We've been taught that the spirit is outside our bodies or above our heads somewhere up in the sky with God. We're supposed to forget that every cell in our bodies, every bone and bird and worm has spirit in it."[83] Anzaldúa further writes that "institutionalized religion fears trafficking with the spirit world and stigmatizes it as witchcraft. It has strict taboos against this kind of inner knowledge."[84] It is this inner knowledge in communication with sacred items that serve as reminders or guides of that which is simple, divine, and provides a clear path to reconnection, remembering, and decolonization.

Estela Román suggests that sacred altars were increasingly built inside the home because Indigenous forms of prayer and ceremony were forbidden in the colonial public space.[85] The solidification of home altares on the land that became known as Mexico formed as a result of Spanish colonization and invasion of this hemisphere and the attempt to destroy and eradicate sacred temples and cultural practices, making it nearly impossible, and life-threatening for Indigenous peoples to live their traditions of ceremony in community.[86] Amalia Mesa-Bains writes specifically about women's use of the family altar and the home altar: "Established through pre-Hispanic continuities of spiritual belief, the family altar functions for women as a counterpoint to male-dominated rituals within Catholicism. Often located in bedrooms, the home altar presents family history and cultural belief systems . . . altars allow history, faith, and personal objects to commingle."[87] What is significant in Mesa-Bains's characterization of the altar is the way family history is incorporated next to spiritual beliefs, providing a space in the home for reflection and connection. Anzaldúa also offers knowledge about the making of home altars by grandmothers: "The making of altars is one of the oldest art forms devised and perpetuated by women. In Mexico, the tradition goes back at least to 1000 B.C. Aztec, Mixtec and Maya women used altars at home." Anzaldúa theorizes that the "tradition of making altars has been for women a means to connect to the speechless part of ourselves . . . that talks in images to express itself."[88]

Because Anzaldúa brought together disparate spirit knowledges in her work with spiritual traditions, her unboundedness or lack of rootedness to an Indigenous lineage and pathway is sometimes questioned as possibly recolonizing. My aim here is to demonstrate that the direct influence of her elder and grandmother, Mamagrande Ramona, including the memories and experiences of her relationship with the land, plants, and energies of the borderlands, and her practice of living in connection with the ancestral knowledges of Mesoamerica all led her toward a sacred path and practices that influenced her vision, writing, and perspective. Activated and remembered in her relation to her grandmother, Anzaldúa's curandera knowledge of traditional medicine was the foundation of her writing and creative expression. In many ways, Anzaldúa's visionary work opened a path—a methodological meditation grounded in spirit, intuition, and creativity—that considers the phases of the moon, planetary positions, eclipses, and sacred interconnected relation with all forms of life, including plants, herbs, animals, insects, water, and intangible or invisible forms of energy. Ancestral altar building and calling on Spirit were part of her process of remembering, of setting intentions, and of envisioning transformative writing. I drew from these heart offerings in my own spirit research, in working with archival research as ceremony—in making time and space to listen to internal guidance, the energy of the Earth in relation to the cosmos, and the presence of sacred elements, fire, water, earth, air. In this spirit research, I learned that the text *Borderlands/La Frontera* is also an altar, an ofrenda that remembers and honors the ancestors of decolonization, those that guide the process of being whole again. I now focus on *Borderlands/La Frontera* as an altar, an ofrenda.

Writing as Ceremony: *Borderlands/La Frontera* as Altar, an Offering

> Writing is the process of exteriorizing interior often vague, voiceless things. . . . That's why it's so close to alchemy and altar-making [*sic*]. Both bring unconscious materials into consciousness. Both make light. Making light (luz) is the same as making soul. Therefore, writing is a way of soul making, or spirit making.
>
> —Anzaldúa, "On the Process of Feminist Image Making"

Anzaldúa's text, *Borderlands/La Frontera*, is an altar, an offering, a site that inspires creativity as spirit work, writing as ceremony, and dialogue across dimensions of time and space. In the Mexicayotl tradition, altares create space to ask permission, and make offerings for specific prayers, as a way to communicate with "Self," the spirit world, ancestors, family members who have transitioned, and with all living relations.[89] The altar holds space for the spiritual trabajo that is needed for decolonization. In *Borderlands/La Frontera*, Anzaldúa's written altar, there are elements of curanderismo, traditional medicine, storytelling, references to la Virgen de Guadalupe, who is representative of Tonantzin Coatlicue, as well as the Mexica/Azteca, Toltec, Olmec peoples, and the tradition of Yoruba, Santería, among other notable traditions.[90] She illuminates a cross-pollination of methodologies from spirit.

For Xicana/x peoples and Chicanx studies scholars in particular, Anzaldúa offered a way of tracing and starting to map Earth-centered and decolonized forms of Mesoamerican or Anahuacan spiritual trabajo and philosophies. At the core of Anzaldúa's decolonial spirit work is her the naming of the importance of *nahualismo*, which is based in the practice shapeshifting.[91] Anzaldúa offered a method of remembering pieces of history and practices that need to be complicated further and that simultaneously compel us to do more unraveling (in particular historical excavando) of what has been forgotten or partially destroyed, colonized, including Indigenous cultures, languages, histories, and worldviews, as well as to interrogate what may have been forgotten or not completely visible in her remembering.

Anzaldúa, as a visual artist, drew, shared, and explained through images and concepts what she witnessed in her life. She created images in her writing that allow you to travel, to the visual beyond of what you think you know. *Borderlands/La Frontera* is in part a significant text because as a curandera and a writer, Anzaldúa was determined to offer *palabra* that would bring justice and transformation. Anzaldúa narrates how her altars were sites and manifestations of her prayers and visions, writing that "I make my offerings of incense and cracked corn, light my candle. In my head I sometimes will say a prayer—an affirmation and a voicing of intent. Then I run water."[92] Anzaldúa illuminates her dedication to her writing and life of prayer:

> I sit here before my computer, *Amiguita*, my altar on top of the monitor with the *Virgen de Coatlalopeuh* candle and copal incense burning. My companion, a wooden serpent staff with feathers, is to my right while I ponder the ways metaphor and symbol concretize the spirit and etherealize the body. The Writing is my whole life, it is my obsession. This vampire which is my talent does not suffer other suitors. Daily I court it, offer my neck to its teeth. This is the sacrifice that the act of creation requires, a blood sacrifice. For only through the body, through the pulling of flesh, can the human soul be transformed. And for images, words, stories to have this transformative power, they must arise from the human body—flesh and bone—and from the Earth's body—stone, sky, liquid, soil. This work, these images, piercing tongue or ear lobes with cactus needle, are my offerings, are my Aztecan blood sacrifices.[93]

In *Borderlands/La Frontera*, Anzaldúa lays out various interconnected pieces that come together in the form of seven key essays and six sections of poetry, as part of the practice and path of remembering ancestry and doing inner work to honor our flesh and bones. These thirteen total pieces ask the reader to search and dig, *excavar*, for historical, political, and spiritual roots, to understand oneself and one's relation to nation-state formations and cultural representations. There are no easy conclusions or remedies—as an altar that contains many connections and representations of visual narratives of familial, political, and ancestral tracings of history, the text is complete. I focus briefly on three short excerpts of the section "By Your True Faces We Will Know You" to illuminate the inter-dimensions of her writing.

> I am visible—see this Indian face—yet I am invisible. . . . But I exist, we exist. They'd like to think I have melted in the pot. But I haven't, we haven't.
>
> The dominant white culture is killing us slowly with its ignorance. By taking away our self-determination, it has made us weak and empty. As a people we have resisted . . . but we have never been allowed to be fully ourselves.
>
> The struggle is inner: Chicano, *indio*, American Indian, *mojado*, *mexicano*, immigrant Latino, Anglo in power, working class Anglo, Black, Asian—our psyches resemble the bordertowns and are populated by the same people. The struggle has always been inner, and is played out in the outer terrains. Awareness of our situation must come before inner changes, which in turn come before changes in society. Nothing happens in the "real" world unless it first happens in the images in our heads.[94]

Through this writing and throughout her text, Anzaldúa encourages dialogue with self in relation to the geographies, landscapes, and borders we exist within. Similarly, Anzaldúa's altares collection challenges the U.S. Southwest centered understanding of her work, especially *Borderlands/La Frontera,* since the ancestors and the sacred items that she works with point to México and larger Mesoamerica as a geographic site where Anzaldúa herself looked for traces of ancestral representations and formations of the cosmic borderlands. Through Anzaldúa's writing and the circulation of this text, she contributed greatly to opening a pathway for recovering and remembering forms of ceremony—while making space for the study of the roots of Chicanx identity formations and shaping Chicana feminisms from a queer Indígena perspective. Anzaldúa opened a path for tracing ceremonial knowledges and practices by creating narratives that challenged colonial understandings of culture, storytelling, and spirit. This is evident through her use of Náhuatl concepts and philosophies.

Anzaldúa took risks to illuminate how spirit is mysterious, and can be unknowable. Her theorizations unravel silences by putting language to that which is often forgotten and unseen, especially the Indigenous ancestry and present day Indigeneity of Chicana/o and Mesoamerican peoples, and queer spiritual consciousness. As Paola Bacchetta notes, "Gloria opens a path for rethinking existence beyond the present forced silenced of racialized, sexual violence of all sorts, through cognitive decolonization."[95] Anzaldúa's writing illuminates how she created a path of knowing through her offerings, writings, with the *enseñanzas* she acquired through her spirit work with Coyolxauhqui.

In her essay, "Putting Coyolxauhqui Together: A Creative Process," Anzaldúa writes of the complex synchronicity of being "blessed and cursed by la llamada," the call to write. "Te espanta el trabajo" (this work frightens you), she offered.[96] Calling to the artist or creator to understand that you can get susto as part of the process, she suggests that it is important to cleanse oneself as a curandera would during a limpeza while inhabiting the creative journey. Anzaldúa continues to name the intensity that arises by articulating how "your struggle to find a methodology, a way of working, is constant. Balancing these aspects of spirit isn't easy. Writing is like pulling miles of entrails through your mouth."[97] Showing her vulnerability in creating her art, Anzaldúa shows us the spirit battle she experiences in her inner world and illuminates the need for a guide through the journey in-between worlds. In this way, working with Coyolxauhqui as a guide for her healing journey during the writing process was key to her spirit methodology. Keating notes that "Anzaldúa's approach to writing was dialogic, recursive, democratic, spirit-inflected, and only partially within her conscious control. She relied extensively on intuition, imagination, and what she describes in this book [*Light/Luz*] as her 'naguala.'"[98]

Anzaldúa's work as a maestra of paths of conocimiento, and as a curandera of the borderlands, provides tools to "de-Indianized" and "detribalized" Xicana/x and Latinx peoples in the cultural, historical, political, and spiritual work of decolonization to remember their Indigenous ancestors and familial relations despite generations and/or centuries of disconnection. Her methodologies, herramientas, of creativity provide a pathway to do their inner work to regain alignment once again.[99] Anzaldúa, along with Moraga and Castillo, is one of the first Chicana lesbian writers to theorize the importance of understanding that Chicanas/os are colonized Indigenous people who have become detached from their roots due to violent suppression over the last five hundred years.[100] Although she does not use the concept of decolonization in *Borderlands/La Frontera*, she is very much guiding the steps of healing work to undo years of self-hatred, shame, vergüenza for being Indigenous, Chicana, queer, other, and for speaking her *verdades* (truths) in multiple languages and worldviews. This is exemplified through her innovative use of three languages—Spanish, English, and Náhuatl—in the text. Mignolo "explores the question of languaging and colonialism," using Anzaldúa's *Borderlands*: "to read *Borderlands* is to read three languages and three literatures concurrently, which is, at the same time, a new way of languaging."[101] Versions of Náhuatl, an Indigenous language of Mesoamerica, are still spoken in parts of Mexico, El Salvador, and beyond. The Náhuatl language was also colonized and made a dominant Indigenous language on the land that became known at Mexico up until 1821 to "simplify" communication for the Spanish colonizers. Forbes notes that, "as surprising at it may seem, Náhuatl actually came into use far to the north of its pre-1522 frontier, partly because of the movement of large numbers of Mexicans and partly because early Spanish policy favored the spread of a single native language."[102]

It is through Anzaldúa's use of Náhuatl that she uncovers traces of Indigenous ancestry and begins to rearticulate sacred energies that were in existence prior to conquest, and thus she contributes to rewriting Chicana/x history through a queer Indígena feminist lens.[103] Saldívar-Hull observes about *Borderlands/La Frontera* that, "by rewriting the stories of Malinali, La Llorona and the Virgen de Guadalupe, Anzaldúa is strategically reclaiming a ground for female historical presence. Her task here is to uncover the names and powers of the female deities whose identities have been submerged in Mexican memory of these three Mexican mothers. . . . In presenting the origins of the Guadalupe myth, Anzaldúa offers new names for our studies—names that we must labor to pronounce: Coatlicue, Cihuacoatl, Tonantsi, Coyolxauhqui."[104] Saldívar-Hull's reference to "names that we must labor to pronounce" signals the struggle that Chicanas/os/xs (and others) have to learn Náhuatl, which became foreign due to conquest and the imposition of Spanish and then English languages. She is also referring to the way that sacred ancestral energies were renamed in Spanish and reconfigured through the Conquest as a strategy for survival for Indigenous peoples.

The chapter titled "The Homeland, Aztlán/El otro México" begins Anzaldúa's classic 1987 text, which is now in its fourth edition. This essay is in direct conversation with the Chicano movement's ideologies and notions of racial oppression, internal colonialism, and struggle from a third-world perspective. Yet, in the poetry that begins this chapter, Anzaldúa illuminates this battle by showing that creation is a stronger force than the imposed racism and constructed political borders that are attempting to dictate peoples' lives:

> But the skin of the earth is seamless,
> The sea cannot be fenced,
> *el mar* does not stop at borders.
> To show the white man what she thought of his
> arrogance,
> *Yemayá* blew that wire fence down.[105]

This is an important example of Anzaldúa's "politics of spirit" and of the knowledge that allows her to see the importance of the Chicano struggle, yet push its boundaries toward an Earth- or creation-centered analysis.[106] She argues that the forms of white supremacy and the imperialist state imposed to divide and separate people from each other—including structures of racism and heteropatriarchy—are not as powerful as the spirit of the vast divine ocean mother and larger universe. Anzaldúa's articulations demonstrate the need for Chicana/x studies as a field to go further in its engagement and praxis with Anzaldúan theories, particular her attention to spirit and ceremony.

Borderlands/La Frontera is an example of a methodological venture into remembering previous ancestors, generations, and knowledges through storytelling, and thus has become a vital text in the curriculum of Chicanx studies. Yet it is important that Anzaldúa's later works also be read to show her evolvement of concepts. The essays in *Light/Luz* in particular show her expansive, spirit-centered theorizations that move beyond mestizaje. Anzaldúa's early work, such as chapter 1 of *Borderlands/La Frontera,* is influenced by core tenants of an early Chicano studies that is nationalistic and patriarchal. What I have articulated here, however, is that Anzaldúa as a philosopher was aware of the controversial logics of appropriation, erasure, genocide, and colonialism. Her work calls for the unraveling of those hierarchies and a move toward decolonization and self-determination.

La Limpeza, the Cleansing

Anzaldúa inspires us to build interconnected analytical frameworks that trace and uncover the connections between the forced removal of a people, rape of women, the feminine, children, and the land, restrictions of Indigenous ceremony and uses of particular curative plants, lack of access to foods from the Earth, and other forms of domination based on gender and racial formations, to see clearly the destruction of peoples, cultures, and languages. Just like the earth and water hold memory, as beings we remember energies, love, and traumas that require spirit work to cleanse and clear. My focus on Anzaldúa's altares collection, an eclectic set of sacred objects, offers an indication of the spiritual practices that informed her writing and visioning.[107] In building *Borderlands/La Frontera* as an altar, Anzaldúa constructed a methodology of spirit, a relation to ancestors such as Coyolxauhqui and Coalticue. As a nepantlera, a writer, a maestra, Anzaldúa's shows us the importance of home and community altars, altars that accompany you while you write, cry, sing, and call to ancestors. These altars provide an opening to ask for guidance, as well as time and space to set down your prayers and give offerings. They offer a place to hold the four elements—water, earth, fire, and wind—and honor the four directions. Through the tools she offered as a curandera to call back the soul, la limpeza, the *curación* (healing), Anzaldúa show us how to move out of "the paralyzing states of confusion, depression, anxiety, and powerlessness and we are catapulted into enabling states of confidence and inner strength."[108] She demonstrates in her writing the need to sanar (heal), to be rooted and grounded, to gain clarity in our path so we can remove what feels toxic or out of alignment with our ancestral truth. Anzaldúa offers us her prayer through her creative spirit work. Through her writing as a dialogue with her inner self and the universe, she is also a guide and, like Coyolxauhqui, an ancestor of decolonization.

This is part of a humble prayer for my search, journey, tracing, excavado, for the liberating evidence that would allow me to feel home, even in my discomfort of new knowledge, my nepantlera fragmentation that reminds me of the moon and her phases—finally coming home to the consciousness of my whole being, full moon. Knowing that my cells, blood, and bones hold more memory than my mind. My politics and ways of being have been based on my remembering whether I have consciously realized this or not. We remember that at every moment we are embodied, even when we are in flight or traveling through time—we come home to our bodies. I am a body. My body is my sacred home in this lifetime. I must remember to get back in my body even when I feel afraid, when los aires (the winds) of susto (fear) or tristeza (sadness) get the best of me. Anzaldúa urges that "you must, like the shaman, find a way to call your spirit home."[109] Remembering the teachings of my ancestors and learning from maestras de la limpeza, curanderas, I burn copal, using herbs, like rosemary and basil, through my tears and with the sound my rattle and drum I call myself home. Susita, come home. Return. Susy, *este es tu hogar. Aqui esta bonito, en tu cuerpo sagrado. Regresa*, Susy. *Regresa*. My spirit returning brighter and in more alignment having shed what no longer serves me especially the toxicity and violence that I absorb as I walk my path, the red road.

And it happens, through this "inner work" as Anzaldúa brilliantly wrote, "you can't stand living according to the old terms—yesterday's mode of consciousness pinches like an outgrown shoe. Craving change, you yearn to open yourself and honor the space/time between transition."[110] I am no longer the same. I am transformed each time. The curación brings me to an intense clarity and distance from institutions that were not made for me or my queer, Indigenous, of color, rebelde ancestors past, present, and future. By focusing primarily on the writing, visual narratives of altars, and healing arts practices of the visionary Gloria Anzaldúa, I align this chapter's argument with the larger vision of the book—by charting a path of knowledge that speaks to understandings through art, culture, creativity, and language inspired by ancestors and remembering. By creating an archive and articulation of the creativity of spirit work—visual culture, storytelling, and ceremony—this chapter makes it possible to see what is hidden in dominant militarized heteropatriarchal narratives while carving out space to imagine connection to ancestors and practices of decolonization.

CHAPTER 3

QUEER INDÍGENA ART

Visual Prayers for Remembering Grandmother Earth through Oral and Visual Storytelling

> When we walk like [we are rushing], we print anxiety and sorrow on the earth. We have to walk in a way that we only print peace and serenity on the earth. . . . Be aware of the contact between your feet and the earth. Walk as if you are kissing the earth with your feet.
>
> —Thich Nhat Hanh, *Peace Is Every Step*

The visual prayers of queer Indígena artists evoke memory that heals the earth. Re-rooting and walking in balance with the earth is a vital praxis of remembering for the cultural producers centered here. Remembering through oral and visual storytelling is particularly important in the historical context of Xicana/x and Latina/x communities who have to differing degrees been displaced, "de-tribalized," and "de-Indigenized" across the hemisphere.[1] I argue that the featured artists evoke spirit and healing as they create, visualize and interconnect the past, present, and future through their narrative representations—they are hxstorians of the contemporary world and the storytellers of ancestors. I build with Laura Pérez's arguments in *Chicana Art*, as she suggests that Chicana artists "engage in *curandera* (healer) work, reclaiming and reformulating spiritual worldviews that are empowering to them as women of color" in order to reimagine possibilities of transformation through art. Pérez envisioned, in her words, "a more serious social role for art," one that is political, spiritual and "concerned for social justice and environmental responsibility."[2] While not everyone within the formulation "queer Indígenas" is Chicana or sees themselves as a curandera, I find this framework significant as a pathway for art as spiritual trabajo that views the artist as healer and facilitator of communal and societal visionary healing.

This work requires a transdisciplinary and transnational frame, as the art forms, artists, and visualities analyzed here answer the call of the praxis of decolonization as it is connected to land, migration, and the formations and contestations of identities, territories, and borders. I intentionally begin this chapter with a quote from Thich Nhat Hanh, a prolific Buddhist Vietnamese monk who was exiled from Vietnam for his antiwar activism. As someone who teaches peace and nonviolence, it is notable that he was nominated by Dr. Martin Luther King Jr. for the Noble Peace Prize in 1967. Hanh's teachings, such as his books *Touching Peace* and *Fear*, have been influential and significant for Chicana and women of color consciousness.[3] His antiwar work reflects the transnational consciousness and coalitional spirit of women of color feminisms and U.S. third-world feminisms that shape the spirit practices for justice of the artists I write about here.

This chapter envisions ceremony and the formation of art work as queer decolonial archives as methods of decolonization, ways to guide us home. I meditate more deeply with the intricacies of remembering through visual storytelling as a form of transformation. I argue that through the articulation of creativity as spirit work—the construction of alternative narratives through visual culture, storytelling, and ceremony—queer Xicana/x and Latina/x Indígena cultural producers make it possible to see ancestral layers of women of color feminist knowledges. Together they create a path toward decolonizing knowledges and critically regaining ancestral memory by acknowledging the traumas that have separated people from who they are and led to disconnection with the land and all their relations. This intentional tracing of oral and visual stories of queer Indígena artists directly addresses colonial forms of epistemic violence or missing memory. I trace how queer Indígena artists enact forms of remembering through the visual prayer of their art. The artwork of queer Indígenas reflects creative and spirit-centered forms of expanding consciousness that are not bound by colonial or state-imposed imaginings of self, community, or the earth. Their visionary work signals a direct intervention into colonial and racist logics that aim to uproot and disconnect people from their cultures, communities, philosophies, and practices.

Decolonization requires recovering, excavating, or breathing life back into knowledges that have been hidden, lost, or silenced. Knowing that prayers and healing are interconnected across time and space, the form of remembering required is not a simple act of locating, uncovering, or reinterpreting what was hidden or violently interrupted, but instead integrating the found, complicated memories, and ever-shifting fragments to be whole in the present moment. The intention is to establish a clear pathway for envisioning a generative and balanced future for generations to come. My analyses therefore focus on visual art as organic and intergenerational generative spaces of ceremony and healing, where forgotten or unacknowledged histories are re-narrated from rooted, anti-racist, non-heteronormative perspectives and practices. The collaborative methodology of this work is reflective of feminist of color knowledges that center the healing of community, the traditional ways of ancestors, and embedded political critiques of imperialism, colonization, and nation-state formations.[4]

In our collective, personal, and familial remembering, there are gaps of memory due to pain and intergenerational trauma. Much of the pain is connected to impositions of violence on the psyche due to forms of colonization, repressive logics of the state,[5] and continued colonial legacies.[6] As visual storytellers who allow spirit to enter their creative work, these artists work in the cosmic realm to offer their sculptures, paintings, and installations as medicine through a soul experience. The queer Indígena artists discussed here, Gina Aparicio and Dalila Paola Mendez—like Gloria Anzaldúa and other queer or lesbians of color in her generation—found a way to bring together their spirituality, politics, and queer or nonconforming sexuality with their respective tracing of Indigenous lineages and racially gendered lives in order to build intentional prayers for collective healing in ceremony as a form of worldwide decolonization. As Anzaldúa theorizes in "Geographies of Selves,"

> For racialized people, managing losses, the trauma of racism, and other colonial abuses affect our self-conceptions, our very identity, fragmenting our psyches and pitching us into states of nepantla. During or after any trauma (including individual and group racist acts), you lose parts of your soul as an immediate strategy to minimize the pain and to cope—hecho pedazos, you go into a state of susto. After a racial or gender wounding, something breaks down; you fall to pieces (you're dismembered). You can't swallow your anger and grief. You struggle to redeem yourself, but you can never live up to the white dominant ideal you've been forced to internalize.[7]

This "white dominant ideal" that Anzaldúa theorizes as an internalized process is in dialogue with Emma Pérez's conceptualizations of the "white colonial heteronormative gaze" of dominant history that must be unraveled or decolonized to heal the susto (soul loss) that trauma brings.[8] This includes the internalizing of shame, vergüenza, tristeza, sadness.

Spirit art or creativity as spirit work does this trabajo in various ways, including providing a visual story through a painting, sculpture, film or other medium of representation that allows the viewer to remember, connect, and touch painful memories as a pathway to acknowledging and releasing any stuck emotion or energy. Anzaldúa writes that "we never forget our wounds." It is important to "acknowledge, mourn, and grieve your losses and violations . . . you learn not just to survive but to imbue that survival with new meaning."[9] This resonates deeply with the trabajo of the artist who is on their healing path and is also creating space for community transformation through their artform. The call to remembering is an instructive form of praxis to unravel imposed oppressive structures, it is the work of decolonization to seek and see—visualize the interconnectivities of subject formations and political contestations, and enact tools of healing and critical reflection that do not allow for absorption or adherence to colonial disease.[10] Spiritual tools and rituals, such as the raising of altars, and work with crystals and stones, can be generative for creativity. Also, reconnection with the earth to feel our own root is a significant way to release wounds.

I center how ceremony and remembering are forms of activism. Community organizing, public outspokenness, and protests are central modes of addressing societal colonial structural injustices. Visual storytelling serves as a vital form of spirit consciousness or spirit work, where the offering of medicine and prayer is a visual and visceral protest. The awareness or conocimiento of the emotion of anger (*fuego*—fire) drives many forms of resistance; however, this research, this Xicana Indígena root work, contributes to building sites of wholeness and balance that integrate the four sacred elements of water, earth, air and fire, and the interconnectedness of relations, courage, respect, love, prayer, and meditation to guide forms of seeking justice and healing.[11] This pathway has been paved by elders and ancestors, including queer and gender nonconforming elders and within women of color feminisms and spaces of ceremony.

I focus on visionary artists who intend for their work to contribute to the sanación of the Earth and of generations of peoples and lineages. They importantly start with themselves to understand what occurred in their own families due to militarized wars, imposed territory demarcations, forced removals, and other violences and forms of harm that come from the dominant mechanisms of genocide, nation-state formations, and the colonization of land and people. I argue for the continued creation of communal spaces, including talking circles, dialogues, and museum exhibits, where art is understood as a visual story and the artists are given the space to share their decolonial visions, as part of transformation and healing. As Anzaldúa writes, "activism is engaging in healing work. . . . It means creating spaces and times for healing to happen, espacios y tiempos [time and space] to nourish the soul."[12] I illustrate this cultural memory work here through two queer Indígena artists, sculptor Gina Aparicio and painter Dalila Paola Mendez, who were both heavily influenced by earlier generations of women of color writers, including Gloria Anzaldúa, Cherríe Moraga, and Audre Lorde, as well as elder Indígena artists, including Yrenia Cervantes and Celia Herrera Rodríguez. The visual narratives these artists put forward offer decolonial cultural representations and practices. Through their methodologies—which are based on intuition-spirit-ancestral memory and prayer—they suggest provocative forms of cocreating intergenerational healing in community and prayers for grandmother earth, Pachamama.

Oral and Visual Storytelling: Creating and Remembering Decolonial Histories through Conocimiento

Visual storytelling and oral tradition are part of Indigenous histories. One important intervention I open here is to imagine how the visual prayers of queer Indígena artists allow us think through the relationship between oral and visual storytelling. I build on the argument I have put forward elsewhere, that "visual culture is a form of storytelling."[13] While there is extensive research on oral history and oral storytelling, there is less written on visual storytelling. I aim to discuss the importance of oral and visual storytelling as a method of transmitting sacred knowledge by examining the tools, herramientas, and analytic frameworks of oral storytelling, oral history, oral tradition, and visual culture and imaginings.

Through this tracing of queer Xicana/x and Latina/x ancestry in queer Indígena art cultural production, I seek to make visible the possibility of oral storytelling as a form of historical memory and knowledge that works to restore violently erased memories through oral traditions and oral histories—cultural knowledge archives for the purpose of transformation. Central questions that drive this methodology include: how is knowledge produced, and what and whose knowledge counts as evidence?[14] Which sites become a part of social memory? Which are erased? Pushing the boundaries of an already innovative method and field of inquiry, I am inspired to explore the connections between the method of oral history and the practices of oral tradition, oral storytelling, and visual storytelling, particularly within the context of histories of colonization and grounded in a particular focus on the roots of queerness, dual energies, balance, and two-spiritedness in relation to queer Indígenas. How can this decolonial feminist methodology open the boundaries of disciplinary theoretical approaches?

The featured artists have a deep spiritual understanding of themselves and a connection to Indigenous ancestries, lands, and peoples of Mesoamerica and beyond, while they simultaneously maintain a critique of the ways that dominant histories have unfolded. Storytelling and oral tradition are part of Indigenous histories. There is a long history of oral storytelling and testimonio among marginalized communities of color. Leyva states that, "as a people who have passed on our *historia* though the sharing of our *historias*, storytelling itself provides a basis for unraveling the multiple meanings of silence."[15] Prior to oral history, archival research was the primary method in historical research. Rarely found in the archives are the narratives of "queer" or "deviant" populations.[16] In many ways, it is through an intentional critique of what is missing or a queering of dominant historical narratives and archives that queer of color studies took form and launched what Emma Pérez eventually called the "queer of color gaze."[17] This gaze shifts the dominant gaze by calling attention to what is outside the "norm" or heteronormative structures.

One of the most intriguing parts about oral history is that there is no intention to generalize a story or narrative; instead, there is an understanding that each story is unique, although there may be interconnections with many other existences or memories. Memories are infused with cultural, social, spiritual, and political imaginings and experiences. Oral history interviews offer an opportunity to "tell" what one remembers of a particular moment or time in history. The very experience of remembering creates meaning through a memory that is contextual (in time and space), while also specific to a topic, genealogy, or legacy. As Perks and Thomson assert, "memory thus became the subject as well as the source . . . of Oral History."[18]

The method of oral history can assist in unraveling historical narratives that have been put forward as dominant historical truths. Feminists of color methodologies search for complex and layered historical truths that are reflective of more than the dominant narrative.[19] Oral history does the work of documenting important alternative histories while mapping the larger social and political contexts. Oral stories are not pulled apart or coded, as in conventional social science inquiry; instead, they are three-dimensional, like a map or story on an ancient wall that when listened to conjures images and shows a path, a direction. Documenting through oral histories works in part to capture what has not been documented, while oral storytelling is a practice more commonly used to name the teachings of elders, Indigenous knowledges, and sacred stories. Connecting oral history with queer of color theory pushes critical inquiry toward an important practice of methodological intersection, of searching for the unseen when we are trained with the dominant eye.[20]

Art-Makers Creating Pathways through Spirit Praxis

> A form of spiritual inquiry, conocimiento is reached via creative acts—writing, art-making, dancing, healing, teaching, meditation, and spiritual activism—both mental and somatic (the body, too, is a form as well as site of creativity).
>
> —Gloria Anzaldúa, "Now Let Us Shift"

> We must create new art forms that support transformation.
>
> —Gloria Anzaldúa, "Geographies of Selves"

These artists, as cultural producers, incorporate ancestral knowledge and practices into their art as a way of decolonizing knowledge and regaining ancestral memory through the praxis of creation and exhibition. The artists and visionaries I focus on are Indígena mujeres, artists, and healers who are on the path of tracing ancestry, "walking the red road," or walking a spirit-centered path that is grounded in an Indigenous vision of transformation and healing. For generations, Indígena and women of color artists have been rewriting forgotten histories through forms of visual storytelling that open up consciousness that destabilizes western ideologies, including capitalism and Christianity, as major destroyers of Indigenous traditions and balanced relations with the Earth. In their art, they move away from Christ-centered religion and move toward spiritual practices that honor the four directions, the sacred elements, and the earth as una abuela *sabia* (a wise grandmother). Central to the context of this chapter is the work of queer Indígena artists and visionaries who are connected to generations of artists and who recreate stories and offer medicines of remembrance through collaborative visions of ancient practices.

This chapter focuses on artists whose work is connection to key collectives—Womyn Image Makers, Cihuatl Productions, a film collective and a two-spirit Xicana Indígena theater collective, and Mujeres de Maíz. These artists work to keep complicated and alive multiple and non-static frames of identity formations, political projects, and methodologies, including but not limited to queer Indígena, queer Latina/x, Xicana Indígenas, and women of color. In this journey, they have mentored each other and younger generations, while they are guided by their ancestors and elders. These artists and collectives are important "role models" or guides in the field of ancestral image making and practices. Other points of similarity are that many of these Xicana and Latina Indígena artists were raised in poor and working-class conditions in California, and many have a history of migration due to violence. Many have dedicated their lives to community activism in avenues that range from mentoring youth in low-income racialized neighborhoods (like Boyle Heights in Los Angeles) to teaching in urban public schools. Multiple forms of community work in various capacities have also been central to their respective formations as community leaders and artists. In the mid-1990s, some of the artists in the mentioned collectives participated in a *circulo de mujeres* (circle of women), where they shared sacred space with younger women of color, burned sage, and held talking circles about consciousness-raising topics. They share a strong connection with Native communities and a deep respect for the land. They also share a practice of honoring the stars (moon and sun), plants, herbs, water, fire, and other medicines from the earth and universe. Part of re-membering the tools was participating in various forms of ceremony, such as sweat lodges, *temezcalli*, altar-making, and danza, as well as practices and prayers that are reminiscent of the "old ways" of connecting with sacred Mother Earth. These aspects directly influence the *trabajo de corazón* (work from the heart) that these artists put forward, and the sacred spaces that are created when their art is exhibited, screened, and viewed, or heard, seen, and experienced in another form. These artists are invested in body-mind-spirit alignment in order to become clear channels for their art, activism, and vision.

In their art, there is a visible constant connection with contemporary Indigenous practices; spirituality, prayer, and ceremony are central elements of their art and existence. They offer a critical transnational consciousness of racist hierarchical logics that maintain the heteronormative United States, particularly as we experience global capitalism rooted in ideologies based on fear and on eliminating, silencing, and/or terrorizing. While they share informed understandings of colonization and of histories of violence and war, each artist and community organizer, does the work to create another way of seeing and existing that moves past destruction to plant seeds of faith and prayer for the earth in the form of action.

Aparicio's Clay Structures as Visual Storytelling: Disrupting Borders of Gender and Nation

Sculptor Gina Aparicio (Xicana/Apache/K'iche'), who regards Rocky Rodriguez, Celia Herrera Rodríguez, and other Indígena and Native American women as her mentors, was a featured artist at the 2006 Thirteenth Women of Color Film and Video Festival titled *Regenerations* on the University of California, Santa Cruz campus.[21] Aparicio self-identifies as a queer Xicana Indígena artist with Apache and Mayan (K'iche') ancestry who was born and raised in Los Angeles. Aparicio's clay sculptures evoke a deep remembering of tragedy and healing for

Indigenous communities of Mesoamerica. Her clay representations are rooted in an intense study of ancient hieroglyphs, a close examination of contested Mexican and Latin American colonial histories, as well as an engagement with Xicana/x politics and spiritual practices.

Aparicio's clay sculptures, although created in the modern day, are reminiscent of ancient art forms that simultaneously disrupt and re-narrate heteropatriarchal stories by centering mujer or gender queer generational memory and knowledge. The creation of her art is a ceremony, beginning with her queer feminist Indígena vision guiding the molding of the clay. Aparicio mixes clay the color of red earth with the blessing of water as she begins to intentionally create a full female-bodied figure that is Indigenous and is adorned with ceremonial elements associated with life and death. She creates an Earth-centered story that is in balance with the four elements (water, earth, air, and fire) and based on her imagination of and connection to ancestors. Aparicio uses a kiln (fire) to harden the clay sculpture before she paints her creation, to further bring her piece to life. Her intentional use of the multiplicity of the color palette, as opposed to other singular-toned sculptures by Aparicio, insists that sacred matriarchs exist in the current dimension walking in vibrant colors on the urban streets of Los Angeles.

Figure 2. *In the Spirit of the Ancestors,* clay. Gina Aparicio, 2005.

Aparicio's sculpture, titled *In the Spirit of the Ancestors* (fig. 2), features an Indígena mujer, sitting in prayer, a sort of replica of Aparicio herself, down to her height (four feet nine). Made of clay, she resembles the red earth and wears moon-shaped earrings to show her connection to the stars and cosmos.[22] She holds both of her arms and hands out to the heavens with her head similarly inclined, signaling a humble connection to the ancestors above and below. A heart-centered necklace lines her yellow-green top, while her belt holds a *calavera* (skull) at her core; she sits cross-legged and rooted in blue jeans and matching green shoes. According to Aparicio, the skull signifies cycles of life and rebirth experienced many times during a lifetime, an idea that directly challenges linear notions of life and death, while the heart of the necklace is representative of the way one connects with spirit, through the corazón (heart).[23] Her hands have a swirl or spiral etched in her palms, a symbol that rethinks time, space, and story, representing non-western, circular ways of imagining those concepts. Her black hair is pulled back in a braid, signaling an *urban diosa en ceremonia*, prayer.

This practice of ceremony is a method of survival that provides growth of spiritual consciousness for Indigenous people who have been "detribalized."[24] In the *Regenerations* display, she sits with burgundy maize in her right hand on top of a layer of red rocks, with ceremonial elements around her, including sage, feathers, a rattle, a lit candle, and a ceramic mug with water—an altar for sacred teachings and cleansing ceremony.[25] Cleansing ceremonies are grounded, traditional ways of doing healing work when someone experiences a form of trauma, especially susto (fear), vergüenza (shame), tristeza (sadness).[26] Using artistic representation and visual culture as a means to pass on stories and sacred teachings is significant for evoking memory and forgotten histories, since practices such as cleansing ceremonies are not easily represented through the written word. The visual offerings provide a pathway to the praxis of decolonization. Aparicio's work encourages remembering sacred healing tools that can be used on an everyday basis to connect with spirit without requiring a connection to an outside institution, for example, a church.

Aparicio's intention for this sculpture was that it would bring together "things that have been passed on from generation to generation, over hundreds and hundreds of years, through our mythology, through our stories, through our oral traditions, and through our spirituality and spiritual practices."[27] As Aparicio explains,

> a lot of times people see Indigenous cultures as something that is dead, as something that no longer exists . . . it is very much alive, and it's alive in us and we

> have a responsibility to keep those things alive for the future generations, so it's an attempt to document our history, to document the lineage that has been passed down and to leave that for future generations. So she's bringing in a lot of these metaphors, but very contemporary, she is like a goddess, but she has on jeans and shoes for instance. . . . She is not the traditional, what you are used to seeing, maybe an unclothed goddess.[28]

In this process of ceremony, she shifts the representational frame for understanding Coyolxauhqui, the Mexica/Aztec moon or Coatlicue, Mexica Earth Mother.

Her efforts to create this piece of visual culture are a direct response to colonization and legacies of forgetting ancestral connections in the contemporary moment. The sculpture creates moments for passing the sacred knowledge represented by this art piece to future generations. A young woman of color from Los Angeles, for example, who traveled to Santa Cruz with Aparicio and other mujeres from Los Angeles, explained to a two-year-old the elements surrounding the sculpture. This young womxn's knowledge reflected a deep wisdom by enunciating the story and uses of the ceremonial elements; she explained to this future ancestor the process of burning sage, sounding a rattle, and lighting a candle, working with fire, as a form of prayer.[29] She explained how anyone could use these tools, giving the young one *permiso* to re-member her own *medicina*. As an observer of this moment, I witnessed the possibility of creating generational knowledge through cultural production and representation created in ceremony. This moment also demonstrated how the formation of an art exhibit in a women of color, Chicana, Latina, and Indígena space allowed for subaltern and sacred knowledges to be remembered in a respectful and interactive way.

Aparicio's art is a form of oral tradition and visual storytelling in the sense that she creates or arguably remembers a narrative that is rooted in gender balance and a time and space where Indigenous women led and continue to lead and practice ceremony today.[30] This production of cultural memory requires a deep focus and belief in something more than what is immediately visible in historical narratives or representations. According to Taylor, "cultural memory is, among other things, a practice, an act of imagination and interconnection."[31] As Taylor argues, "sometimes memory is difficult to evoke, yet it's highly efficient; it's always operating in conjunction with other memories."[32] For Aparicio, constructing memory through her clay structures is a disruption of male-centered Indigenous narratives, such as Chicano cultural nationalism or Chicano assertions of Aztlán that dis-remember the significant role of female or queer counterparts of Mesoamerica.

Through Aparicio's careful and intentional art piece, she creates a space of connection and ultimately healing from colonial legacies. In this sculpture, Aparicio is remembering the process of re-rooting, or creating an Indigenous centered ceremonial space for Xicanx/as and Latinx/as who are in diaspora. As Patrisia Gonzales argues, "Indigenous Mexican practices in Mexico and the United States are examples of how communal peoples maintain ancestral practices without a defined communal base." Gonzales further suggests that "Indigenous/traditional medicine creates a relationship with nature, the place-cosmos. Through activating Indigenous values of respect, responsibility, and renewal, disconnected original peoples can restore their teachings and cultures. They can change the effects of domination."[33] Aparicio's work creates a pathway for restoration and re-Indigenization.

DECOLONIZATION OF AZTLÁN

Although the decolonization of Aztlán is a complicated task, Chicana feminists have theorized critiques of heteropatriarchy, exclusivity, and male dominance that have led to a reconceptualization of Chicano cultural nationalism. As part of a framework and a movement, Chicana feminists have challenged imperialism and structures of racism. Aparicio's work is an example of honoring the land through ceremony, without continuing the colonial legacy of territorial regulation through borders; her remembering asks for permission as she honors the four directions. Through a queer Xicana Indígena methodology, there is intentional respect and solidarity building with original Indigenous peoples who are connected to, and in some cases rematriating, the land in colonial United States, Mexico, and respective homelands. This framework situates property as a white supremacist notion rooted in colonization. A structure based on the elimination or disappearance of Native American, Indian, and Indigenous peoples.[34] Morgensen argues that "white supremacy and settler colonialism are interdependent and must be theorized together."[35] The decolonization of Aztlán therefore contains the possibility for a reconstructed relationship to the land that is not based on ownership or recolonized borders when the myth of Aztlán is delinked from the southwest being homeland.

Aztlán, like Chicano nationalism, has been contested and disrupted by Chicana and Latina feminists.[36] The mythical homeland of Aztlán was based on a notion of territory that positioned the ancestors of Chicanos as the original peoples of the U.S. Southwest, seemingly disregarding other Indigenous peoples and histories. The logic of Aztlán was central to the formation of Chicano cultural nationalism. As chapter 1 discusses, it emerged as the result of the 1848 Treaty of Guadalupe Hidalgo and Mexican "loss of land," which ended the war between the United States and Mexico. The treaty made legal the "transfer" of land from Mexico to the United States, including California, Texas, Arizona, Colorado, New Mexico, and Nevada. In addition to land that was taken by force and the subsequent reconstructing of political nation-state borders, the 1848 treaty also established racial hierarchies through divisive language.

A critical Xicana Indígena methodology asks what focusing on the "loss of land" in 1848 obscures in terms of ancestry in Mesoamerica and a shared interconnected history with Native and Indigenous people on this continent. The mythical formation of Aztlán was an important strategic political formation for Chicanos who had been forcibly displaced during conquest and thus denied access to Indigenous historical narratives, languages, and cultures. Still, the ownership claim to the land known as the U.S. Southwest must be uprooted within Chicano/a consciousness.[37] Employing Native studies frameworks as a methodology facilitates the disrupting of the settler colonial logic emphasized by Chicanos who claim Aztlán as a literal territory without the acknowledgement of other tribes and peoples. The focus on the legacies of the United States–Mexico War is limited because it overlooks the Spanish Conquest in central Mexico as a significant moment of colonization for Chicanos. Critically revisiting the history of Mesoamerica, particularly from a feminist perspective, makes Indigenous and gender queer ancestry become increasingly central to forgotten stories of the "Mexican-American." As Blackwell argues, Aztlán made women "invisible through the construction of nationalist patrimony that universalizes masculine subjects through the category of 'Chicano,' encoding a gendered mode of remembrance."[38]

Aparicio's vision and creation of *In the Spirit of the Ancestors* shows the layers of sacred knowledge that are informed by a spirit of resistance to the annihilation of Indigenous cultures. Central to Aparicio's narrative is a concern for future generations and their knowledge of non-heteronormative Indigenous cultures, histories, and spiritual practices that most importantly honor Mother Earth but are disappeared, or read as nonexistent, in modern-day colonial society. Her effort to produce this representation allows the viewer to integrate ancestry in the present day with contemporary forms of an urban Xicana who is walking a spiritually connected road. This idea of remembering forgotten histories is of particular significance because, according to Gonzales, "the ceremonial discourse and rites were precisely the spaces of Mesoamerican knowledge that the Spanish sought to annihilate."[39] Through continued analysis of Aparicio's clay structures, I move now to the Conquest of Indigenous people of Mesoamerica or Anahuac by the Spanish Crown.

CUICA MAQUIXTIA, NÁHUATL LANGUAGE, AND "INDIAN" IDENTITY

Cuica Maquixtia is another clay sculpture exhibited at the *Regenerations* exhibit, which features "a woman crucified on the cross," and "impregnated and her womb is the earth" (fig. 3).[40] She is blindfolded, unclothed, and her hair is in a long braid. Her hands and feet are literally crucified, nailed and tied, on the large cross behind her. This representation is reminiscent of an outcast who challenges dominant structures. Cuica Maquixtia is a Náhuatl name, which according to Aparicio, "translates into she who sings to be free."[41] In this extraordinary political sculpture, Aparicio expresses her critique of "issues from institutionalized religion to patriarchy," formations of dominance that were central to the conquest of Indigenous people in Mesoamerica.[42] This sculpture visually represents the colonization by the Spanish Crown in the early 1500s, particularly those subjected to the imposed practices of the Friars and priests. *Cuica Maquixtia* illuminates the resulting disruption with grandmother Earth, spiritual practices, and ways of life that threaten extinction of the people and land through forced disconnection. It is significant that Aparicio created this artwork to remember the trauma experienced by the ancestors of "detribalized"

Figure 3. *Cuica Maquixtia* (She who sings to be Free, in Náhuatl), clay. Gina Aparicio, 2004.

and "de-Indigenized" Xicana/x and Latina/x. *Cuica Maquixtia* opens a path for healing for those who have experienced historical trauma and for the Earth, which has endured the repercussions of colonial disbalance.

In this case, Aparicio creates a stunning piece of art as a response to layers of complicated histories that caused multiple forms of destruction through forced dislocation, sexual violations, and intentional erasures of feminine spiritual practices. Through a queer Xicana Indígena tracing of colonial historical occurrences it is possible to bring sanación or healing to the ancestors of displaced peoples, by remembering the dominant forces of conquest. Maori scholar Linda Tuhiwai Smith identifies "Remembering" as one of "twenty-five indigenous projects."[43] She writes that "the remembering of a people relates not so much to an idealized remembering of a golden past but more specifically to the remembering of a painful past and, importantly, people's responses to that pain." As part of what Smith describes as "crucial strategies" for healing and transformation, Aparicio's work "asks a community to remember what they may have decided to unconsciously or consciously forget," in terms of song, language, spirit practices, origin stories, and their relations.[44]

Within this layered and complex piece, Aparicio critiques the imposition of Christian ideology and a white-centered racial hierarchy, while honoring lineages of life-givers by presenting a cis-gendered woman's body that holds the earth in her womb.[45] As Alexander suggests, "if healing work is a call to remember and remembering is embodied then we want to situate the body centrally in this healing complex."[46] Aparicio's sculpture accomplishes this by centering the naked body of a full-figured Indigenous mujer that is rarely seen in a respected and dignified form or honored site of creation in connection with the balance of the earth and her resources. As Bonfil Batalla details, "the colonial enterprise engaged in destroying Mesoamerican civilization and stopped only where self-interest intervened. When necessary, whole peoples were destroyed. On the other hand, where the labor force of the Indians was required, they were kept socially and culturally segregated."[47] Aparicio's piece is therefore a resistance to the de-Indianization that resulted from colonization.

As argued in chapter one, in what became New Spain or colonial Mexico (1821–48), colonial power was maintained through the fictive spectrum of "purity and impurity." In her writing about la "*limpeza de sangre*" (purity of blood), historian Maria Elena Martínez documented a system in which the mixed-blood mestizo had more authority than the Indigenous (pure blood), who was said to have "stained ancestry."[48] Aparicio challenges this process of de-Indianization and fiction based on blood hierarchies by remembering and creating the striking Indígena representation of Cuica Maquixtia that offers a direct response to oppressive racist and colonial institutions.

COMPLEXITIES OF NÁHUATL LANGUAGE AND "INDIAN" IDENTITY

Because Aparicio's earth-toned and provocative sculpture intentionally holds a Náhuatl name, it also works to remember language. Language and song are significant forms of remembering, in this case the Náhuatl language is significant since it was a dominant Indigenous language of Mesoamerica.[49] It is often associated with the Aztec, since the Aztec were the ruling power during the Conquest in the early 1500s.[50] In making a striking argument about the language of Náhuatl in relation to domination and conquest, Batalla suggests that "Náhuatl was the preferred tongue, and its teaching was proposed as a general method of facilitating preaching in all of New Spain. To a large extent the 'Náhuatlization' that can be observed in many parts of the country resulted more from missionary action than from Aztec expansion. . . . The ability to communicate was converted into a means of control and domination."[51] Náhuatl was used widely in New Spain and among Indigenous people in the Americas until 1821, the year that Mexico became a nation.[52] Although the widespread use of the Náhuatl language was not necessarily by choice, the Spanish rulers, to reduce the effort of learning multiple Indigenous languages, mandated the use of Náhuatl by all the tribes as the language of communication.

This example shows the complexity of co-optation and language. It is a layered and complicated history that surrounds the Indigenous language of Náhuatl. Its reclamation—despite the misuse by colonial forces—is significant, as is the tracing, honoring, and learning of other Indigenous languages that have been disappeared or are currently marginal to the Spanish language (a colonial language).[53] Because language holds knowledge, worldview, memory, and culture, Anzaldúa argues in "How to Tame a Wild Tongue" that "a language to remain alive must be used."[54] She simultaneously critiques the way Chicanas will "speak English as a neutral language."[55] Aparicio's artwork links this analysis of colonization to the ever-receding access and fragmented or forgotten knowledge concerning Indigenous languages, cultures, and spiritual practices that were disrupted with the formation of the Mexican nation-state. Purposefully naming this piece in Náhuatl to remember and re-root the language in its Indigenous context through a strategy of decolonization, Aparicio describes the language as "one of the Indigenous languages from the central valley of Mexico, and so in an attempt to try to preserve those Indigenous languages . . . so many have been lost. Not lost, but . . . very violently taken away . . . so it is an attempt to preserve that and to reintroduce that into the community . . . in Los Angeles."[56]

Ipan Nepantla Teotlaitlania Cachi Cualli Maztlacayotl (Caught between Worlds, Praying for a Better Future)

Aparicio's more recent art installation, *Ipan Nepantla Teotlaitlania Cachi Cualli Maztlacayotl* (Caught between Worlds, Praying for a Better Future), offers a distinct prayer for Mother Earth. Birthed in 2014, this mixed-media installation has traveled and been exhibited in three significant geographical and chronological variations and iterations—Florida 2014, Los Angeles 2017, and Davis, California 2019.[57] Aparicio's starting point or imagined space of ceremony for this installation is nepantla, which reflects Anzaldúa's final works as Keating argues that she moved in a "geographical-theoretical shift" from her early work on "Aztlán to the borderlands" toward her later work theorizing nepantla.[58] Aparicio fittingly names this ceremonial space nepantla, as Anzaldúa wrote, "In nepantla we hang out between shifts, trying to make rational sense of this crisis, seeking solace, support, appeasement, or some kind of intimate connection. En este lugar we fall into chaos, fear of the unknown, and are forced to take up the task of self-redefinition."[59] Clearly illuminating a moment of self-autonomy, after being in this space of nepantla, just as there is much learned during ceremony when one does the work to go deep into their trabajo. I see Aparicio as nepantlera, particularly as in Anzaldúa's definition: "Nepantleras such as artistas/activistas help us mediate these transitions, help us make the crossings, and guide us through the transformation process—a process I call conccimiento."[60]

Aparicio created a sacred space of conocimiento through the medium of mixed media in the museum in order to disrupt the idea that art should be removed from the viewer in a glass case. She invites us into ceremony with four tall structures, naguales (bear, owl, jaguar, and deer), placed in the four cardinal directions praying with an eight-foot-wide circular wooden cut representation of Coyolxauhqui in her dismembered state, most commonly known as the Mexica moon energy representing the rising of feminine energy, at the center. Each nahual (standing animal figure) *en las cuatro direcciones* (the four directions) of the circle is holding a ceremonial instrument (a rattle, drum, or flute) prepared to offer traditional song, while one holds a sacred pipe. I asked Aparicio where she would place the fire in her installation if she could, when we spoke about the sacred elements. She replied: "*If* they [the museum] let me, in the ombligo of Coyolxauhqui"—her navel, the center of the circle.[61]

Ipan Nepantla Teotlaitlania Cachi Cualli Maztlacayotl is, in Aparicio's words, a "communal prayer for social justice and a better world for our future generations."[62] As an artivist and visionary of peace, Aparicio's aim is to create and contribute to a dialogue that can lead to a shift in cosmic consciousness. This is reflected in her raising of the tobacco prayer altar, also referenced as "a tobacco prayer for peace." Before entering the circle of the larger installation, Aparicio brings together the sacred and the political by inviting visitors to "make a prayer," an intention, with the tobacco prayer ties on the interactive altar for "what they feel needs to be changed, where they see injustice," for example, with the environment, the earth, relation with other human beings, internal changes, or changes in structures, governments, or nations. Ofrendas of gratitude and permiso. Aparicio builds on the teachings learned from her maestrxs and elders in ceremony, walking the red road.

Her tobacco prayer altar that begins the installation encourages the viewer to reconnect with an Earth-centered conscious way of life and invites a practice of meditation and prayer, instead of the capitalist colonial detached entitled way of life. She invites the viewer to transform their consciousness of the moment by reflecting and making an offering with this sacred plant and a small, red square of fabric that becomes a prayer tie (fig. 4). Placed on a cork board with peyote flowers, made of fired clay—sacred earth—creating a space to rest prayers. The altar held the elements of sage, a feather, and water. There are four

Figure 4. Tobacco ties, *Ipan Nepantla Teotlaitlania Cachi Cualli Maztlacayotl*. Gina Aparicio, 2019 iteration.

nahuales, one in each cardinal direction, following Lakota teachings, imparted to Aparicio by elders: Bear woman in the East (yellow), Owl woman in the West (black), Jaguar woman in the South (red), Deer woman in the North (white). Aparicio's placards guide the viewer: "Tobacco is one of the sacred medicines for Native Peoples. Prayer ties are used to make special intentions. Take a pinch of tobacco into your left palm. Say a prayer or make an intention for the world you'd like to see. Place the tobacco onto the center of the cloth and pin it to the wall and join our communal hope for a better world."[63]

Aparicio's *Ipan* represents what resembles or can be understood as a peyote ceremony, where ancestors are invited for the night, in a respectful way, to join in collective prayer. Aparicio intentionally offers a place to *teotlaitlania* (pray) and heal for another world by providing people with a space for reflection and pause, where they feel held by the elements, song, and smell of the Earth from the mulch on the ground. A public, yet intimate space to unravel intergenerational traumas from colonization through the experience of her mixed-media installation. Her Mesoamerican spirit-centered structures work to shift our senses to the present moment enough to be able to time travel and visit with and remember our antepasados through our breath, prayer, and ceremony. Aparicio's "offering" is a re-centering of memory through song, prayer, and material connections to earth. With the earth-colored lighting, she disrupts

Figure 5. *Ipan Nepantla Teotlaitlania Cachi Cualli Maztlacayotl* (Caught between Worlds, Praying for a Better Future). Gina Aparicio, 2019 iteration.

the white walls and creates the sensation of ceremoniously entering Mother Earth: "It is a prayer for the healing of ourselves, our community, our Madre Tierra. . . . It is an act of self-determination. It is meant to transform the white walls of an institution into sacred space. These prayers are arrows fighting for the children we will never know. The vision is to unify the red, black, yellow, white, all the races, all peoples, to be part of a new beginning."[64]

Aparicio's *Ipan* installation echoes Anzaldúa's writing and reverence of Coyolxauhqui as a matriarchal ancestor of decolonization. Aparicio accomplishes this by placing grandmother moon at the center of the prayer ceremony. Her prayer of this installation is manifested through her method of intuition and connectedness and wisdom. The four nahuales each have their own energy, but positioned together they are in dialogue and relation with each other and in prayer together for the rising of the feminine energy at the center, the moon (fig. 5). Aparicio told me that

> [*Ipan*] was a prayer for the feminine energy to resurface. The world has been for many many years dominated by male energy . . . it's destroying our planet and its destroying humanity. I think the feminine has to rise . . . I don't have any children . . . but the woman [or person with a womb] gives birth to life and so it relates to life in a very different way than the male energy and [cis-gendered] males. In the way they see the world. I invited people to come into the space and be in prayer. Together.[65]

As viewers walk through the installation, we hear songs on a loop, featuring Grupo Tribu, In Lak Ech, Cihuatl Tonali, and Aparicio herself reciting a spoken prayer and playing a hand drum. The song supports the feeling or remembering of ceremony as one walks through. All the music is by and voices are of cis-gendered women, except Grupo Tribu. Their song, "Fecundación Sagrada," however, is about mujeres, mujeres who transform into nahuales. The lyrics prompt introspection, asking and evoking: "¿Que mujer eres tú? . . . Mujer serpiente, Mujer venado, Aguila mujer, Mujer jaguar, mujer, mujer . . . Mujer de tierra, Mujer de mar, Mujer montaña, Mujer de arena, Geografia de mujer" (Which woman are you? . . . Serpent woman, deer woman, eagle women, jaguar woman, woman, woman . . . Women of the earth, women of the sea, mountain woman, sand woman, geography of woman). The significance of these ceremonial songs is that they allow for another modality to travel and open one's heart to the memories of ceremony and the teachings of ancestors. The heartbeat of the drums, palabra, traditional song resonate as tools, as pathways, to unthreading legacies of patriarchy, colonialism, and imperialism. Aparicio's visual art as activism is a praxis of decolonization, a visual storytelling of transformation.

Womyn Image Makers: Creativity as Spirit Work or "Stories from Spirit"

The four mujeres who make up Womyn Image Makers (WIM) joined forces in May 2000 and created a sacred space to build collective trust for storytelling through film, "with the intentions of opening up dialogue and documenting their art and methodologies of collaboration and visual art production."[66] This collaborative of queer Indígena Xicanas and a centroamericana, with roots in El Salvador, Guatemala, Mexico, the San Francisco Bay Area, and East Los Angeles, collaborated and conspired together for over ten years. The members who made up this non-hierarchal, Indígena-centered filmmaker collective were Maritza Alvarez, Aurora Guerrero, Claudia Mercado, and Dalila Paola Mendez, who is the focus of this section of the chapter. According to Mercado, "these urban Xicana, Indígena, Mestiza filmmakers and visual artists . . . share a passion for representing our stories: sensual morena narratives, obsidian experimental digital collages, slice of life adventures and herstorical ancestral portraits."[67] They build on a Xicana Indígena subject formation that is hemispheric, in the sense that it defies the boundaries of nation-state demarcations. Many of them were involved in Xicana Indígena projects that supported Native and Indigenous women's rights and struggles at the United Nations level; therefore, their perspectives are intercontinental and embedded with a steadfast critic of nation-state formations and imposed political borders. As Guerrero explains, "Latinos who identify as Xicanas are starting a resistance to mainstream culture and colonialism and have a spiritual base that is rooted in their Indigenous ancestry."[68] In their films, there is a visible and constant connection with Indigenous practices—with spirituality, prayer, and ceremony as well as politics that are conscious of the earth as central elements of their storytelling.

Their form of collaboration is a manifestation of ceremony. WIM's filmmaking was groundbreaking, as queer Indigenous identified mujeres who collectively burned sage and copal, participated in traditional ceremony, and mentored a youth circle. Their intentional collaboration defied Hollywood's individualistic film industry strategies, as well as Hollywood's whiteness and heteronormativity. WIM also defied dominant structures through critiques of colonization and imperialism by retelling histories of violence, and addressing the complexities of war and police brutality. As independent filmmakers, WIM managed not only to put the stories of Indigenous-identified queer women of color on the big screen, but intentionally worked to create a space for women and people of color to be part of the filmmaking crew. As a result, they open doors for aspiring artists to develop their creative talents and receive guidance in the process of film production.

Womyn Image Makers' methodologies for creating art and storytelling are reflective of a larger collective vision that can be encapsulated in what Mendez named the philosophy or legacy of Indigenismo, which she also referred to as "people of the land." Mendez, who handles the production design in the collective, suggests that "*indigenismo* or people of the land" is "reflective of our working-class backgrounds, and how we realize that we have to work together as a whole and that each of us has our strengths and we can build upon that. . . . The way that we are doing it is through visual communication, a visual language."[69] It is insightful to see how this philosophy of Indigenismo, as conceptualized by Mendez, is distinct from the Mexican nationalist formation of this concept and praxis.[70] What is most impressive about this film collaborative was their dedication to breaking with the hierarchies of filmmaking and working as a collective to tell their personal stories as mujeres Indígenas, what Mendez called, "stories from spirit," narratives that have meaning and purpose.

Dalila Paola Mendez: The Two *Diosas Enamoradas*

These stories from spirit are present within Dalila Paola Mendez's visual art, which includes painting and serigraph, among other print media. Mendez, who was raised in Los Angeles, inherited from her abuelita—grandmother—who is from Guatemala, her *sabiduría de las plantas y crecer comida*—growing one's family's food in relation to the cycles of the earth, elements, and seasons. She offered, "as an artist, I am first generation born here in the U.S. and through my grandma's teachings, I've also learned a lot about plant medicine or different old traditions."[71] As a queer Indígena, raised in a matriarchal family, Mendez is also a master gardener, a muralist, Buddhist, and photographer.[72] Her vibrant interdimensional representations hold at their center her life experiences and *enseñanzas* received to visually story tell and guide people doing the work to reconnect with the earth and remember balanced relations. The paintings of the *Diosas Enamoradas* features two sacred beings reimagined in story by Mendez. This poignant artwork transports the viewer to inter-dimensions of time and space where relations and genders are sacred and circular, fluid, and constantly in formation. Although we do not know the exact dialogue between these *diosas abuelas*, we are told a story through the Mayan glyph inspired shapes that narrate an untold queer love story, connecting and honoring present-day praxis on earth to cosmic prayers from ancestors.

Mendez, as a detribalized Mayan Indígena artist, grounds her gaze—her way of seeing—in her abuela's forced migration to the United States and Mendez's required travel to the British Museum in London to view a significant collection of Indigenous art from precolonial Mesoamerica since many sacred ancestral items are held in European museums.[73] Inspired from an image Mendez encountered there of an ancient structure near her maternal homeland of the Yucatán, Guatemala, Mendez leads us through a journey of creativity as spirit work heavily influenced by the Mayan codices to create her acrylic painting series, which includes *Diosas Enamoradas* (fig. 6) and *Diosas Enamoradas II* (fig. 7), and that intentionally evoke amoxtlis. According to maestra Patricia Juarez, founder of the danza calpulli Huey Papalotl, "amoxtli" is a Náhuatl word that is more accurate than "codices." In addition, the name of the codex is usually connected to the colonial relation of the sacred texts. Such is the case with the Dresden Codex, one of three or four existing Mayan codices. In their coauthored scientific report, Böhm and Böhm show important evidence to underscore the arguments of this chapter.[74] Their study signals significant contradictions in the honoring of and extracting from the Mayan people and culture. Their analysis is achieved through reporting on the sacred codex, one of a handful of sacred Mayan archives that survived the decimation of ancient codices. Böhm and Böhm reveal that the Dresden Codex is held in the Saxon State Library in Dresden, Germany and is named after the location in which it resides—showing continued colonial domination. This "stolen" archive in diaspora leads to disconnection from its roots, peoples, and rightful home. This amoxtli is a historical document of the Yucatán area (Chichén Itzá).

Mendez reflects on the ancestral creative formation of this painting by emphasizing the role of sacred geometry and the vertically narrow orientation of the canvas that inspired her to create hieroglyphs. The central representation on the right is a queering of Kukulkán, the Mayan *energía* or god who is usually portrayed in the male form. Here, Mendez portrays the *serpiente* in their full feminine representation—opening a spectrum of gender balance reimagined in relation to the cosmos. The queering of Kukulkán that Mendez manifested through the shifting of gender mirrors the decolonizing of gender structures in our present day to unthread from strict colonial gender binaries. An intergenerational tension exists around gender and sexuality that is increasingly being opened by younger generations who are remembering who they are as they enter this dimension. Earlier generations of lesbians of color and transgender people of color laid a critical foundation for current critiques and formations yet there is a disconnect among communities that Mendez's artwork addresses.[75]

Mendez noted that it was her intention to make this a codex visually connected to ancient time—an image or symbol of "mujeres amando mujeres

Figure 6. *Diosas Enamoradas*, acrylic on canvas. Dalila Paola Mendez, 2005.

[women loving women] with the connection grounded to this earth" that could appear on a mural or on a wall in her ancestral homeland.[76] While the acrylic painting *Diosas Enamoradas* is in two colors, "black ink with red earth color," *Diosas Enamoradas II* holds the sacred colors of turquoise, gold, shades of brown, and pronounced bits of white that represent the moon. This sacred and profound image of two ancient "mujeres amando" portrays "the spirit of love."[77] She maintained during our discussion that "we are all creating, doing things and some of us, I think are conscious and try to do our art to raise consciousness or share

Figure 7. *Diosas Enamoradas II*, acrylic on canvas. Dalila Paola Mendez, 2017.

a story . . . connected . . . through spirit."[78] She explained that, in the process of creating this painting, she entered "this whole other dimension . . . nothing else was around."[79] She arguably entered another dimension of re-membering ancient time. In many ways, this form of remembering is necessary when tapping into ancestral knowledge systems that were colonialized, disrupted, and reformulated, and this is particularly significant in non-heteronormative or queer narratives of Mesoamerica. Taylor underscores the importance of knowledge and time in the amoxtlis in Mesoamerica: "Through *in tlilli in tlapalli* ['the red and black ink,' as the Nahuas called wisdom associated with writing], Meso-americans stored their understanding of planetary movement, time, and the calendar. Codices transmitted historical accounts, important dates, regional affairs, cosmic phenomena, and other kinds of knowledge."[80] Mendez's art does the work of mapping implications and interpretations of these ancient wisdoms critically and consciously, since "histories were burned and rewritten to suit the memorializing needs of those in power."[81] There is a refusal to romanticize the existence of the amoxtlis or put a contemporary misplaced meaning on them, while simultaneously honoring those who have direct connection and understanding due to their lineage, culture, tradition, language, and way of life, including ceremony. As Taylor says of the codices, "the images, so visually dense, transmit knowledge of ritualized movement and everyday social practices."[82]

These forms of knowledge are often the subject of solely scientific Christian research-based analysis, which, while practical, continues a legacy of colonization; it restricts access to ancestral knowledge and re-membering. Astronomers Böhm and Böhm refer, for example, to the "Dresden Codex," a misnamed Mayan amoxtli:

> The results of Mayan observations and calculations of astronomical phenomena are concentrated in the Dresden Codex. It is a band of paper 3.5-meter-long set up into 39 sheets marking up 78 pages 8.5 × 20.5 cm. The paper was obtained from the bark of wild-growing species of fig tree. It is supposed that it originates from Yucatan as a latter transcription of an elder original. It contains calendrical data, written in the Mayan dating system, concerning astronomical data and the sky mechanics, and tables of multiple integers that are to be used for calculation of planetary movement ephemerids and tropical years, next to the hieroglyphic texts and numerous depicturings of the Mayan gods and ritual scenes.[83]

Böhm and Böhm's findings emphasize that they were able to obtain a "new co-efficient" that allowed "for the conversion of the Mayan dates to our [Christian] dating system by a complete analysis of the mutual relation between the time intervals of all the Mayan dates in the Dresden Codex and 400 inscriptions from the cathedral cites."[84] The Mayan cosmic observations include dates for Venus and Mercury visibility, solar eclipses, full moons and new moons, next to equinoxes and solstices, and planetary conjunctions.[85] There is no doubt that these days and planetary happenings were directly linked to ceremonies practiced by the Mayan, which continue today among Mayan people who are re-membering and on their ancestral paths. However, this is not found in this report. They geographically describe and date the "Mayan settlement" as forming, "the so-called early phase of the initial period placed between 1500–800

BC. It was spread step-by-step to the regions of Guatemala, south-eastern Mexico, Belize, Salvador and north-western Honduras. The construction of beautiful and splendid cathedral cities, fine arts of sculpture and painting, use of their own hieroglyphic script, success in astronomy, existence of the literature and the development of handicraft and trade were the outer expression of this cultural-economic rise."[86] Many, like Mendez, whose familial lineages and roots are in Guatemala and El Salvador, experience tensions in ancestral remembering and practicing cultural traditions when there is a detachment to the rooted sabiduría of spirit work, prayer, and ceremony.[87]

Mendez's paintings then are a pathway home—to remembering sacred relations of spirit, and blessed cosmic love through visual storytelling. In *Diosas Enamoradas*, the two quetzal birds are facing each other, "dando la bendicion," giving the blessing, honoring this queer love.[88] At the top we see what Mendez describes as "different Mayan stars," while the bottom features three phases of the moon: a crescent moon, quarter moon, and full moon. A lotus flower appears in the center as an ofrenda to the love of the diosas, and in connection with Buddhist beliefs of illumination. On the side of the two diosas, three Mayan symbols are visible that travel vertically; they incorporate the Mayan number system. *Diosas Enamoradas II* has six phases of the moon, more pronounced geometric shapes, and hands on the top giving the blessing. *Diosas Enamorados II* was featured in 2017 at the Los Angeles Plaza Cultura y Artes, *¡Mírame! Expressions of Queer Latinx Art*, an exhibition exploring issues of identity in the LGBTQ Latinx community. In 2019, the work was featured in the *Cosmic Matriarchs Exhibition* at Taller Arte del Nuevo Amanecer (TANA).

Balam Huipil Remix Serigraph

Mendez's *Balam Huipil Remix* serigraph is a politically conscious visual story that critiques global structures of war and violence, with a direct focus on forms of corporate and colonial exploitation that cause destruction of the earth and her people (fig. 8). She contains these political toxins spatially within a spirit-centered intergenerational prayer for peace, protection, restoration, and balance. Mendez's visual representations of capitalist life-threatening formations include images of melting glaciers and rising water, AK-47 machine guns, genetically modified organisms (GMOs) in corn, drones and other distracting technologies, as well as processes of petroleum oil offshore drilling, deforestation, and corporate exploitation with the symbols of Nike and McDonald's. Each representation or image holds a deep critique of global politics that enact violence over the earth, her water and land, and the right to live peacefully and in balanced relations.

Figure 8. *Balam Huipil Remix*, serigraph. Dalila Paola Mendez, 2013.

Curated by Victoria Delgadillo at Self-Help Graphics, Mendez created *Balam Huipil Remix* serigraph in 2013, an urban and contemporary woven textile reflecting the wisdom that *huipiles* are a "weaving" of stories. *Huipil* comes from the Náhuatl word *huipilli*. Mendez was a contributing artist to *Communication Threads & Entwined Recollections*, which describes itself as "a textile inspired silk screen print atelier."[89] Mendez articulates her conocimiento of huipiles by offering that "there are always these symbols that are woven into the textiles to tell a story of an area of el Salvador or Guatemala, different woven textiles look different depending on what region you are in."[90] In this case, her hand-drawn serigraph was created with six color separations that each took fourteen hours to draw to "create the effect of woven string. This work honors the creation of typical woven blouses loomed by Mayan Guatemalan women."[91] Mendez created this artwork while her uncle was in his transition to the spirit world, and her abuela, who guided Dalila in her lifetime, had fallen ill. She expressed how it gave her a meditative focus to work so intensely while hand drawing the lines of this "visual prayer."

Mendez's *Balam Huipil Remix* was exhibited at the *Entre Tinta y Lucha: 45 Years of Self Help Graphics & Art* exhibition in 2018. There she was part of "Maestras," an intergenerational panel with Yreina Cervantez, Barbara Carrasco, and Judy Baca, held at the California State University, Los Angeles Fine Arts Gallery.[92] Mendez blogged about this exhibit: "My serigraph *Balam Huipil Remix* is on exhibit with an amazing list of artists. I am so humbled to be a part of this. When I was a junior in high school I first learned Xicanx/Latinx artists in LA existed and Self Help Graphics was the place they were making really great art, inspiring youth to create art and working with community. I wanted to be an artist and make art. 25 years later my serigraph is part of this retrospective."[93] Since her early twenties, Mendez has had an intergenerational relationship with artist, professor, and activist Yrenia Cervantes. In this *Entre Tinta y Lucha* exhibition, Cervantes's "Danza Ocelotl, 1983" was positioned next to Mendez's *Balam Huipil Remix*.[94]

In a 2019 interview, I asked Mendez if there were other elders who she felt have carved a path for her in the art world as a centroamericana. Mendez recalled meeting Rosana Pérez, whose words appear on Yrenia Cervantes's 1989 mural, *La Ofrenda*:

> I met Rosana Pérez who is an elder, Salvadorian poet, but she was also part of the FMLN in El Salvador and was a freedom fighter. . . . She had to escape, she had to leave because her life was in danger. She was part of *Epi Centro*, we called Epi Centro the group (of Central American activists and artists) . . . we had a good relationship, she was the elder of the group. . . . [S]he worked with Yrenia Cervantes, so Yrenia [herself] has done a lot of work with Central American artists and . . . when I have been on panels with her, she always brings that up I am a Central American artist. She is sweet to acknowledge to carve out the space and to pushes me to talk about this. She [Yrenia] worked a lot of Central American authors and writers during the '80s, when the whole civil war was happening in El Salvador. She did a mural that actually has Dolores Huerta in the middle, it's in Echo Park, and it has Rosanna Perez poetry along the mural and Yrenia painted it. She did a lot of work with Central Americans.[95]

Mendez concludes by noting the "intersecting ways" that she and Cervantes both work with the next generation. Both work with jaguar spirits, yet from their own imaginings. Dalila acknowledges the pathway that Cervantes as a visionary elder walked by making intentional connections with the next generation of artists who would be shaping consciousness. Through the 2018 acquisition of *Self Help Graphics & Art* prints by the Los Angeles County Museum of Art (LACMA), Mendez's *Balam Huipil Remix* print became a part of their permanent collection.[96]

Remembering and Planting Visual Prayers

How do generations remember when records and memories have been destroyed or mutilated for the purposes of cultural extinction and domination?

I argue, as others have, that memory or remembering what is painful opens space for the healing of historical traumas.[97] It builds possibilities for seeing and uprooting what has caused harm for an extended amount of time, particularly when communities have been focused on survival. This is helpful in thinking about queer Xicana/x and Latina/x Indigenous histories, and histories of people of color more generally, because as argued in the previous chapters, the misrepresentations, dominant narratives of history before and after 1848 and the colonization and misuse of the land, have caused the people of the Earth and grandmother Earth herself, great despair and various forms of disease, *maldad*. As Sturken suggests, hegemonic historical narratives do not honor the truths of multiple peoples across time and space: "The writing of a historical narrative necessarily involves the elimination of certain elements."[98] The written word and discourse has been dominated by the western imperialist gaze in our colonial modern world; therefore, this artwork opens a pathway to revision and visual and oral storytelling.[99]

To have the courage to remember in the midst of forgetting is not an easy task. To heal the heart often includes feeling generations of pain; one must touch the pain in mindfulness and peace so healing can occur.[100] To continuously remember that Indigenous peoples of Mesoamerica and many other lands have been displaced, sexually violated, and desecrated is significant historical work that resonates with contemporary forms of "racialized sexuality"; nevertheless, there must be a simultaneous healing energy or space created in order for transformation on a larger scale to occur.[101] I believe this is the risk that the artists featured in this chapter take with their work—they offer us a way to enter into what feels painful or difficult and make it visible and manageable through their ceremony of creating or creativity as spirit work.

The featured cultural producers participate in various forms of ceremony and actively work to evoke, spark connections, and unravel ancestral knowledge, historical discourse, and political memories in shared spaces and through practices of creative ritual. According to Taylor, "cultural memory is, among other things, a practice, an act of imagination and interconnection." It requires a deep focus and belief in something more than what is immediately visible. As Taylor argues, "sometimes memory is difficult to evoke, yet it's highly efficient; it's always operating in conjunction with other memories."[102] While Taylor focuses on cultural memory, Sturken makes an important distinction: she differentiates "between cultural memory, personal memory, and official historical discourse," arguing that "when personal memories of public events are shared, their meaning changes."[103] They become a form of cultural memory or collective remembering that can become a form of collective story. Like Sturken, I am more concerned and attentive to multiple forms of cultural memory, and I build on her framework by illustrating the ways in which spiritual and political spaces of collaboration and collective remembering are important to the process of restoring or inciting ancestral memory and imagination.[104] The work of collective remembering and imagining makes it possible to piece together expressions, perspective, and theories through manifestations of spirit-centered methodologies. The remembering I focus on occurs through various forms of cultural production, including media-film, theater, music, poetry, painting, sculpture, or a fusion of these.

This chapter focuses on the insights of "organic intellectuals" or art-makers who are aligned with a vision of creativity and hemispheric justice—a transformative and transnational impulse within feminists of color consciousness that is rooted in dismantling colonial and imperial forms of displacement and violence. My work is not exhaustive of the artists who are creating this spirit work; instead, my writing on two artists is intentional to show the intricacies of each, while also showing their interconnections. The organic and intergenerational efforts of queer Indígenas to construct their ancestral narratives and histories through oral and visual representations is a form of restoring collective and cultural memory that has previously been denied to them.

I offered an integrated approach that keeps in tension oral history interviews, archival spirit work, and visual readings of artistic production to show a formation of cultural artists and visionaries who contribute to queer Indígena discourse of remembering. The next and final chapter, "Tracing Latina Lesbiana *Historias* of Resistance, Solidarity, and Visibility," connects to this chapter by showing another distinct community that has done the work to build memory. Latina lesbianas, like other communities, have used solidarity as a site to build historical knowledge around a disappeared community of social actors. Through their own recognition of missing memory and exclusion from dominant forms of social and political knowledge, Latina and Chicana lesbians did the work to create spaces of creativity to tell stories from their own critical perspectives, as well as to create archives and forms of print to document these stories. Anthologies became an important site to build this knowledge, particularly because they are a collective theorization of relevant politics and forms of expression. Chapter 4 argues that, because of racist and heteropatriarchal structures of oppression, Latina lesbians have become visible mostly through their own efforts to gain visibility and create historical memory with the purpose of building a cross-border movement of resistance. In a parallel form to the artists discussed here, their articulations make it possible to envision alternative routes of hxstorical and cultural memory.

CHAPTER 4

TRACING LATINA LESBIANA HISTORIAS OF RESISTANCE, SOLIDARITY, AND VISIBILITY

Genealogical Archives of a Generation of Gatherers and Guardians of Knowledge

This chapter traces a genealogy of Latina lesbiana historias to illuminate the significance of archivists, scholar-activists, and artists who collectively birthed a political formation based on lived experiences and narratives of visibility that counteract the detrimental heteropatriarchal idea that lesbians of color or lesbianas de color do not exist or contribute significantly to philosophies of transformation in our social world.[1] I build with transnational feminist thinkers Mohanty and Alexander, who innovatively articulate that the "use of words like 'genealogies' or 'legacies' is not meant to suggest a frozen or embodied inheritance of domination and resistance, but an interested, conscious thinking and rethinking of history and historicity."[2] The genealogy is not linear or one-dimensional. This chapter maps a shift in the historical terrain that renders queer Latinx visible and significant to historical analysis by focusing on a generation of Latina lesbiana gatherers and guardians of knowledge.

Through their respective efforts to manifest anthologies, establish political formations, reconstitute library databases, and create photographic documentation of Latina lesbians, I argue that there has been a collective establishment of creative and historical archives that focus on Chicana and Latina lesbiana stories and feminist perspectives. This chapter is centered around a generation of cultural knowledge producers, including Laura Aguilar, Gloria Anzaldúa, Jeanne Córdova, Cherríe Moraga, Juanita Ramos, Yolanda Retter, tatiana de la tierra, and Carla Trujillo.

Although they vary in age, geographic location, and familial origins, these Latina lesbianas are central to a groundbreaking generation for Latina lesbian or queer Latina knowledges. Calvo and Esquibel argue that "research on Latina lesbians" demonstrates they are "an understudied population in the social sciences" and reveals some significant tensions over representation and visibility.[3] As scholars, Calvo and Esquibel chose to use the terms "queer Latina" and "Latina WSW" (Women who have Sex with Women) due to the exclusion of bisexual and transgender Latinas that can occur with the use of "Latina lesbian."[4] Gloria Anzaldúa is among the activists, writers, and scholars who also argue that the word "lesbian" has a homogenizing effect that is similar to the term "Hispanic," which "whitens" Black and Indigenous populations. Instead, Anzaldúa prefers the terms "dyke" or "queer" because they are more representative of her working-class background.[5] For this reason, as well as the historical time frame I am working with, I articulate this formulation as "Latina lesbianas," not "Latina lesbians," but also not "queer," to most accurately attempt to represent a generation that came into their sexual consciousness at a time when "lesbian" (read: white) was a term in circulation that preceded the politicization of "queer" in a radical form.

I carried out oral history interviews with six of the eight women for this project. Although I did not formally interview Anzaldúa or Moraga, I spoke with both informally, on separate occasions, about this research. Together they are a generation of elders who greatly contribute to legacies of cultural memory that have opened up and paved a pathway for political praxis for gender, sexuality, matriarchal relations, spirit work with ancestors, and interconnectivity in fields such as feminist studies, women's studies, and critical race and ethnic studies.

This chapter analyzes a historical archive organically created by and about Latina lesbianas. It continues the work of this book by specifically unsettling the patriarchy, nationalism, and homophobia that at times plagues knowledge formations, for instance in Chicanx studies. It centers the intellectual and political activism of important social actors that critically engage in radical transnational feminist, lesbian of color, and anti-patriarchal theory and praxis. Specifically, I focus on Latina lesbiana archivists, artists, writers, and scholars, who have creatively built forms of resistance and solidarity. Following the radical transnational impulse of uncovering subjugated queer knowledges,[6] Latina lesbiana social actors centered and cited here have carved out a space for the marginalized or the unseen, in various community and public spaces, including academia, the world of visuality, and cross-border social movements based on solidarity. I am most interested in how Latina lesbiana archivists, scholar-activists, and artists did the work of tracing and archiving unseen or unrecognizable intersectional knowledges. There is focus on the methodologies used to negotiate structures of power and to create spaces of solidarity.

I trace Latina lesbiana root knowledges and particular strands of women of color feminist social movements in order to disrupt silences around queer historias and to document communities who work within and across the politics of identity formations. Cindy Cruz offers a generative revised articulation of narrative as collaboration: "Narrative gives order to our multifaceted worlds and helps us grasp our lived experience to give it new meanings. Narrative is a collaborative sense making activity, socially constructed, where the mediation of lived experience happens with others in larger ideological structures and dominant value systems."[7] Coalitional terms manifest through lived tensions and struggle, including Chicana lesbians, Latina lesbianas, lesbians of color, women of color, and queer people of color, and more recently transgender Black and Indigenous people of color, which all emerged in particular social and political contexts. The narratives and cultural producers engaged here worked within and across multiple formations to create networks, collaboratives, and lasting legacies of political solidarity. My work does not attempt to be all inclusive, nor can it be. Instead, I engage with particular Latina lesbian creative critical work to illuminate interconnections and generational tensions among social actors in a generation of Latina lesbianas whose praxis is reflexive of women of color feminisms, a collaborative methodology. This chapter offers a genealogy that is connected to the coalitional term "Latina lesbianas" despite its potential limitations as an identity formation and a political space of possibility and creativity.

Latina Lesbianas in Resistance and Solidarity: Walking a Subversive Path

The political formation of Latina lesbianas is based on women of color lived experience and collective narratives of resistance that critique forms of imperialism, racial hierarchies, and modern technologies that are rooted in legacies of colonialism, including war, capitalism, enforced borders, genocide, and systems of imprisonment. Social movements and political struggles in the late 1960s and early 1970s provoked an upsurge in consciousness within Black, Chicano, Asian, and Native communities, based on historical racial tensions of civil rights struggles and movements of decolonization worldwide.[8] As a result, political identities that focused on racial and class struggles were shaped, at times in the form of cultural nationalism with a necessary focus on racialized exploitation at the center. While within this rising consciousness connections were made across race and class, what was largely lacking was a consistent interwoven analysis of gender hierarchies and sexual formations outside of heteronormativity and patriarchy. Forms of oppression—namely racist patriarchal formations and legacies that systemically and detrimentally impacted women, children, the feminine, the queer, the Earth, and in particular Indigenous peoples and communities of color—were not always seen as violence.[9] As social theorist Roderick Ferguson argues, "a national liberation movement like the Black Panther Party inserted itself into hegemonic waters as it normalized heteropatriarchal culture and revolutionary agency. Hence, despite its antagonisms to liberal ideology, it—like the civil rights and women's movements—facilitated liberalism's triumph."[10] He suggests mining "the history of women of color feminisms" as a site of emerging knowledge that disrupted "racial domination from the normative grip of liberal capitalism."[11] This rupture, or theoretical entry way, contributes to a pathway of tracing Latina lesbiana historias of resistance, solidarity, and visibility—to uplift a political understanding of knowledge production and praxis that is intentionally complex, dynamic, and spiritual.

Social movement discourses of the 1960s and 1970s tended to categorize participants and their activism through narrow or exclusive analysis and heteronormative frames. In this context, the connections between queer sexuality and the radical become invisible.[12] It became necessary to complicate the notion of one unified movement in order to document the narratives of the "marginal" or "other" forms of subjugated knowledges.[13] In particular, the lives and complex perspectives of lesbians of color or Latina lesbianas remained mostly hidden and/or silenced due to widespread homophobia and the chastisement of queers or gender nonconforming people in struggles for racial justice. The decade of the 1980s brought visible and critical interventions from women of color feminists and lesbians of color that wove together an analysis of race, class, gender, and sexuality under the rubric of what Chela Sandoval later named oppositional consciousness.[14] Together with the formation of women of color feminisms, "U.S. third world feminisms," as conceptualized by Sandoval, emerged as an international feminist politic of solidarity. Chicana historian Antonia Castañeda notes that "most women scholars of color who research and write the history of women of color look not to the women's liberation movement, but to third-world liberation movements," observing that these movements "identified with global struggle of third-world peoples for economic and political freedom.[15]

The interconnections in women of color feminisms became the foundation of a new way of theorizing difference and possibility. The roots of Sandoval's theorizations of U.S. third-world women theory and method are found in her report on the racism of the 1981 National Women's Studies Association (NWSA)

Conference, "Women Respond to Racism."[16] Sandoval, as the secretary to the National Third World Women's Alliance, explains that the three hundred women of color who attended were offered only one option for the consciousness-raising session that was required of all attendees. "White" women "were offered a series of lists signifying their diversity and emphasizing their choices," such as "'white/immigrant,' 'white/upper-class,' 'white/working-class' . . . and so on."[17] Sandoval documents the conflict that arose when women of color were placed "under one, seemingly homogenous category" at this predominately white conference that was attempting to confront racism.[18] According to Sandoval, there was no ready-made framework to dialogue for those three hundred women in 1981. What ensued was a critical discussion that interrogated the category "women of color" next to "third-world" women. They asked, "Is it possible that our similarities and differences be named under a single name?"[19] Within this intensive space of dialogue they acknowledged "a solidarity amongst the group."[20] This political solidarity or "common ground"[21] destabilizes simple forms of unity and sisterhood, frameworks that view differences as blocks to liberation. In fact, liberation is only possible when differences are understood as the building blocks.

The site of women of color and U.S. third-world feminisms has historically been a site of coalitions and alliances, where there are no simple answers or frameworks, the only constants are conflicts, negotiations, and collaborations and an openness to learning, unraveling, and cleansing previously internalized narratives. As Sandoval wrote about the limitations of the 1981 conference, "Our differing opinions seemed to place us in opposition to one another. *We managed this seeming conflict by considering our differences, not as idiosyncratic and personal, but as a rich source of tactical and strategic responses to power.* This positive perception of difference is not divisive, so there is no need to deny our differences or make them invisible. Instead these once personal responses to racism and oppression can be recognized as new weaponry in the ideological warfare necessitated by power struggle."[22] We see a formation of women of color and U.S. third-world feminism that interrogates and maps power through a coalitional methodology that centers difference in an international or global context. But also, and maybe more importantly, we see a politicized identity formation that does not posit experiences of race, class, gender, and sexuality as the place to name individual or collective *victims*; instead, this formation works to map the interconnections based on a vision of eradicating interweaved injustices through the everyday experiences with local, state, and global structures in relation to inequalities, injustices, and sites of struggle. Although the concept varied depending on geopolitical location, this politic of solidarity consisted of a complex analysis that held the United States accountable for historical atrocities toward people of color and Indigenous people in the United States and beyond.

It is important to note that the term "lesbians of color" predated the emergence of the term "women of color."[23] The term "third-world women" was constructed within the frame of first world-third world struggles; it is a gesture of solidarity with women of the so-called third world outside of the United States and third-world communities inside the United States. It is to an in-depth discussion of the constructions of these terms that I now turn. In their preface to *Third World Women*, editors Mohanty, Russo, and Torres offer a critical positing of the term "third world." They prefer "third world" over "postcolonial or developing countries" with all its complications:

> *Third world* refers to the colonized, neocolonized or decolonized countries (of Asia, Africa, and Latin America) whose economic and political structures have been deformed within the colonial process, and to black, Asian, Latino, and indigenous peoples in North America, Europe, and Australia. Thus, the term does not merely indicate a hierarchical cultural and economic relationship between "first" and "third" world countries; it intentionally foregrounds a history of colonization and contemporary relationships of structural dominance between first and third world peoples. In drawing on histories of antiracist, anti[-]imperialist struggles around the world, the term *third world* is also a form of self-empowerment. However, the unproblematized use of a term such as *third world women* could suggest the equation of struggles and experiences of different groups of women, thus flattening and depoliticizing all internal hierarchies. The term could also suggest that "third world" cultures or "ethnicity" is the primary (or only) basis of the politics of third world women. We intend neither.[24]

With this bold and thorough statement, Mohanty, Russo, and Torres guard against any all-encompassing moves that would potentially categorize third-world women into any sort of simplicity.

Similarly, Sandoval reports that "Third World" signals three things: "first, to have been de-centered from any point of power in order to be used as the negative pole against which the dominant powers can then define themselves; second, to be working politically to challenge the systems that keep power moving in its current patterns, thus shifting it onto new terrains; and third, such a name would work to underline the similarity between our oppression in the U.S. and that of our international sisters in Third World countries."[25] In both Mohanty, Russo, and Torres and Sandoval, there is an alliance or solidarity with women in third-world countries, as well as the stark recognition that there is an impinging third world within the land stolen by the United States.[26] It is based on a consciousness of unequal power relations that critique U.S. imperialism, colonialism, and other formations of empire. Because the "intersectionality" practiced by women of color relies on interconnections and links among systems of domination—it follows that mapping U.S. imperialism and hierarchies of race would require a global understanding of race, class, gender, sexuality, and nation, to name a few. It is this multilayered and always-shifting critique of heteronormative patriarchal dominance that historically informed the solidarity of Chicana and Latina lesbianas, lesbians of color, and women of color feminisms. Within these coalitional and collaborative communities there was a vision of solidarity that moved across constructed, binary, and policed borders.

Queering Women of Color: Origin Stories and Anthologies as Traceable Archives

> I was not a part of the sweat and fire that birthed a woman of color politics in this country in the 1970s and 1980s. This is why I want to remember that I have been shaped by it. It is why I am indebted to the women who literally entered the fire for me, on my behalf.
>
> —Jacqui Alexander, "Remembering *This Bridge Called My Back*"

It is significant that in the historical time frame I am addressing, many lesbians of color took issue with the term "queer" because it can erase gender specificity, similar to the category or label "gay." Women choose to name themselves to not be erased or remain unseen. Anzaldúa says: "My labeling of myself is so that the Chicana and lesbian and all the other persons in me don't get erased, omitted, or killed. Naming is how I make my presence known, how I assert who and what I am and want to be known as. Naming myself is a survival tactic."[27] Catriona Rueda Esquibel's *With Her Machete in Her Hand: Reading Chicana Lesbians* is an important contribution to research on Chicana lesbian fiction and thinking through formations of identity rooted in legacies of sexuality, race, and gender spectrums. She argues that "Chicana lesbian writing has yet to be studied as a distinct field . . . with definable characteristics, themes, paradigms, and contradictions." Her text undertakes this research by primarily focusing her analysis on "plays, short stories, and novels that feature Chicana lesbians."[28] Esquibel argues that "the work of Moraga and Anzaldúa is rarely perceived as being situated within a genealogy of Chicana lesbian writing. Instead they are decontextualized" as *the* Chicana lesbian representative of the whole community, or their lesbianism is detached from their work.[29] Her book reflects this significant theme or finding. Chicana lesbians did the work to piece together their histories through story and creativity, so that their complexities, contradictions, and multiplicities would not be written out of history. I build and extend this idea to Latina lesbianas cultural production and archival work in the 1980s and 1990s. This generation of Latina lesbianas, who were in collaboration with many others (people of color, queer communities, working class, communists, etc.), did the work to contribute to the roots of a queer women of color radical body of knowledge.

The emergence of this field of study is in response to the lack of historical knowledge about Latina lesbianas and other queer communities of color who are not often the subjects of inquiry in queer or Latina/o studies or acknowledged as part of the genealogies of these fields. Muñoz writes of this obliteration that "Cherríe Moraga and Gloria Anzaldúa's 1981 anthology *This Bridge Called My Back: Writings by Radical Women of Color* is too often ignored or underplayed in genealogies of queer theory."[30] He argues that *Bridge* "serves as a valuable example of disidentification as a political strategy."[31] Esquibel, through her queer "reading" of Chicana lesbian fiction, notes the establishment of the historical proof of existence for this complex community of artists, visionaries, and healers, through their own writing, an important breakthrough for a community that is often rendered marginal in historical narratives, at times even in queer studies.[32] Emma Pérez and Leyva, along with several other queer Latinx and Chicana lesbian scholars, have proposed important alternative methodologies for "locating" queer Latina and Chicana lesbianas in history and theoretical discourse.[33] Muñoz's *Disidentifications* is an early contribution to this field that, along with Ferguson's *Aberrations in Black*, articulates and builds with the complexities of women of color feminisms.[34] It is difficult to draw strict boundaries around Latina lesbiana knowledges and women of color feminisms since they exist in multiplicity; however, tracing offers a way to find connections and relations within this dynamic site of knowledge production. Women of color and Latina lesbiana thinkers made integral contributions to formulations of transnational, cross-border, and intercontinental feminisms and practices of solidarity through visual and textual representations.[35]

An important source of Latina lesbiana or queer Latinx knowledges is "creative production." Calvo and Esquibel suggest that "despite the paucity of empirical studies on this population, there is a rich body of Latina lesbian creative work circulating at film festivals, poetry readings, and comedy shows and in short stories, anthologies, theater, performance art, and a significant number of novels. This creative production has inspired an equally rich body of critical work on Latina lesbian culture and identity."[36] To illuminate a pathway of "creative production," I focus on the classic *This Bridge Called My Back: Writings by Radical Women of Color* next to a brief discussion of other key anthologies, which are relevant to queer Latinx and Latina lesbiana legacies. I draw attention to the long line of collaborative anthologies (collections of writing) that hold a dialogue between various authors, artists, and social actors of distinct perspectives, genres, and social positions.[37] Muñoz models this direct engagement with the legacies of women of color feminisms through his analysis of *Bridge*: "I . . . consider the critical, cultural, and political legacy of *This Bridge Called My Back*."[38] Another prime example of his engagement is with filmmaker Osa Hidalgo de la Riva's 1996 video, *Marginal Eyes or Mujería Fantasy 1*. Muñoz's analysis of Hidalgo's film shows a rescripting of a dominant narrative, a disidentification with patriarchy, where scientific evidence is unearthed to illuminate the existence of ancient matriarchal societies and thus leads to a women of color–centered state.[39]

Women of color offered alternative ways to conceptualize social transformation. Much of this work was sprouted from a vision of collectivity that aimed to disrupt racism and was in connection with politics of worldwide decolonization. Yarbro-Bejarano writes that "women of color thinkers such as the writers in *Bridge* and [Chela] Sandoval were developing notions of multiple subjectivity in a context of political resistance in the early 1980s."[40] According to Norma Alarcón's view of *This Bridge Called My Back*, "the editors and contributors believed they were developing a theory of subjectivity and culture that would demonstrate the considerable difference between them and Anglo-American women, as well as between them and Anglo-European men and men of their own culture."[41] To trace this intervention further and trace the growth of women of color feminisms, it is important to consider the legacy of *This Bridge Called My Back: Writing by Radical Women of Color*, a book project that inspired generations of women of color scholars, writers, and activists.[42] The call for submissions to *Bridge* began to circulate in April 1979: "We are planning a Radical Third World Feminists' Anthology: A Woman to Woman Dialogue of essays by women of color on their perspectives of the Feminist Movement." It was signed, "Sincerely, Cherríe Moraga Lawrence, Gloria Anzaldúa, and friends."[43] Significant in this call is the productive tension held between third-world and women of color. This political debate was an important concern and critique for feminists of color who were actively confronting racism in various institutions and everyday experiences in the United States while simultaneously seeing connections with racist and sexist forms of oppression in so-called developing or underdeveloped countries.

This Bridge and other women of color anthologies have been particularly instrumental in mapping revised politics of identity formation, difference, and solidarity. Although *This Bridge* was centered on radical women of color writers, it is significant that the two editors were Chicanas and lesbianas who consciously framed this offering with women of color at the heart of the writing. It is not a Chicana-centered text or a lesbian-only text, as are other edited collections or anthologies I discuss here. Moraga and Anzaldúa did the work of conceptualizing beyond the confinements of nation-states, places of origin, sexualities, classes, or racial physical features, in order to build solidarity and chart interconnections among women of color feminists without losing specificity. Moraga and Anzaldúa were part of a larger network of women of color and lesbians of color whose cultural creativity and forms of resistance were constantly in solidarity with other artists, scholars, activists, cultural producers, theorists, and writers. Their vision to create community is demonstrated in the postscript to the original call of *This Bridge*: "We are also compiling a list of Third World Women writers, artists, scholars, performers, and political activists. We hope to set up a network of women of color who may be called upon to give presentations, readings, workshops, or participate in conferences. We hope to make this list available to women's studies departments and other interested feminist organizations. If you would like to be included in this list, please send a short biographical sketch."[44] This vision and praxis of collectivity—the building of a network of women of color and a larger community of knowledge, resistance, and multiplicity—is integral to the continued relevance of this text and the contributors who together carve out a visible and viable pathway and form of knowledge.[45]

Women of color anthologies, particularly *This Bridge Called My Back*, became a forum a generational expression, formulation, and politicization of radical women of color feminisms that address the limitations and complexities of social movements that work toward liberation.[46] Sandoval argues that "the social movement that was 'U.S. third world feminism' has yet to be fully understood by social theorists."[47] In the introduction to the first edition of *This Bridge*, Anzaldúa explains the naming of the text: "we named this anthology 'radical' for we were interested in the writings of women of color who want nothing short of a revolution in the hands of women."[48] Therefore, the qualifier "radical" signals a vision of transformation that was rooted in ongoing activism at multiple sites and critiques of systems of domination. This is reminiscent of Sandoval's arguments about "differential consciousness." Sandoval argues that "U.S. third world feminism" is driven by a differential consciousness and "new subjectivity"—a "political revision that denied any one ideology as the final answer, while instead positing a tactical subjectivity with the capacity to de- and re-center, given the forms of power to be moved.[49] Sandoval's concept of "tactical subjectivity" provides a framework of negotiation for those subjects that are oppositional to multiple dominant ideologies and cannot be located under one singular rubric of identification. U.S. feminists of color, like the "radical" contributors to *Bridge*, brought together multiple ideologies and an interconnected analysis to shape the theory and method of differential consciousness.[50]

Bridge contributors create language.[51] Critiques of racism, colonialism, homophobia, and articulations of resistance were central to the story line of the feminists of color writing featured in *Bridge*. Alarcón says that "*Bridge* leads us to understand that the silence and silencing of people begins with the dominating enforcement of linguistic conventions, the resistance to relational dialogues, as well as the disenablement of peoples by outlawing their forms of speech."[52] There was an engagement of various erased and hidden histories within the text. For Moraga, *Bridge* was a coming home: "I didn't have to choose between being a lesbian and being Chicana; between being a feminist and having family."[53] Responding directly to the homophobia and heteronormativity imposed by the Chicano movement, this concept of being whole is radical because it challenges the fragmentation of the self that queer women of color have historically faced, including the dangers of being out to one's family or community, in a homophobic society. Through the creativity and collaborations within *Bridge* came the urgings for alternative movements or spaces to center the worldview perspectives of queer women of color among many others who are not always visible, a revised modality: "The vision of radical Third World Feminism necessitates our willingness to work with those people who would feel at home in *El Mundo Zurdo, the left-hand world*: the colored, the queer, the poor, the female, the physically challenged."[54] *El Mundo Zurdo* was conceptualized as a world that actively negotiated injustices of racism, homophobia, and other forms of hatred and harm based on difference, a world where the interconnected relationships among all forms of life are honored and understood in their own manifestation.

Another significant contribution of this anthology is the way *Bridge* illuminates the groundbreaking concept of "theory in the flesh." As Moraga explains, "a theory in the flesh means one where the physical realities of our lives—our skin color, the land or concrete we grew up on, our sexual longings—all fuse to create a politic born out of necessity. Here, we attempt to bridge the contradictions in our experience. . . . This is how our theory develops."[55] Moraga's idea of "a politic born out of necessity" is part of the legacy that fused an understanding of how radical transformation is linked to everyday experiences of being of color, queer, working-class, migrant. Anzaldúa writes that "the danger in writing is not fusing our personal experience and world view with the social reality we live in, with our inner life, our history, our economics and our vision."[56] The contributors in each essay, letter, manifesto, poem, and interview in *Bridge* do the work of linking their particular personal perspective and struggle with larger social critiques of systems of domination, namely global capitalism and classism, racist hierarchies, structured violence, and homophobia. Alexander explains: "For me, *Bridge* was both anchor and promise in that I could begin to frame a lesbian-feminist-woman-of-color consciousness and at the same time move my living in a way that would provide the moorings for that consciousness. Neither anchor nor promise could have been imaginable without the women in *Bridge* who gave themselves permission to write, to speak in tongues."[57]

This Bridge, although not necessarily a transgender space, is ample enough to hold the tensions, shifts, and spectrums of gender and sexualities. It is significant to note that contributor Max Wolf Valerio, "a transman, and an American Indian (Blackfoot)/Latino poet, performer, and writer," published as Anita Valerio in the original 1981 anthology.[58] Valerio's essay, "It's in My Blood, My Face—My Mother's Voice, The Way I Sweat," courageously and unapologetically critiques "traditional cultures" for the tendency to be "conservative" and his Blackfoot family lineage for being "patriarchal," as he recounted a story his mother shared of what it meant to be a "holy woman."[59] Simultaneously, Valerio does the critical work to show the healing he received in his first sweat lodge, where, as he explains, the "weeping was all of our pain—a collective wound—it is larger than each individual."[60] He continues: "in the sweat it seems as though we all remember a past—a collective presence—our past as Native people before being colonized and culturally liquidated."[61] Struggling with the shame of not speaking Blackfoot, being "half blood Indian and half Chicana," and the desire to go back home and learn songs, his Native language, and "how to set up a sweat," there is an underlying dimension of his sexuality and the rift it causes.[62] Valerio, alluding to a time when colonial binaries of gender did not overdetermine people's way of life, wrote that "perhaps in the old days, in some way or other I could have fit in there. But today, my lesbianism has become a barrier between myself and my people."[63]

Significantly, fields of study, such as feminist of color studies and Chicana/Latina studies, have witnessed an outpouring of anthologies that mirror the legacy of *Bridge*.[64] One such intergenerational echo is *Colonize This! Young Women of Color on Today's Feminism* by Daisy Hernández and Bushra Rehman, who say in their introduction that, "despite differences of language, skin color and class, we have a long, shared history of oppression and resistance. For us, this book is activism, a way to continue the conversations among young women of color found in earlier books like *This Bridge Called My Back* and *Making Face, Making Soul*."[65]

Such anthologies point to the continued relevance of race, class, gender, sexuality, nation, and other categories as important frameworks of analysis and intervention despite historic efforts to eradicate systems of discrimination that perpetuate violence in the United States.

Anthologies are unique in that they hold space for collective expression and contradictory voices that create a forum for dialogue and engagement.[66] As articulated by the Santa Cruz Feminist of Color Collective, "anthologies reflect a conscious method of solidarity across difference."[67] The "theory in the flesh" that Moraga theorized is connected to lived experience, living memory, and storytelling. Subsequent anthologies, such as Juanita Ramos's *Compañeras: Latina Lesbians*, Carla Trujillo's *Chicana Lesbians* and *Living Chicana Theory*, and Anzaldúa's *Making Face, Making Soul/Haciendo Caras*, set the tone for theorizing from a place of deep, intimate knowledge "of the flesh."[68] They also offer a genealogy or legacy of politics for Latina lesbianas. These anthologies are an offering, a collective analytical self-disclosure and critical reflection that speak, write, and theorize through lived experiences of systems of inequalities. These texts were created in spaces of collaboration and through visions of solidarity and resistance.[69] Anzaldúa, like other feminists of color scholars and visionaries, saw paradoxes and contradictions in the social movements around race and feminism as places to critique and build alternative forms of social transformation.

Anthologies matter because they document the transnational social movements of Latina and Chicana lesbians. In 1988, Cherríe Moraga and Ana Castillo edited a Spanish-language edition of *This Bridge*, titled *Esta Puente, Mi Espalda: Voces de mujeres tercermundistas en los EEUU*, translated by Ana Castillo and Norma Alarcón. This edition was a gesture toward an emerging third-world consciousness that reflected worldwide decolonization politics and a desire to build international solidarity to disrupt constructed political borders and violences. Critical writings from women in Cuba, Veracruz (Mex.), El Salvador, and Watsonville (Calif.) were brought into this anthology in an effort to acknowledge larger political struggles, especially in connection to resistance, survival, and the spread of U.S.-based imperialist militarism and war in Latin America.

Latina lesbianas also employed oral histories as archives to construct alternative sites of knowledge production for marginal or subaltern subjects. Juanita Ramos started the New York–based Latina Lesbian History Project in an attempt to fill gaps of knowledge about Latina Lesbian histories. Ramos compiled and edited the anthology *Compañeras: Latina Lesbians*. This anthology was groundbreaking in the sense that it spans the spectrum of Latinas, which included Gloria Anzaldúa, but it is not focused on Chicanas by any means and it uses *autohistoria*, oral history, and poetry as the primary forms of expression. *Testimonio* (testimony) or autohistoria are the related ways in which the political stories of Latina and Chicana lesbians have been documented and circulated.[70] Writer and editor Carla Trujillo, in her introduction to *Chicana Lesbians: The Girls Our Mothers Warned Us About*, says that, when *Compañeras* was published in 1987, it "gave presence to the voices of Latina lesbians who, with the exception of Cherríe Moraga and Gloria Anzaldúa, had been largely unheard."[71] In my interview with Trujillo, she discussed the important influence of both Moraga and Anzaldúa on her writing when she saw them speak at an antiracism conference during her graduate school years. She recalled that both women told her to write, even if she didn't consider herself a writer.[72] Trujillo went on to formulate and edit two anthologies that contributed greatly to setting the foundation for the emerging site of knowledge by Latina lesbianas: *Chicana Lesbians* and *Living Chicana Theory*.[73]

The production of these anthologies, from historian Deena González's perspective, is pivotal for recognizing lesbian women of color in the academy: "without some of our work in print, we face total erasure, and risk not being present in historical and cultural memory."[74] This presence and production of the texts is at the cost of still not being fully heard, since "they now have or own our words; they think they 'hear' our voices, our languages, but we are still absent."[75] González's review of two key Latina lesbiana forms of cultural production, Anzaldúa's *Making Face, Making Soul/Haciendo Caras* and Trujillo's *Chicana Lesbians*, argues that these anthologies "give radical lesbian women of color a forum" of expression, resistance, and visibility.[76] She further argues that Chicano and feminist intellectual spaces rarely acknowledge the work of lesbians of color and instead "impose upon these works a heterosexual genealogy."[77] González describes *Making Face, Making Soul/Haciendo Caras* as a text in which "cultural criticism unifies the essays and creative selections, as do expressions of rage against colonization, and the problem of de-colonization in the academic malestream and in mainstream feminist circles."[78] Of Trujillo's anthology, she says that "this work challenges Eurocentric organizational schemes and, by extension, Euro-Americans and heterosexual people of color who accept those methodologies unquestioningly in 'their' canons."[79] If Anzaldúa and Trujillo's anthologies are not seen as queer or lesbian women of color texts at their core, then the layers of analysis that complicate heteronormativity in Chicanx/Latinx and women's studies are no longer viable, which in turn flattens the critique these authors are asserting within and about these fields of study. Collaborative interventions and political formulations such as the ones articulated in these archives—anthologies and stories—allow for queer lesbian of color theorizations based on lived experiences and narratives of visibility to contribute to dismantling the logics of colonization, global capitalism, and imperialism while taking rooted steps toward decolonization and asserting a critical place in the canons of Xicana/x and feminist studies.

The Work of Tracing: Rewriting Early Latina Lesbiana Historiographies

This tracing of Latina lesbiana history is an active response to colonial legacies in modern forms of knowledge that silence or homogenize racialized queer histories of color through unintentional exclusion and fragmentation within, for example, the fields of Chicano/a studies and women's studies. Mainstream women's studies rely on frames from "the women's liberation movement," which tend not to represent women of color histories, ancestries, or realities. Similarly, a gap in knowledge exists in Chicano studies due to widespread adherence to homophobia, whether conscious or unconscious, resulting from the internalization of colonial logics of gender and sexuality. Carla Trujillo, in her classic essay, "Chicana Lesbians: Fear and Loathing in the Chicano Community," argues that an attention to sexuality, lesbianism, and queerness consistently poses a threat to "revolutionary" or "alternative" political agendas that were male-centered or race-based and in turn skews the way this knowledge is presented.[80] Emma Pérez's queered "decolonial framework" is useful in the tracing of Latina lesbiana historias.[81] Her work facilitates questions about oral history and archival analysis, which signals the need for decolonized historical narratives of queer, lesbiana, dyke, jota, *marimacha*, butch, trans, gay, gender nonconforming, two-spirit pathways that are attentive to the paradoxes of silence and the possibilities that open when building collectively.[82]

> She called me diosa one day
> And I believed her
> I mean, she was a librarian
> She wrote encyclopedia entries
> Archived important papers
> Surely, she was an authority on diosas[83]

Long-time activist and archivist Yolanda Retter, a Latina dyke of Peruvian ancestry, responded to the call for *This Bridge* with her information and biographical sketch to be a part of the women of color network. In a 2006 interview with Juanita Ramos, Yolanda Retter noted that she began her early activist work "intentionally and consciously" in 1971. Further noting the trajectory of her activism, she said during a radio interview that "when I came

Figure 9. "Yolanda Retter from *Latina Lesbian* series." Laura Aguilar, 1987. Photographic collage.

out publicly, I began working with a group called Lesbian Feminists in Los Angeles. Which was a politicized lesbian group that was primarily white and later in the '80s with a group called Lesbians of Color in Los Angeles. And then after that in the '90s when the movements had sort of abated, I began working in archives and libraries on behalf of lesbians, women, and people of color."[84] Retter's narrative trajectory is an example of how women of color feminists have historically struggled for visibility and connection with other women of color. In Retter's case, although she did not submit her writing for consideration to the editors of *This Bridge*, her life's work and activism demonstrates her dedication and solidarity with the creation and establishment of this form and legacy of knowledge production that centered a radical women of color consciousness, where the radical signaled an uprooting of systematic forms of domination. Retter credits the release of Moraga and Anzaldúa's *This Bridge Called My Back* as a historic moment when out Latinas started to be more visible, "and different groups emerged across the country, including . . . Lesbianas Unidas."[85]

In a 2005 interview, Retter spoke about her awareness of the Chicano movement as well the reasons for her non-interest in that space of organizing and community:

> I am not Chicana, I am half-peruana. And I grew up in El Salvador, although I was born here [in the United States]. But I remember very distinctly when I was at Pitzer College, that would be late '60s and beginning of '70s, I wasn't going join the Chicano movement. Why? Homophobia and sexism. Who needed that? When I finally decided to come out to the public, tell everyone that I was dyke,

> my first political *familia* were the white girls at the Lesbian Feminists group that met in the 1970s, [specifically] 1971 at the women's center. There were maybe 5 women of color in that group, 3 Latinas, a couple of Black women and a couple of Asian women.[86]

Retter's narrative shows how her process of coming out was supported by being a part of a white women's lesbian feminist group instead of a race-based movement. This is revealing in terms of the lack of lesbian of color or women of color spaces in the 1970s where an analysis of gender, race, sexuality, and class could simultaneously exist. When I asked Retter about out Chicana lesbians during the 1970s, she informed me that I was going to have a very hard time finding Chicanas who identified as lesbians within the movement. This has proven to be an intense truth.

At the USC ONE Gay and Lesbian Archives, where Yolanda Retter was an archivist for years, I spent most of my research time with the Lesbian Legacies Collection (LLC). In the 2006 radio interview, Retter commented that the ONE, which was seen as very white and male, established the LLC because it wanted "to be credible." With a "lesbian legacies" collection, there would be a gender balance. Within this collection, at the time of my visit, only a disheartening eight folders focused on the "Lesbians of Color" category, which is sadly impressive. Although very limited, this is more than what is usually found in the archives, which is next to nothing. There was enough repetition in the folders to ensure that even if you viewed only one folder, you had a chance to catch a connection with the material in another folder. The collection had one general folder, and the remaining seven were titled "LA, National Conference, 1983," "California," "Los Angeles," "Network," "New York," "U.S.," and "Writers."

Retter's dissertation, "On the Side of Angels," is based on her own participant observation in the lesbian feminist community in Los Angeles as well as on oral histories, with people such as Jeanne Cordova.[87] What is notable about the dissertation is that Retter pointedly highlights when lesbians of color or women of color are involved in an action, event, or scene. This focus is reflected in her work of building archives, which was clearly a central part of scholar-activism. It is largely due to her stubbornness that the Chicano Studies Research Center at UCLA has the LGBT and Mujeres Initiative Archival Project. This effort was significant in reformulating histories that had been marked by a norm that was not inclusive of lesbian of color, butch, or genderqueer histories. Much of Retter's early work was dedicated to studies focused on Latina lesbians in the Los Angeles area, especially their histories. Retter, who died at the early age of fifty-nine, contributed to the building of archives on women of color and lesbians of color by working with Walter Williams on the ONE USC International

Lesbian and Gay Archives. They also coedited *Gay and Lesbian Rights in the United States: A Documentary History*.[88]

Besides Retter's research, publications and archival work, her collaboration with Lillian Castillo-Speed, ethnic studies librarian at UC Berkeley, is one of the most significant indicators of her contributions toward shifting institutional formations of knowledge. In 2005–6 the two worked on a revision of the Chicano Thesaurus funded by a grant from the Librarians Association of the University of California.[89] The revision added two resources to the online Chicano Database used in Chicano studies: "List of LGBTIQ Terms Added to the Chicano Thesaurus" (twenty-four terms) and "List of Non Chicano People of Latino Heritage" (sixty-five terms). A major effort to make visible or at minimum make "searchable" people outside of heteronormative Chicano studies. tatiana de la tierra who was also a library science specialist with concerns similar to Retter's. In her poignant 2008 article, "Latina Lesbian Subject Headings: The Power of Naming," de la tierra discusses the complications of her search for Latina lesbianas and finding "Homosexual" and "Hispanic.[90]

Castillo-Speed and Retter had conversations for some time about the desire to collaborate, since they were both working in the Chicano studies research centers on their respective campuses (UCB and UCLA). Castillo-Speed recalled that Retter had a lot of critiques about the Chicano Database, the major one being the limited terms to name Chicanx and Latinx LGBTIQ communities; prior to this revision project, "homosexual" was the key term.[91] As of 2007, one can enter terms such as "lesbians of color" and "transgender people" into the database for more accurate and inclusive research searches. The other major shift is the sixty-five terms to search for research connected to non-Chicano people; terms such as Costarricences, Dominicanos, and Salvadoreños were added to acknowledge in the database people of Latino heritages (the terms reflect Latin American nation-states and migrants in the United States). Still, as important as this work is, language, terms, and categories are not static and are constantly evolving. For example, traces of the formulation "queer Xicana Indígena" may not be easily searchable in archives and databases. This intervention in library systems speaks to the underlying vision of this chapter: illuminating narratives of visibility through a collectively birthed political formulation that allows for the transformation of social worlds.

Collaboration with Laura Aguilar

The art of photography is yet another method or form of creative or cultural production that documents what is under erasure, particularly when a Latina lesbiana is holding the camera. Laura Aguilar brilliantly captured the black-and-white photo series of Yolanda Retter (see fig. 9). Another version of this 1987 photo shoot, titled "Yolanda," appears in the 2017 *Laura Aguilar: Show and Tell* exhibition publication. For her *Latina Lesbian* series, Aguilar included a short quote by each featured Latina lesbiana. Retter's quotation read: "My Latina side infuses my lesbian side with *chispa* and *pasión*. I am a lifelong lesbian and I think that women hold powerful promise for changing conditions on the planet. You think I look hostile? Maybe it has to do with a passion for and an impatience with a vision. Maybe it comes from comparing what could be with what is. *¡¿Y que?!*"[92] Sybil Venegas writes that "the 'Latina Lesbians' series took an early documentary view of professional Latinas whose portraits were augmented by personal texts regarding their sexual preference and self-esteem."[93] These portraits, taken by Aguilar primarily in the late 1980s, establish a visibility to affirm the formation of this complex community and dynamic political formation that could otherwise remain below the heteronormative radar.

Laura Aguilar—whose "ancestral maternal lineage ran deep into the Mexican and Native populations of the San Gabriel River basin" according to Venegas and who "possessed a significant oral history of her maternal line"—became a well-renowned Chicana lesbian photographer whose final photographic works document nature, spirit, and body, yet was largely invisible to the mainstream art world during her lifetime.[94] Retter and Aguilar shared a friendship, where Aguilar was a mentee of Retter's. When I asked Aguilar about Retter and her presence in her life, she explained to me that Yolanda was the first and most consistent person in her life to pronounce her name in Spanish, *Laura Aguilar*. Laura discussed how "Aguilar" evokes the eagle (*águila*) in her family name, so Retter's pronunciation evoked a remembrance of the eagle in her family lineage.[95] This affirmation of her name in Spanish and *cultura* is another layer of tracing and remembering ancestral roots.

Aguilar's photographs of Yolanda Retter (see fig. 9) were the first in her *Latina Lesbian* photographic series.[96] Aguilar reflected in our interview about Retter's significant presence in her life in terms of her racial formation and understanding herself as a lesbian of color.[97] Retter encouraged Aguilar to connect her racial identity formation to the visual representation of her art form. Insisting that she assert being Latina with the recognition of also being a lesbian and artist. As a visionary activist, Retter also influenced Aguilar to dedicate herself to developing her art practice and applying for funding to support her work. Aguilar remembers that there were not a lot of Chicana photographers at the time; often, she was the only Latina or woman of color among white women in a photo exhibition. The mentorship of Yolanda Retter, among others, helped

Laura Aguilar break barriers of racialization, gender, disability, sexuality, and spirituality. As a result of Yolanda Retter's influence on Aguilar and their mutual trust, the UCLA Chicano Studies Research Center has a substantial archival collection of Aguilar's photography and other works.

When I asked Aguilar what made her decide to put her work in the UCLA archive, she responded with a nervous chuckle, revealing that it was because she was suicidal.[98] She later shared that she had a difficult conversation with Retter about these feelings and that Retter insisted Aguilar's work be documented and archived with her vision guiding the process. Affirming this incredible gesture of care, Christopher Velasco of the Laura Aguilar Trust noted that the trust was created through Yolanda Retter and Laura Aguilar's friendship. Retter supported Aguilar to work with a lawyer to attend to all of her tax and legal matters.[99] Aguilar had consistently struggled with economic hardship, acceptance in society, and toward the end of her life with severe illness. She was born to a Mexican American family in 1959, raised in Rosemead, California, and was aware from an early age that being a dyslexic person resulted in her having difficulties with learning and with language. Aguilar turned to a visual format to express herself and contributed greatly to rethinking standards of beauty, creativity, and possibility for Chicana lesbians through this medium. Her contributions to Latina lesbian histories are significant on multiple dimensions (including political visibility for queers of color) through various projects. I focus on two relevant photographic projects: Aguilar's *Latina Lesbian* series, and her *Plush Pony* series. Within these photos we see a telling of historias de la gente.

The *Latina Lesbian* series documents a variety of mujeres from various geopolitical locations and peoples who are part of a network of Latina lesbianas. Yolanda Retter commissioned Aguilar for this project, and she was the first to be photographed for this series. Aguilar began this groundbreaking photographic series in August 1986 with a grant from Connexxus, an organization led by women of color.[100] A short narrative on each photo offers a particular palabra or message from the featured Latina lesbiana, a moment of self-representation for each mujer in which they name themselves and dismantle the ways they can be feared or unseen in society. Many of the women featured were genderqueer, making these visible representations even more groundbreaking as they expanded the possibility of what a Latina and a lesbian in her power looks like. According to Aguilar, the *Latina Lesbian* series captures women who were part of an activist, creative, and/or professional world, a network. The *Plush Pony* series, on the other hand, is an intentional documentation of a working-class bar in the LA area where Aguilar set up to photograph the bar patrons. In these images, we see various representations of sexuality and gender, including variations of masculine butches and femmes. The images document roles and bodies that were rarely seen or curated as a photographic series due to many factors. As an artist, Aguilar was unsatisfied that she had only captured a particular circle of lesbians who had access to institutions, education, and other privileges in the *Latina Lesbian* series. With *Plush Pony*, according to Aguilar, her intention was to capture nontraditional bodies of working-class mujeres who are not usually represented in visual images or the public world in beautiful ways. Her photographic works, which are extensive beyond what is discussed here, represent Aguilar's fierce political vision and critique of the inequalities in the world.[101] Aguilar's brilliant use of black and white offer a gentle pause to *see* the depth of the subject or subjects with a genderqueer nonnormative gaze.

Just as Laura Aguilar photographed Yolanda Retter as the first person for the *Latina Lesbian* series, in 2005 Retter was my first oral history interview for this project. A foundational guiding question at the core of this project is how you trace a something or someone under erasure. This was the impulse of my desire to be in dialogue with Retter, an outward Latina lesbian archivist—one of the few I could locate in my trace of queer ancestry. In many ways, my research journey for this work was initiated with a conversation with Yolanda Retter. I sat with her at the Chicano Studies Research Center at the University of California, Los Angeles. She talked through the possibilities of my project with me from an archivist-scholar-activist point of view. At that time, Retter was doing the work of conducting oral histories with Latina Lesbians of early generations (1970–90s), and she reinforced what I was slowly understanding about my research trajectory—I was going to have a very difficult time locating archives and even people to conduct oral histories with. The loudest echo I heard in her guidance was that many of these knowledge holders are elders, and their stories need to be heard and have a place in *our historias*.

In this way, Laura Aguilar's photography is a reconfiguration of "Latina lesbianas," building visual conceptual tools and formations full of dynamism, contradiction, and different forms of silence. The collaboration between Laura Aguilar and Yolanda Retter explicates that Latina lesbianas created their own representations through a necessary disruption of normative images of Latinas and lesbians.

After I learned of Retter's sudden death in 2007, I returned to the UCLA CSRC archives intending to listen to the oral histories she had conducted. To my surprise, grouped with her oral histories on Latina lesbians is a tape labeled "Chicana lesbians of the 1960s and 1970s." I became curious about its contents, since this was exactly what I had been searching for. I put the tape into the recorder and within seconds was shocked to hear my voice in a dialogue with Yolanda

Retter from some years earlier. This moment sent me, as a spirit-centered researcher, into deep pause, a methodological reflection on the critical articulations and praxis of navigating "evidence," archives, narratives, and efforts of intervention to locate, document, and trace what is seemingly unknowable or erased from the colonial logics of our social world.

Remembering my own study of silences around sexuality, lesbianism, and queerness, as well as the guidance I received from Retter, I made the critical decision to imagine cross-border, hemispheric interconnections as a methodological way to unravel imposed border of nation-state separations and instead ground in movements and mujeres that traversed rigid political boundaries. The formation of Latina lesbianas as a political project opened my focus to trace beyond Chicana lesbians, and facilitated the visibility of a transnational solidarity rooted in issues of land, forced removal, migration, colonization, and social and economic crisis due to imperialist wars and the subjugation of the people of the land. To trace queer ancestry, it is necessary to unsettle colonial tendencies. Deep listening, truth telling, and oral storytelling emerge as key queer Xicana Indígena root work methodologies that facilitate the seeing, tracing, and recognition of sabiduría (wisdom) and knowledge keepers. To the question "how do you find something under erasure?" this work responds by understanding the tenets of the imposed colonial silence, the uplifting of resilient ancestors who guide traditional praxis, and the weaving of decolonial or liberation movements from distinct social locations without homogenizing or aiming to unify differences that can spark alternatives we have never imagined.[102]

Gathering the Multidimensional Archives

What I signaled in this chapter are the gatherers and guardians of knowledge who contributed greatly to the movement of making Latina lesbiana communities visible and recognizable to society by resisting the norms imposed and creating alternatives that honored their complexities, distinct positionalities, and working-class identities. Latina lesbianas, for generations, have done the work to create visibility through a feminist critique of inequalities, including patriarchy and homophobia. This network of women of color worked to create spaces that opened up possibilities for a radical feminist politic, particularly positions that could take on the difficulties of analyzing violences on multiple levels, while building visual stories of resistance, solidarity, and visibility. The intersectional analysis within women of color and lesbians of color articulations and activism facilitated an analysis of larger systems of subjugation and sprung forward as an important site of tension from which to build theory, map praxis, and re-create a space of resistance within institutions that rarely recognized the complexities of women of color.

Through the building of archives, the reconstituting of databases, the photographing of Latina lesbians, along with the creation of anthologies, art exhibitions, and organizations focused on Chicana and Latina lesbiana stories and feminist perspectives, this chapter maps a shift in the historical terrain that renders queer Latinas visible and significant to philosophies of transformation. Following the radical impulse of uncovering subjugated knowledges, the Latina lesbiana social actors, scholars, artists, and archivists centered and cited here have done the work of carving out a space for the marginalized or the unseen, in various spaces, including academia and cross-border social movements. Latina lesbianas, through their visual representations, although distinct in their efforts, create an important visibility and feminist critique of inequalities, particularly interconnected global forms of capitalism and heteropatriarchy through the articulations of their gender, sexuality, class, and racialization in unapologetic ways.

EPILOGUE

Coda of Enseñanzas

In this coda, as a way to come full circle, I want to breathe life into the *Xicanx Futurity* exhibition that took place on the homelands of the Patwin peoples at the Manetti Shrem Museum of Art, territory designated as the land grant institution of University of California, Davis. There, the late Jack Forbes (Lenape) was an original faculty member of the Native American Studies Department, as well as a founder of DQ University (Deganawidah-Quetzalcoatl University), one of the first tribal colleges in California. It lies about nine miles away from the UC Davis campus.

This exhibit was one moment in time that makes visible how art and cultural production are pathways toward decolonization. Here I make an argument for the fire. The need to sit with the abuelo fuego and our own internal fire to cleanse. The tension that I opened this book with regarding Chicanx people having the right to reclaim and self-determine their Indigeneity is a pathway to unraveling truths that need to be spoken. It is a divisive debate that began with colonization, and for Mesoamerica with the arrival of Christianity in the form of the Spanish Crown. Xicana/x peoples have always been people of the Earth. However, through legal systems based on fictive notions of race, and militarized borders, dominant narratives of who Chicanx and Latinx peoples are activated. It is important we tell our own stories, and it is perhaps more important to learn our stories. It is also important to learn how to listen with an open heart, to yourself, the collective, and the ancestors. This book attempts to contribute to expansive methodologies that open pathways and imaginations that give permission to be Xicana Indígena or a detribalized Indigenous person. To shift the narrative out of the state imposed rhetoric of "immigrant," "Hispanic," "foreigner," "Mexican." What follows aims to illuminate how *Queering Mesoamerican Diasporas* has intentionally centered matriarchal lineages, Indigenous medicine, and balanced relationship with the Earth. Dialogues with visionary artists, ceremony, spirit work, truth-telling, and tracing have been central to the formations of this text. I turn to the artwork of elder Celia Herrera Rodríguez, whose work weaves through this text.

Building on the theorizations I established previously (see esp. chapter 3), in particular the focus here is on the visual storytelling of queer Xicana Indígena artists as a site of wisdom and knowledge that addresses colonial forgetting by creating present day visual narratives of traditional spiritual practices that have been sustained despite colonization. The artwork and vision of queer Xicana Indígena artists, namely sculptor Gina Aparicio and elder Celia Herrera Rodríguez, who were featured in the exhibition along with four other Indígena artists, serve as explicit sites of analysis and reflection. The intention of the exhibit worked to connect Indigenous roots, familial lineages, memories and pratices of traditional healing modalities, to relationships with medicinal plants, and ceremonies to support sustenance and life. For Xicanx and Latinx peoples living in diaspora, visual culture that opens the senses to remembering has the capacity to awaken sacred seeds and prayers planted by ancestors. This trabajo can lead and guide a path of conocimeinto and sanación, a healing of intergenerational traumas.[1] It does this while also facilitating the building of reciprocal and respectful relations with all beings on Earth and the cosmos. One of the most significant and provocative components of the *Xicanx Futurity* exhibition was how it provided a pathway into ceremonia, nearly a thousand people were present at the exhibition opening in early 2019.[2] The intentional prayer was felt. People were moved through the presence of smells, songs, and textures, alongside the visual blessings. When open, it is possible for the viewer to be transported into an open-hearted space of remembering, ceremony. Gonzales theorizes "birth as ceremony" and therefore our first ceremony; according to her cosmological worldview, we have all experienced a moment when time, space, and the cosmos aligned to bring transformation and new life, a new beginning.[3] This exhibit provided a way to re-member and realign the body, mind, and spirit.[4]

Here I focus on enseñanzas of queer Xicana Indígena root work, philosophies and practices, in particular relation to the *Xicanx Futurity* exhibition, which ran from January 2019 to early May 2019. In this brief coda, I focus on one part of Celia Herrera Rodríguez's contribution of the exhibit. As a whole, this art exhibition was rooted in an intergenerational prayer. Carlos F. Jackson invited Maria Esther Fernandez and me to cocurate an intentionally sacred and inherently political space, where visual culture was a form of storytelling and those stories and visual prayers lead to a deep remembering. I say "inherently political" because Xicana Indígena art and artists as the central focus in a university museum exhibition is rare, an intervention to the white colonial walls and racist heteropatriarchal structures. For two of us, as faculty in Chicanx Studies at the University of California, Davis, this exhibit was an opening to address deep tensions our students and communities struggle with in terms of identifying or dis-identifying as Indigenous and the implications of Indigeneity in Chicano/a/@/x identity formations or Xicanx praxis. As Patrisia Gonzales writes, "sometimes because detribalized people have lost communal structures, there is a sense of the need to name oneself."[5] Fernandez, a well-established leading Chicana curator, had previously collaborated with Celia Herrera Rodríguez (Xicana/O'dami) in multiple art exhibitions and held space for Indigenous women and artists of color in museum spaces. All three of the cocurators had previously established yet differing relationships with maestra Celia. Like the artists in the show we collectively view her as a respected elder and wisdom carrier—a queer mujer artist who walks the red road with dignity and generosity. The remaining featured artists of the exhibit were Margaret "Quica" Alarcón (Otomí and Taino), Gina Aparicio (Xicana/Apache/K'iche'), Melanie Cervantes (Xicanx), Felicia "Fe" Montes (Xicana Indigenous), and Gilda Posada (Xicana). The *Xicanx Futurity* exhibition held the presence and worldviews of queer, nonbinary, Central American (including Guatemalan and Salvadoran), Puerto Rican, undocumented, femmes, and Indigenous peoples (including Odami, Taino, Apache, K'iche', Otomi, Xicanx, and Xicana Indígena). It argued that hemispheric dialogues on Indigeneity on the University of California, Davis, campus and beyond must include Chicanx and Latinx people who are Indigenous to this continent.[6] A significant controversy arose around "the sacred" in this art exhibition. The implications are significant for Xicanx and Latinx Indigenous peoples and all relations.

Mi Camino, My Methodology: Queer Xicana Indígena Root Work

Here I offer a bit of my own autohistoria to locate myself as a curator, professor, and researcher. During my time as a Chicana/x studies faculty member at the University of California, Davis, as a person who self-identifies as a queer Xicana Indígena and who walks a decolonial spirit-centered path, I have encountered many contradictions in the colonial academic world. I have witnessed exclusions, silencing, and the upholding of hierarchies that inflict violence, all at the cost of honoring all our relations and interconnectedness. When I first arrived to campus, I was met with students who were intensely frustrated, confused, and at a loss. Several expressed that they were tired of existing in a hybrid space and needed to feel grounded. In the first class I taught in the Chicanx studies department, I presented frameworks of decolonization. An undocumented Indígena student, along with two Chicana-identified students, approached me to ask me to consider teaching a whole class focused on decolonial-centered knowledge—this was the birth of a course I currently teach, Decolonizing Spirit. The syllabus, themes, and readings were cocreated with the first cohort of this course in 2016. I started to ask myself more and more: How does a student who is Chinantec, Zapotec, Mixtec, Purépecha, Rarámuri, Yaqui, or Otomi find their alignment or truth in a field that signals to a foundational myth that has settler colonial tendencies with Aztlán as a homeland? What is the conversation and unthinking about land as property, forced migration, and colonial borders that needs to take place? Similarly, I acknowledged the profound presence of "detribalized" students who know they are Indigenous, have Indigenous blood, lineages, and roots, and are connected with the traditional medicine practiced in their families and communities, yet are met with knowledge and frameworks that insist they are hybrid, mestizo, at an institution that is aspiring to be a Hispanic-serving institution. This can be very disorienting.

The exhibit then became a space to wrestle with and weave some of these tensions by uplifting Xicanx and Indigenous Latinx artists who are deeply rooted in community and Indigenous thought, practice, and philosophies, including forms of healing and ceremonia. Gonzales writes that "colonization is permeable. The potential of human beings does not have to be limited by oppression or limiting paradigms that may not factor the power of prayers and ceremonies left by earlier generations or the spirits of memory in the foreground."[7] In the case of *Xicanx Futurity*, through prayer as praxis, the representations created by the six Xicana/x artists opened space for deep introspection and inquiry of history, lineages, ancestry, medicine, foods, language, and other forms of traditional Indigenous wisdom, with the vision of reconnecting and restoring "teachings and cultures." Xicana/x people have arguably created a dignified path to self-determination that honors Indigenous roots and familial legacies across the hemisphere. Art, that is, visual storytelling—gives us access to remember what we have lost especially when grounded in prayer and ceremony—to reacquaint ourselves with practices and philosophies we feel connected to and were disconnected from over generations due to colonization and forms of trauma, such as de-Indianization.[8] Xicana Indígena Art brings fragments of memory back together (like Coyolxauhqui at the full moon).

In order to do the work of healing from intergenerational traumas of susto that have been internalized over generations due to colonial state logics of racism and projects of de-Indigenization, a focus on creating spaces of ceremony and spirit work are necessary. The consequences of soul loss, particularly the susto of de-Indigenization, can be as severe as a disconnection with one's ancestors and family lineages, disruption in the sabiduría of traditional medicine, and missing memory of Indigenous languages and concepts that can sever knowledge of cosmological worldviews. I am guided by Moraga's words: "We must ask ourselves: *what do we know? We know more than we know we know. What is the way back to knowing?*"[9] Art, visual storytelling as a pathway to remembering, in the case of *Xicanx Futurity* was an interweaving of visual stories and prayers across generations, lineages, and geographies to tell of complex narratives connected to what Gonzales names "traditional indigenous medicine."[10]

Enseñanzas of *Xicanx Futurity*

I vividly remember that the day of our first meeting with Manetti Shrem Museum of Art staff, I heard the reminder to offer tobacco. I prayed this way, honored the original peoples and asked permission for the work ahead, in front of the railroad tracks on this day in June 2018, and almost every day that I visited the Patwin land that the museum is situated on. I would make my offerings to the Earth, sacred Tonanztin Tlalli Coalticue, and often encountered hawks that flew nearby, above, or en route to the water tower. Through the experience of the *Xicanx Futurity* exhibition, I encountered many enseñanzas, lessons that arrived from elders, community, and ancestors, to show and teach us an expansive *aprendizaje* (teachings) about the moment we were living and experiencing.

Earlier in this book I discussed queer Xicana Indígena root work, with the aim of complicating what is understood or misunderstood as "Chicanx Indigeneity"—a phrase that has been established in key debates. George Hartley outlines some of these tensions.[11] He makes note of the differing positions and perspectives of Chicanx peoples claiming Indigeneity. Through Hartley's thoughtful analysis he suggests "inter-tribal" relations, instead of "pan-tribal" solidarity to shape forms of "networking" to honor distinctions among Indigenous peoples, "just as the peoples of Turtle Island had done before colonization and conquest."[12] He also articulates key tensions that require deep analysis and are significant to critiques Chicanx and Latinx Indigenous identified people are faced with: "This self-definition of Chicana indigenism has not always sat well, nevertheless, with some Native North American critics or with other Chican@ critics of such representations of Indianness and indigeneity. Reasons given for resisting the identification of Chican@ as indigenous generally hold in common the insistence that there are major, perhaps irresolvable distinctions between the two groups that need to be maintained."[13] Hartley continues: "these distinctions fall under three main concerns: (1) the living legacy of the Spanish Conquest, (2) the differing ways in which the US government relates to and defined the two groups, and (3) the claim that Chican@ appropriations of markers of indigeneity differ little if at all from the exploitative appropriations of all things Indian by the dominant Anglo culture."[14] I argue that this point of departure presented by Hartley about Chicanx Indigeneity invites further meditation for Chicanx studies scholars—to move away from a homogenizing mestiza/o identity formation that excludes Indigenous and African lineages, as well as the need to decenter the Conquest as the start of our history, origin, or raza (people). Perhaps, more importantly, it invites a move toward a rooted existence in Indigenous lineages on this continent that, according to Roberto Cintli Rodríguez, dates back at least seven thousand years.[15] It is time to remember our maíz narratives.

New Fire and *Xicana Codex* as a Weaving Toward *Xicanx Futurity*

At a 2012 reading and panel discussion at Stanford University, playwright and author Cherríe Moraga described the theater production of *New Fire: To Put Things Right Again* as a "three-dimensional" version of her book, *A Xicana Codex of Changing Consciousness: Writings, 2000–2010*.[16] This articulation moved me. *New Fire* is a multimedia theater production that features ceremonial song, dance, music, healing, performance, and video. Moraga's book is, as its title indicates, a codex, amoxtli, a collection of Moraga' sacred writings, images, and stories over a decade, speaking to the growth of Indigenous awareness in daily life. The 2011 publication of *Xicana Codex* and the January 2012 world premiere of *New Fire* at Brava Theater in San Francisco mirrored each other in presentation and production, and inevitably were a pathway of ceremony for Xicanx Indigenous peoples.

New Fire was a collaboration of Cihuatl Productions.[17] In a collective "Open Letter" written by the artists and founders of Cihuatl Productions, Moraga, Anthony, and Rodríguez describe *New Fire: To Put Things Right Again* as "the sacred geography of Indigenous American mythologies" that tells "a 21st century story of rupture, migration and homecoming."[18] This is evidenced in the play through the presence of many Indigenous peoples and their practices, including Filipino, Peruvian, Xicana/os, Native American (Oglala Lakota), Black, and

African lineages. It was a sacred collaboration among healing people with the purpose of representing tools of transformation in a public space. *New Fire* is rightfully described as where "theatre meets ceremony."[19] The theater production of *New Fire* features Celia Herrera Rodríguez in multiple ways.[20] In some scenes, she appears on stage as "Roadwoman," leading the ceremony as a grandmother "who brought the medicine." At times, she is simultaneously featured on video panels on either side of the theater's stage, where the audience sees representations of various moments of ceremony with Indigenous people in locations such as Chicago, and South Central Los Angeles, and with original people, such as Zapotec migrants. Rodríguez and her prayers, her *voz* (voice), her cooking, and her sabiduria indígena (Indigenous wisdom) are captured through visual representation on the screen. This brings another layer of reality and social context to the play. There is a particular striking and instructive segment in which Indigenous is redefined as "knowing where you come from." Particularly in the context of Chicanas/os/xs, this is significant since a history of displacement and erasure of Indigenous cultures plagues this consciousness.

These urgent themes for Chicanx and Indigenous peoples explored in the theater production *New Fire: To Put Things Right Again* are analytically explored in Moraga's 2011 text. At the 2012 Stanford panel discussion on Cherríe Moraga's *A Xicana Codex of Changing Consciousness*, religious scholar David Carrasco said, "stories come alive in ceremony," referencing Moraga's work in the theater. He asserted that "fire is about change" and "new fire is about radical change," speaking of the *New Fire* theater production. Similarly, he drew a parallel between Xicana consciousness and radical consciousness. He acknowledged the strand of Buddhism within Moraga's text, eastern teachings that connect to or speak of "the old ways."[21] The expression "the old ways" refers to traditional and ceremonial Indigenous ways, although its use is not limited to the past *only*; conversely, the use of "the old ways" in this context shows the pertinence of spiritual forms of being that have existed for thousands of years and do not resemble colonial legacies or adhere to western modes of existence. "The old ways" were very present in *New Fire* and the enseñanzas within her writings.[22]

Moraga as an artist, author, mother, playwright, and fire-keeper presents her writings humbly, and yet the offerings within are illuminated visions, images, and intellect. Moraga's knowledge and writings span the decade from 2000 to 2010 and offer Xicanas and Xicanos a way to remember. In one essay, Moraga writes of her mother's Alzheimer's: "She had forgotten all stories, suffering from Alzheimer's. Still she remembered me, although at times she referred to me (and my lesbian niece) as 'he' instead of 'she.'"[23] Moraga continues: "I have other butch Latina lesbian friends (my age) who tell me the same," that is, who say that their abuelas or mothers refer to them by a male pronoun.[24] For Moraga, forgetting is a form of remembering. She suggests that her mother is remembering when she calls her "he." Moraga understands this to mean a remembering of her "two-spirit" self, and she rethinks her mother's supposed error in naming: "some part of me feels that in this great show of intuitive knowing, our 'demented' mothers and grandmothers may not be forgetting so much as remembering."[25]

The strength of the *New Fire* production emerges from the way Moraga and Rodríguez brought the deep wisdom of ceremony that activate your senses onto the stage. At times it was the prayer offered by Rodríguez that brought the audience clarity and peace, and in others, it was the performance itself, which included music, song, and drums to guide the ceremony on stage. The stories, visual narration in bright colors, and geometric patterns through song and movement do the work of decolonizing storytelling by explicitly representing a healing ceremony in which the audience is privileged to see and hear sacred knowledge at work.

In addition, *New Fire*'s themes offer a break with western patriarchal gender-sexuality systems and move toward regaining matriarchal sacred memories in which nonbinary and two-spirit genders and sexualities were honored. Besides the important role of Coyote as a two-spirit character, in the *New Fire* theater production El Caminante, the male elder storyteller, takes gentle issue with the ceremony being run by a Roadwoman or grandmother rather than by a Roadman or grandfather. Across the duration of the play we see his consciousness shift: he begins to wonder if Creator could be two-spirit. Toward the end of the play, he turns and asks Vero, the fifty-two-year-old character who is being honored at the ceremony, "do you think Creator is two-spirit?" and he follows this by instructing, "don't tell anyone I asked that." Showing how his curiosity and question are taboo, this scene reveals how Indigenous cultures and spiritual communities are not free from patriarchal narratives, including homophobia and male-centricity in language and conception.

This elder male character, who is guided by wind in his storytelling, was not quite comfortable with the idea that a medicine woman could lead and guide ceremony, a role that he was used to being fulfilled by the grandfathers. Yet, what we see on stage are two-spirit women and grandmothers guiding, particularly through the Roadwoman and Cedar Woman in a peyote ceremony. A peyote ceremony is especially significant to re-create in a Xicana Indígena theater production due to the restrictions on "Mexicans and Mexican Indians," who "are often prohibited from using this potent medicine because they cannot prove they are Indian." This occurs even though "many in Texas are the descendants of

Chichimeca tribes and other Native peoples with an ancestral connection to this medicine."[26] Gonzales complicates the colonial history of peyote medicine: "In colonial Mexico, peyote medicine was so revered and useful, female midwives and healers were prosecuted by the Holy Office of the Inquisition for employing it, and colonial records document its widespread use among Indigenous peoples of Mexico. Despite religious persecution of its users, its medical and ritual use continues today among numerous Mexican Indians from Huichol and Tarahumara, Native peoples of the north, and detribalized Mexicans and 'Chicanos indígenas' who use it medicinally in homes with families as part of prayers or in large ceremonies."[27] The courage and guidance that is offered in *New Fire* and *Xicana Codex* assist in planting the seeds of sanación, a pathway for Xicanx who are doing the spiritual trabajo to find their way home.

Acoyaliztli Tlachpana Xicana (To Raise Our Voices in Prayer to Clear the Obstacles in Our Path), Mixed Media, 2019

> As Chicana/os, we are a displaced people of many nations of origin, living in diaspora in the United States. Our mestizaje—perhaps more a political idea rather than a fact of biology—was forced upon us. How do we recover from the shock of displacement, the loss of Indigenous memory? How do we rekindle the home-fire? The painting is the record along the road. It allows me to think, meditate, to assume the posture of ceremony, to pay attention in that deep way. The door opens to us, just by spending time looking at the images, the symbols. And we begin to understand. These paintings and installations are a conceptual language, a suggestion of how to find our way back to home.
>
> —Celia Herrera Rodríguez, interviewed by Cherríe Moraga (2011)

Maestra Celia Hererra Rodríguez, who is an artist, philosopher, and ceremonial leader, through her visionary art installations intentionally creates a way to pray, remember, honor, and seek justice. In her platicás, she often asks people to reflect on their values, Indigenous values present in their daily life; she also provokes Xicana/x to think critically about the way we are encouraged to surveil each other. Through her liberatory social practice of creativity of spirit, she illuminates how the most important herramientas (tools) we have to fight structures of oppression is our spirit work, our prayer, our ceremonia. This articulation is reminiscent of Celia Herrera Rodríguez's artwork featured in the *Xicanx Futurity* exhibition, which offers her prayer, a pathway to remembering and coming home. Honoring those who have given Chicanas/os/xs, Xicana/x, Latinx detribalized and de-Indigenized peoples sacred space to heal and be in ceremony. Celia Herrera Rodríguez's featured installation was titled *Acoyaliztli*

Figure 10. *Cihuacoatl: Prayer for Our Future*, part of *Acoyaliztli Tlachpana Xicana* (To Raise Our Voices in Prayer to Clear the Obstacles in Our Path). Celia Herrera Rodríguez, 2019.

Tlachpana Xicana (To Elevate Ourselves in Prayer to the Open Road), 2019. It was a mixed-media offering that wove together watercolor painting, handmade structures of Earth-based materials, beaded staffs, and feathers. The piece that I focus on here is *Cihuacoatl: Prayer for Our Future*, a prayer for the Central American migrant *caravanas* that started heading to the United States in 2018 from Honduras, Guatemala, Nicaragua, and El Salvador.[28]

In the summer of 2018, Maestra Celia asked me for support in creating a part of what would become her installation for the upcoming art exhibit. I agreed and met her early morning at the Cache Creek Conservancy in Woodland, California, the original homeland of the Patwin people. She guided me to wear long sleeves and long pants to avoid being bitten by rattlesnakes, although the temperatures were expected to be above a hundred degrees that day. She shared with me about her long relationship with Cache Creek Conservancy, including her relationship with local elder and cultural practitioner Diana Almendariz of Maidu, Wintun, Hupa, and Yurok descent and bringing her students there from the University of California, Berkeley. We unpacked Maestra Celia's car and walked directly to the creek. Before I knew it, we were asking permiso, offering prayers with tobacco to

Figure 11. *Cihuacoatl: Prayer for Our Future*, part of *Acoyaliztli Tlachpana Xicana*. Celia Herrera Rodríguez, 2019.

the willow that would assist in creating a structure for holding the sacred. I soon understood why we needed to be in close proximity to the flowing water as we built the prayer structure. Rodríguez has explained that what she has created was capturing the "conversations" we were having "about what is happening politically and culturally."[29] We worked under the blistering sun for five days, fearing heat stroke especially as we got into the afternoon, yet many of our conversations were extremely humbling and gave us courage to continue. There was a lot of focus on the next generations, the children, and in particular the migrant children of the caravans, as well as on mothers, and the possibilities of motherhood, including queer parenthood. It became clear that part of Celia's prayer was for the present and future of those young ones. The flow of the water, the presence of the sun, the smell of the willow, and blessing of the birds allowed for the prayers to be felt, voiced, and weaved with all elements present.

In installation form, *Cihuacoatl: Prayer for Our Future* (fig. 10) features a corn mother holding an elder's staff at the center, with cedar and turkey feathers at her crown. This is a collaboration with artist Suzy Hernandez, a mother of twins, ceremonial sister, and former student of Maestra Celia. *Cihuacoatl* which translates literally as "woman serpent," *mujer serpiente*, is often likened to the legend of La Llorona, who is in perpetual search of her children due to patriarchal atrocities, as well as Tonantzin Coalticue, earth mother. In Rodríguez's installation, this association aligns with the grief, *susto,* rage of knowing the potential tragedies that the migrant Indigenous children are experiencing due to economic poverty, structural abuses, corrupt neoliberal governments, and colonial legal frameworks that keep people undocumented and detained asylum seekers. At the base of *Cihuacoatl: Prayer for Our Future* is a mat with hand-sewn child-sized clothes with the word *caravana* woven into them. Next to this are two pairs of children's huaraches, wooden sticks for fire, a ceramic pot, and an offering to the four directions that contains cedar, sage, and tobacco. The intergenerational collaboration in Rodríguez's social practice was ever-present in an important prayer that manifested in the form of Maestra Celia, Suzy Hernandez, and cocurator Maria Esther Fernandez—three generations of mothers—sewing the clothes for the future, the children, *las semillas del futuro* (the seeds of the future).

Interestingly, the *Xicanx Futurity* exhibition was closed a few days early because this particular willow structure—often referred to as the "feminine structure" in description of Celia's structures—was being eaten by beetles, which can have a range of meanings. What is clear is that the prayer of the exhibit and Maestra Celia's *Acoyaliztli Tlachpana Xicana* was powerful enough to close down a museum, after much needed reflection, provocation, and awakening in Xicana/x, Latinx, and Indigenous communities around the sacred, ceremonia, and spiritual consciousness that is rooted in seeking justice for all relatives. In many ways, this exhibit created space to ask difficult questions that are in alignment with the root work of this book: How do we open up space for healing and listening across distinct communities when there is a need to acknowledge intertwined and complicated historical traumas, genealogies of Indigenous knowledge, and violence that separate ourselves from each other? How do we create spaces that can hold unresolvable tensions? In closing this book, I propose that there is intention put into emerging difficult dialogues to open up circles of healing and justice to create stronger relations and interconnectivity.

I also propose the concept of cross-pollination offered by an elder of mine, as used in ceremonial circles, as a concept to interrupt the accusation and idea of appropriation that often falls on Xicana/x peoples. The goal is not to appropriate another's culture, yet there must be an acknowledgment of the hemispheric migration, interaction, exchange, and interconnectivity before the imposition of the border, missionization, conquest, and other forms of colonization. This is particularly important as many Xicana/x peoples are in the process unraveling centuries of de-Indigenization. The echoes of tensions are legacies of colonial wounds that are not new. Yet there is an awareness that capitalist nation-states and racist structures rooted in the hierarchies of white supremacy benefit from the people of Earth staying in a state of perpetual fear and conflict. How do we intentionally manifest alternative pathways? How do we move in dignity and respect as we are all learning and experiencing difficult enseñanzas? I believe this is especially significant for people doing the work of decolonization, self-determination, and sovereignty. It is important to imagine and work toward the abolition of prison systems, detention centers, and militarized nation state borders, as well as to dismantle all forms of heteropatriarchy and violence, to restore balance and vital lifeways. Finally, it is important to ask: What type of legacies are we leaving our next generations? What is the role of traditional medicine? What is the role of the sacred?

NOTES

Foreword

1. See Keating 2013 for more on post-oppositionality.
2. Keating 2008.
3. Keating 2008: 54–55.

Introduction

1. A. Smith 1999.
2. Champagne 2014.
3. Leyva 2002b: 6.
4. Leyva 2000a: 10.
5. Anzaldúa et al. 2003: 8.
6. Anzaldúa et al. 2003: 9.
7. Anzaldúa et al. 2003: 12.
8. Anzaldúa et al. 2003: 19.
9. Anzaldúa et al. 2003: 6.
10. Hernández-Ávila 2003–4.
11. See Mignolo 2007.
12. Miranda and Keating 2002: 202.
13. Miranda and Keating 2002: 203, 204.
14. Miranda and Keating 2002: 204.
15. Miranda and Keating 2002: 204.
16. Miranda and Keating 2002: 203.

17. Anzaldúa et al. 2003.
18. Miranda and Keating 2002.
19. Miranda and Keating 2002: 203.
20. Avila 2000: 28–29.
21. Luna 2012a: 10.
22. Luna 2012a: 11.
23. Gonzales 2012a.
24. Gonzales 2012a: 37. See also Román 2012.
25. Gonzales 2012a and Calvo and Esquibel 2015.
26. Castañeda 2001: 118.
27. Santa Cruz Feminist of Color Collective 2014.
28. Hall 1996.
29. E. Pérez 1999.
30. Latina Feminist Group 2001.
31. Miranda 2010.
32. Spivak 1999. Also see Muñoz 2009.
33. See R. Rodríguez 2014: xxv.
34. Leyva 1996.
35. Leyva 1996: 145. See also Leyva 1998.
36. Spivak 1999. For more on methodological interventions in queer historiography, see Boyd 2008, Kennedy 2006, among many others.
37. Moraga and Anzaldúa 1983. Mohanty, Russo, and Torres 1991. Trujillo 1991. Ramos 1994. Alexander and Mohanty 1997. Trujillo 1998. Santa Cruz Feminist of Color Collective 2014.
38. See, for example, Bonfil Batalla 1996, Gonzales 2012b, Martinez-Cruz 2011, S. Garcia 2021.
39. Román 2019.
40. E. Pérez 2003: 124.
41. E. Pérez 2003.
42. Gonzales 2012a and 2012b.
43. Alexander 2005 and A. Smith 2010.
44. Anzaldúa 2015c: 156–59. See Moraga and Anzaldúa 1983, esp. section 6, "El Mundo Zurdo: The Vision"; Alexander 2005; and more recently, Lara and Facio 2014, and Medina and Gonzales 2019.
45. Gonzales 2012b acknowledges the Judeo-Christian origins of the concept of "prayer." My use of the notion of prayer is distinct from any type of structured/imposed religion.
46. Alexander 2005.
47. Alexander and Mohanty 1997, E. Pérez 1999, L. Smith 1999, and Cruz-Malavé and Manalansan 2002.
48. L. Smith 1999.
49. J. Rodríguez 2003: 22.

50. It is important to note the contributions of scholars who have theorized a queer of color critique, including Muñoz 1999, Ferguson 2004, and Soto 2010.

51. On "borderlands," see Anzaldúa 2007.

52. Sandoval 2000.

53. Alexander 2005. Also see Keating 1996.

54. Santa Cruz Feminist of Color Collective, 2014.

55. Quijano 2000.

56. Davis 1981, A. Smith 2005, Blackwell 2011. Grewal and Kaplan 2006, Shohat 2001, INCITE! 2016.

57. See Mohanty 2003.

58. Retter 1997, Cruz 2001, Retzloff 2007, Córdova 2011.

59. H. Ramírez 2005: 116.

60. H. Ramírez 2005: 113.

61. Colonization, genocide, and violent dislocation are not unique to the geographic landscape known as Mexico, but for purposes of this book, there is an inherent focus on the histories of Mexico (Bonfil Batalla 1996, Gonzales 2003).

62. Miller 2009.

63. Keating 2000: 187.

64. Gonzales 2012b.

65. Taylor 2003: 34.

66. Taylor argues that "Although the Aztecs, Mayas, and Incas practiced writing before the Conquest—either in pictogram form, hieroglyphs, or knotting systems—it never replaced the performed utterance. Writing, though highly valued, was primarily a prompt to performance, a mnemonic aid" (2003: 17).

67. Sturken 1997: 7.

68. Sturken 1997: 7.

69. A. Smith 2005.

70. This logic follows that of post-traumatic stress, when one becomes aware of what caused the trauma, and that knowledge facilitates the path of overcoming the memory.

71. Martinez 2017: 192–93. Maestra Cuauhtli Cihuatl articulates: "I think that my path through all these years, from birth to sixty, has been to guide people to re-remember that *we are* the medicine. That we *are* the earth, that we *are* the fire" (Cihuatl and Muñoz 2021).

72. Alexander 2005: 293–94.

73. Alexander 2005: 262–63, emphasis original.

74. Gómez-Barris 2009: 78–89.

75. Warner 1993.

76. Muñoz 1999.

77. Estrada 2007, Hernández-Ávila 2006, Moraga and Rodríguez 2007, Driskill 2016.

78. Tello 2018.

79. Some important examples of this include Ferguson 2004, Seidman 1996, Gray and Gómez-Barris 2010.

80. Brown Childs 2003.

81. Anzaldúa 2007: 29. See also Guidotti-Hernández 2011.

82. Waziyatawin 2008.

83. Omi and Winant 1994.

84. Alexander and Mohanty 1997: xxvii.

85. Waziyatawin and Yellow Bird 2005. Also see Fanon 2004.

86. L. Gómez 2007.

87. Miller 2008: 15.

88. Anzaldúa 1987, Bonfil Batalla 1996.

89. Thiong'o 1986: 11.

90. Mignolo 2007.

91. Mignolo 2007: 156.

92. Mignolo 2007: 164. Also see Grosfoguel, Maldonado-Torres, and Saldívar 2005.

93. Lugones 2008: 2.

94. Lugones 2008: 2.

95. Lugones 2008: 1. See DiPietro 2020.

96. E. Pérez 1998.

97. Blackwell 2003: 81. Also see Ruiz 2008, Castañeda 1992, and A. Garcia 1997.

98. A. Garcia 1997.

99. Warner 1993: xvi.

100. Muñoz 2009.

101. Some notable articles and essays written about or within the legacy of *This Bridge* are N. Alarcón 1990b, Short 1994, Duffield and Cespedes 2002, M. Gonzalez 2002, Sudbury 2003, and Alexander 2005.

102. Moraga 1993, Moraga 2011, Galarte 2014 and 2020, Muñoz 1999 and 2009.

103. For example, I was fortunate to interview Juanita Ramos, editor of *Compañeras: Latina Lesbians* (1994), and Carla Trujillo, editor of *Chicana Lesbians: The Girls Our Mothers Warned Us About* (1991). See chapter 4.

104. L. Zepeda 2018.

105. There is a continuously growing, yet relatively still emergent body of work, in the field of queer Latinx sexualities. See Cantú 2000, Acosta 2008, Mitchell 2010.

Chapter 1. Decolonizing 1848

1. On a land-based heteropatriarchal Aztlán, see Anaya 1989.

2. Gonzales 2012b: 28.

3. Forbes 1973, Moraga 2011, Gonzales 2012b, Luna 2012, R. Hernández 2005, R. Rodríguez 2014, Alberto 2016, Lara and Facio 2014, Román 2012, and Medina and Gonzales 2019.

4. The formulation "theory in the flesh" first appeared in Moraga and Anzaldúa's (1983) groundbreaking *This Bridge*, 22–23. It is Cherríe Moraga who theorized this

powerful articulation that has shaped Chicana feminist, Xicana Indígena, and women of color feminist knowledge production.

5. Gutiérrez 2004.

6. Moraga 2011: 95.

7. Pulido 2018: 7.

8. Rowe 2017: 525.

9. Rowe 2017: 535.

10. Pulido 2017: 2.

11. Wolfe 2006.

12. Gonzales 2014.

13. R. Hernández 2005: 131.

14. Gonzales 2012b: xxv.

15. Anzaldúa 2002a: 540.

16. Moraga 2011: 81.

17. Leyva 2002a, Leyva 2002b.

18. Moraga 2011: 81.

19. Moraga 2011, Celia H. Rodríguez 2011, Moraga 2011. See also Luna 2012a.

20. Gonzales 2012b: 5.

21. Gonzales 2014, River Rose Apothecary 2014.

22. Gonzales 2012a: 27.

23. A temascal or temazcalli is a Mesoamerican form of an ancient ceremonial steambath, or baño, usually heated by sacred rocks that are activated with fire, water, and the intention of cleansing and detoxing the body-mind-spirit. For more, see Falcón 2009. Also see, Estela Román in Medina and Gonzales 2019.

24. Gonzales 2012a: 28–29.

25. A. Smith 2006.

26. A. Smith 2006: 71, 72.

27. Contreras 2008, Cotera and Saldaña-Portillo 2015, Pulido 2017.

28. Keating 2000: 184.

29. Ines Hernández-Ávila in Keating 2000: 186. When "Aztec" is used as a stand-in for the Mexica tradition, ceremonies, and knowledges, it can produce an erasure of the depth of traditional practices often offered through story in the language of Náhuatl and Mexicayotl traditions; therefore, the in-depth study of philosophies, worldviews, food, canto (song), and ceremonial practices must be considered.

30. Luna 2012b.

31. Keating 2000: 188. See 184 for Hernández-Ávila's contradictory way of aligning and then dividing Native and Chicanx peoples; as Deborah Miranda 2002 points out, these are different forms of colonization that are dependent on geography, empires, and migration.

32. R. Gómez 2003–4: 69.

33. Martínez 2004.

34. Gonzales 2012a: 39.

35. R. Gómez 2003–4: 76.

36. R. C. Rodríguez 2014: 62.

37. "Missing memory" is from Alexander 2005. Martínez 2004.

38. Alarcón 1990a, Alarcón 1990b, Castillo 1994, Moraga 2011.

39. Anzaldúa 2007.

40. Anzaldúa 2007: 27. Translation: "In 1521 a new race was born, the mestizo, the Mexican."

41. Contreras 2008.

42. Pérez 2020: 166. The danger of José Vasconcelos's articulation was the aim to eliminate the specificity of Blackness, Indigeneity, and Whiteness to create a new superior race. *La raza cosmica* has been critiqued as a racist logic that heavily influenced Mexican state politics.

43. Fregoso and Chabram 2006: 26.

44. Fregoso and Chabram 2006: 27.

45. Fregoso and Chabram 2006: 28.

46. Fregoso and Chabram 2006: 28.

47. Fregoso and Chabram 2006: 29.

48. Anzaldúa 2007.

49. Martínez 2008: 129, 61.

50. Martínez 2008.

51. Martínez 2008: 101.

52. LGBTQ2S is an acronym for Lesbian Gay Bisexual Transgender Queer Two Spirit relatives.

53. Trujillo 1991.

54. Moraga 2017: 261.

55. R. Rodríguez and Gonzales 1998.

56. Building on Chicana historian Emma Pérez's (1999, 2003) work of "the decolonial imaginary," I move toward a decolonized queer feminist of color frame or lens for the purposes of tracing ancestry.

57. Anzaldúa (2007) argued for the consideration of ancestry and spirit in the form of ancient female diosas in *Borderlands/La Frontera* (and other key works) for an alternative historical analysis of identity formations, cultures, and knowledges.

58. Anzaldúa 2007: 41. Anzaldúa translates "mita y mita" into "half and half"—someone who is between genders (41).

59. See Galarte 2014 and Galarte 2020 for excellent discussion.

60. E. Pérez 1999, Castañeda 1992.

61. Morgensen 2011a, Morgensen 2011b.

62. See Miranda 2010, Williams 1986, Brown 1997, Roscoe 1988, Roscoe 1991.

63. Anzaldúa 2007: 25. Bonfil Batalla 1996 was written in a similar timeframe, "between May 1985 and April 1987" (xix).

64. Mexico gained independence from Spain on September 16, 1821. Mexico had only been a nation for twenty-five years before the official beginning of the war between the United States and Mexico in 1846. The "boundaries of Texas" were being

negotiated as early as 1828, a mere seven years after the new nation of Mexico had been granted rule over the land (Griswold del Castillo 1990).

65. Tuck and Yang 2012: 7.

66. I was taught that speaking an Indigenous language of this hemisphere is more supportive of building a connection with the land than using a colonial language, especially when in prayer.

67. Brown Childs 2003. Also see Dunbar-Ortiz 2014 for a retelling of Indigenous history.

68. Luna 2012a, Miner 2012 and 2014.

69. Castillo 1994 and Hernández 1975. The author first encountered Cherríe Moraga and Celia Herrera Rodríguez's 2007 La Red Xicana Indígena "Mission Statement" in April 2007 at Cherríe Moraga's "Indígena as Scribe" talk at UC Santa Cruz (Ohlone Land).

70. Mesa-Bains 1991: 137.

71. Yarbro-Bejarano 1999: 336.

72. Yarbro-Bejarano 1999: 339.

73. Yarbro-Bejarano 1999: 341.

74. Griswold del Castillo 1990: 14.

75. R. Ramirez 2002: 7.

76. D. Alarcón 1997: 24.

77. Blackhawk 2006 discusses the process of westward expansion and shows evidence of detrimental impact of the Spanish invasion on Native tribes. He convincingly argues tribes went into battle with each other due their access to colonial technologies, such as armor and weapons. Also see Denetdale 2007 for a decolonized history of the U.S. Southwest.

78. Coyolxauhqui's stone was uncovered in a 1978 dig near the Templo Mayor. Carrasco, Luján, and Moctezuma 2007: 87.

79. Anzaldúa 2007: 119.

80. Griswold del Castillo 1990 explains, "The Hopi people, for example, presented a statement at the 1981 Geneva Conference where they cited Article IX and XI of the treaty to support their opposition to the relocation of the Navajo (Dineh) and Hopi elders from their ancestral lands near Big Mountain Arizona" (148). In the statement, the Hopi "assert that their rights as Mexican citizens under Article VIII of the treaty had been violated by the U.S. courts and that their religious rights under Article IX had not been protected" (149).

81. Forbes 1973: 28.

82. Griswold del Castillo 1990: 48.

83. Griswold del Castillo 1990: 70.

84. Griswold del Castillo 1990: 70. For another critical definition of genocide of Indigenous peoples, see Waziyatawin 2008.

85. Anzaldúa 2007: 29. See also Guidotti-Hernández 2011.

86. L. Gómez 2007: 5; original emphasis. For more on New Mexico and Land Loss, see Zentella 2009.

87. Griswold del Castillo 1990: 59.

88. Almaguer 1994 builds closely on George M. Fredrickson's work—a comparative study that was "international" in the sense that he compared white supremacy in the contexts of the United States and South Africa (219–20).

89. Almaguer 1994: 7.

90. Carrigan and Webb 2003: 418.

91. Carrigan and Webb 2003: 417.

92. Almaguer 1994, Smith 2006.

93. Bonfil Batalla 1996.

94. Weber 1973: 12.

95. Weber 1973: 12.

96. General Stephan Watts Kearny quoted in Weber 1973: 161.

97. Weber 1973: 162.

98. L. Gómez 2007.

99. L. Gómez 2007: 5.

100. L. Gómez 2007: 5.

101. Carrigan and Webb 2003: 412. Mariscal 1999 makes a similar argument in discussing the difficulty of identifying accurately how many Latinos fought in the Vietnam War because there was no classification for people of Latino, "Hispanic," or Mexican origin.

102. Almaguer 1994: 2.

103. Almaguer 1994: 3.

104. Brown Childs 2002, Brown Childs 2003. Also see Forbes 1981.

105. Brown Childs 2002: 58.

106. Brown Childs 2002: 57.

107. D. González 1991: 91. This association has been renamed the National Association for Chicano and Chicana Studies (NACCS) due to the struggle to make Chicana scholarship visible within this intellectual space. D. González 1991.

108. D. González 1991: 92. A similar case is found in the narrative of Anna NietoGomez. In her letter in response to being fired from the Chicano studies department at California State University, Northridge alluded to being let go, despite her success in teaching Chicana studies, due to rumors that she was a lesbian. Blackwell 2003 and others have labeled this a form of "lesbian baiting."

109. D. González 1991: 93.

110. The theme of NACCS 2018 was "the Queer Turn." Many participants had a lot to say about how the legacies of the queer were already a part of the thread in NACCS, noting the firm standing Joto Caucus and LBMT Caucus.

111. D. González 1991: 96.

112. See R. Rodríguez 2014.

113. Anaya 1989: 230.

114. Anaya 1989: 232.

115. Anaya 1989: 230–1.

116. N. Alarcón 1990a, Alarcón 1990b, Anzaldúa 2007.

117. C. Ramírez 2002: 50–51.

118. C. Ramírez 2002: 51.

119. C. Ramírez 2002: 52.

120. C. Ramírez 2002: 52. Ramírez emphasizes a pan-Latina representation, situated as, "third, trans-or-extranational space when situated between the nation-state." She notes that in many ways the "borderlands feminism" put forward by theorist like Chela Sandoval are the "antithesis" to Aztlán (57).

121. Carrasco 2008: 236.

122. N. Alarcón 1990a: 250.

123. E. Pérez 1999: xiii.

124. E. Pérez 1999: 5.

125. D. Alarcón 1997: 20. He wrote of the narrowness of the myth of Aztlán: "In restricting Aztlán to just one version, the leaders of the Chicano movement created a nationalist myth so narrow that the nation it offered suffocated many within, and excluded many without, causing them to reject it" (32).

126. D. Alarcón 1997: 19–20.

127. Marez 2001: 269.

128. R. Rodríguez 2014: 48.

129. Anzaldúa 2009b: 243.

130. Anzaldúa 2002a.

131. Lara and Facio 2014.

132. R. Rodríguez 2014: 42.

133. R. Rodríguez 2014: 43.

134. A. Smith 2010: 52–53.

135. R. Gómez 2003–4: 68.

136. R. Gómez 2003–4: 76.

137. Grande 2008: 9.

138. Grande 2008: 10.

139. Grande 2008: 11.

140. Grande 2008: 13.

141. Alberto 2016: 108.

142. Alberto 2016: 108.

143. Forbes 2013: 2. Jack Forbes, "The Mestizo Concept: A Product of European Imperialism," unpublished manuscript, 2013, Department of Native American Studies, University of California Davis.

144. Bonfil Batalla 1996: 62.

145. R. Ramirez 2002: 75.

146. R. Ramirez 2002: 71.

147. R. Ramirez 2002: 71.

148. Bonfil Batalla 1996: 17.

149. Bonfil Batalla 1996 states: "It is difficult to comprehend many characteristics of Mesoamerican civilization if one does not take into account one of its most profound dimensions: the conception of the natural world and the human being's place in the

cosmos. In this civilization, unlike that of the West, the natural world is not seen as an enemy. Neither is it assumed that greater human self-realization is achieved through greater separation from nature. To the contrary, a person's condition as part of the cosmic order is recognized and the aspiration is toward permanent integration, which can be achieved only through a harmonious relationship with the rest of the natural world" (27).

150. Bonfil Batalla 1996: 59.

151. Bonfil Batalla 1996: 9.

152. Carrasco 2008.

Chapter 2. Enseñanzas con la Maestra Gloria, in Ceremony with Anzaldúa

1. Anzaldúa 2015b.

2. This includes the visual representation aspect that activates forms of spirit travel that can facilitate healing.

3. Joysmith 2007.

4. Anzaldúa's specific essays focused on Coyolxauhqui in Anzaldúa 2015b include "Let Us Be the Healing of the World: The Coyolxauhqui Imperative—La sombra y el sueño," and "Putting Coyolxauhqui Together: A Creative Process."

5. Anzaldúa 2015c: 124.

6. In recognizing Coyolxauhqui as a sacred energy connected to the Méxica, often named the Aztec moon diosa, I want to bring this name into relation with the Mayan sacred energy Ixchel often associated with the moon, and Coyolxauhqui's other sacred name in Nahua cosmology, Meztli, grandmother moon.

7. Hartley 2010.

8. Moraga 2000: 147.

9. Anzaldúa 2015b: 8.

10. E. Pérez 2003: 123.

11. Celia Herrera Rodríguez "Nepantlera" (drawing) in Moraga 2011: 115.

12. Luna and Galeana 2016: 8.

13. Galeana 2012: 1.

14. Galeana 2012: 5. See also Luna and Galeana 2016: 14, on Nahua ideology.

15. Tello 2018.

16. Galeana 2012: 16.

17. Galeana 2012: 21.

18. Anzures 1991. Galeana 2012: 41–42.

19. Luna and Galeana 2016: 27.

20. Luna and Galeana 2016: 8.

21. Luna and Galeana 2016: 8–9.

22. Luna and Galeana 2016: 7, 27.

23. Luna and Galeana 2016: 23.

24. Luna and Galeana 2016: 24.

25. Luna and Galeana 2016: 18.
26. In Lak Ech 2007, Gorocica 2019.
27. Gorocica 2019. Author's translation.
28. In Lak Ech 2007. Author's translation.
29. Luna and Galeana 2016: 23.
30. Moraga 2000: iii.
31. Moraga 1993: 74.
32. Keating 2009b: 304.
33. Hartley 2010: 141.
34. Pérez 2005: 3.
35. Keating 2008.
36. Keating 2008: 54. Díaz Sánchez 2013.
37. Keating 2008: 54.
38. This "spirit terrain" was perhaps first articulated in print in Anzaldúa's theorizations in "El Mundo Zurdo" in Moraga and Anzaldúa 1983.
39. Anzaldúa 2007: 41.
40. Lara 2005b: 48. Also see Vakalahi and Starks 2011.
41. Lara 2005b: 48.
42. Facio 2014: 70.
43. Facio and Lara 2014: 8.
44. Facio and Lara 2014: 3.
45. Facio and Lara 2014: 13.
46. Facio and Lara 2014, 17n15.
47. Anzaldúa 2002a: 574–76.
48. Hartley 2010: 137.
49. Hartley 2010 builds with Avila 2000.
50. Hartley 2010: 138.
51. Anzaldúa 1995: 6.
52. "Rue" is English for *ruda*, a potent plant often used in curanderismo and other healing traditions.
53. Anzaldúa 1995: 3.
54. Hartley 2010: 137.
55. See also Rebolledo 2006.
56. Lara 2005a: 26.
57. Castillo 1994: 146. See also Avila 2000, Román 2012, Falcón 2009.
58. Gloria Anzaldúa, "Altares: On the Process of Feminist Image Making," unpublished essay, box 57, Gloria Evangelina Anzaldúa Papers.
59. Anzaldúa 2009a: 183.
60. Anzaldúa 1997. Also see Delgadillo 2011.
61. Anzaldúa 1997.
62. Keating 2000: 180.
63. Gonzales 2012a: 30.

64. Reti 2017. Irene Reti, the curator the Gloria Evangelina Anzaldúa Altares Collection, was also Anzaldúa's upstairs neighbor and writing comadre for ten years. Reti did the work to preserve and find a new home for Anzaldúa's sacred objects. See also Reti 2005.

65. Anzaldúa, "Altares: On the Process," 1.

66. Anzaldúa, "Altares: On the Process," 1.

67. Anzaldúa "Altares: On the Process," 2.

68. Gloria Evangelina Anzaldúa Altares Collection.

69. Gloria Evangelina Anzaldúa Altares Collection.

70. Anzaldúa, "Altares: On the Process," 8.

71. For more on nahaules, see Anzaldúa 2015b: 26.

72. Also see Díaz Sánchez 2013.

73. Reti interview 2010. I interviewed Irene Reti in 2010 on two occasions, once at the Women's Center at UCSC, where she guided me through a viewing of Anzaldúa's sacred objects that were on display. Key in this collection was a bright yellow-and-red wooden jaguar woman, which Reti informed me sat in a visible place in Anzaldúa's home. The other interview took place at McHenry Library on Ohlone land.

74. Román 2012.

75. Anzaldúa "Altares: On the Process," 9.

76. L. Pérez 2008: 341.

77. Anzaldúa 2009b.

78. Anzaldúa, "Altares: On the Process," 16.

79. Anzaldúa, "Altares: On the Process," 10.

80. Anzaldúa, "Altares: On the Process," 10.

81. Anzaldúa, "Altares: On the Process," 13.

82. Miller's (2008) concept "Indigenous Paradigm" illuminates the historic significance of recognizing a relation with the cosmos and forms of consciousness in the construction of knowledge.

83. Anzaldúa 2007: 58.

84. Anzaldúa 2007: 59.

85. Estela Román, ongoing conversations with author, Temixco, Mexico, 2007–10, 2016–20. Also see Román 2012.

86. Bonfil Batalla 1996. Martínez 2008.

87. Mesa-Bains 1991: 132.

88. Anzaldúa, "Altares: On the Process," 12.

89. Anzaldúa 2007: "I am the dialogue with my Self and el espíritu del mundo. I change myself, I change the world" (92).

90. Lara (2008) argues "re-memberings, Tonantzin-Guadalupe becomes a decolonial figure capable of healing the virtuous virgen/pagan puta split perpetuated by Western patriarchal thought" (103). She suggests that "the relationship between Guadalupe and Tonantzin is alive in the cultural memory and practices of many Mexicans and Chicana/os, particularly those who are still connected to their indigenous identi-

ties in spite of a colonial legacy that attempts to erase or delegitimize the indigenous link" (104). This is significant then because within a spiritual icon that is known, there is a possibility to tap into ancestral knowledge by renaming Guadalupe: "Tonantzin-Guadalupe can be a powerful force of healing and creativity" (106).

91. Anzaldúa 1997: viii.

92. Anzaldúa 2007: 89.

93. Anzaldúa 2007: 97.

94. Anzaldúa 1999: 108–9.

95. Bacchetta 2007.

96. Anzaldúa 2015b: 96.

97. Anzaldúa 2015b: 102.

98. Keating 2015: xi.

99. Gonzales 2012b.

100. Moraga 2000. Castillo 1994, in particular the chapter "Brujas and Curanderas: A Lived Spirituality," also makes significant contributions to open this pathway.

101. Mignolo 1996: 189.

102. Forbes 1973: 24.

103. Saldívar-Hull 1999: 6.

104. Forbes 1973: 24.

105. Anzaldúa 2007: 25.

106. Keating 2008.

107. Gloria Evangelina Anzaldúa Altares Collection.

108. Anzaldúa 2009b: 122.

109. Anzaldúa 2002a: 547.

110. Anzaldúa 2002a: 549.

Chapter 3. Queer Indígena Art

1. Gonzales 2012b.

2. L. Pérez 2007: 21–22.

3. See Laura Pérez, "Writing with Crooked Lines," in Facio and Lara 2014.

4. Santa Cruz Feminist of Color Collective 2014.

5. INCITE! 2016.

6. Alexander and Mohanty 1997.

7. Anzaldúa 2015a: 87.

8. E. Pérez 2003: 123, 129.

9. Anzaldúa 2015a: 88.

10. Forbes 1992.

11. Anzaldúa 2015b: 19.

12. Anzaldúa 2015a: 90.

13. S. Zepeda 2014: 120.

14. This question is influenced by Foucault's (1980) "Power/Knowledge" formulations.

15. Leyva 1998: 430.

16. E. Pérez 2003. L. Zepeda 2018.

17. E. Pérez 2003. L. Zepeda 2018.

18. Perks and Thomson 2006: 4.

19. Blackwell 2011, Gluck et al. 1998.

20. See Ferguson 2004, Muñoz 2009, J. Rodríguez 2003, Driskill et al. 2011.

21. The Research Cluster for the Study of Women of Color in Collaboration and Conflict film festival organizers coordinated with the Nineteenth Annual MALCS (Mujeres Activas en Letras y Cambio Social) Summer Institute, Transfronteras: Generations and Geographies. Activistas en la lucha! (August 2–5, 2006), to host an artist exhibit at the University of California, Santa Cruz, featuring Aparicio and other women of color artists.

22. Aparicio interview 2013.

23. Aparicio interview 2013.

24. Gonzales 2012b.

25. Halfmoon 2006.

26. Román 2012.

27. Halfmoon 2006.

28. Halfmoon 2006. Aparicio worked on this piece and others addressed in this article at California State University, Northridge facilities.

29. The burning, lighting, or offering of sage is primarily a Northern Native American practice that has been adopted by Xicanas/os/xs and Latinx. In Mesoamerican or Anahuacan tradition, mainly copal is burned, lit, and offered during ceremony. The Roman Catholic Church uses frankincense (copal) during occasional services, showing how a colonial institutional force co-opted ceremonial elements of the people.

30. Boone and Mignolo 1994.

31. Taylor 2003: 82.

32. Taylor 2003: 82.

33. Gonzales 2012b: 235.

34. A. Smith 2006 and Wolfe 2006.

35. Morgensen 2011a: 109.

36. C. Ramírez 2002; Fregoso and Chabram 2006; Blackwell 2011.

37. Saldaña-Portillo 2003, Contreras 2008, and Cotera and Saldaña-Portillo 2015 all make similar arguments.

38. Blackwell 2011: 95.

39. Gonzales 2012b: 71.

40. Halfmoon 2006. This image appears in Hidalgo de la Riva 2006: 64.

41. Halfmoon 2006.

42. Halfmoon 2006.

43. See L. Smith 1999.

44. L. Smith 1999: 146.

45. See Martínez 2004.

46. Alexander 2005: 316.

47. Bonfil Batalla 1996: 62.

48. Martínez 2008 argues further that, in the Americas, "the colonial discourse of purity of blood was . . . initially propelled by the Christianization project and by Spanish distrust of the religious loyalties of Jewish converts—by religious utopias and anticonverso sentiment" (129).

49. León-Portilla 1988 speaks of movements to defend languages, including Náhuatl speaking communities. He cites an "English version of a Náhuatl declaration by a native leader, Joel Martínez Hernández from Chicontepec, Veracruz," which begins with this telling stanza:

> Some non-Indians say
> we Náhuatl-speaking people will disappear
> we Náhuatl-people will vanish,
> that our language no more will be heard,
> our language no more will be used.
> Non-Indians rejoice with this,
> non-Indians are looking for this.
> Why is it so,
> that they are looking for our destruction? (38).

50. As Bonfil Batalla 1996 suggests, "Mexico City is the place with the largest number of speakers of indigenous languages in all the Americas" (52).

51. Bonfil Batalla 1996: 87.

52. Forbes 1973.

53. Leon-Portilla 1988 writes: "More than fifty Mesoamerican languages still resound in Mexico and the Central American countries. They are the means to communicate all that has to be expressed in the life cycle, from birth to death, in subsistence activities, agriculture, arts and crafts, markets and commerce, as well as in the sphere of spiritual concerns" (37).

54. For an important discussion of Chicanos/as and variations and uses of the Spanish language, see Anzaldúa 2007, ch. 5.

55. Anzaldúa 2007.

56. Halfmoon 2006.

57. This communal prayer, originally exhibited in 2014 at the Museum of Fine Arts in Tallahassee, Florida, was part of Aparicio's Graduate Student Thesis Exhibition, and subsequently became in 2017 a variation exhibited as part of the Mujeres de Maiz 20th Anniversary Retrospective Art Exhibition.

58. Keating 2014: 533.

59. Anzaldúa 2015b: 17.

60. Anzaldúa 2015b: 17.

61. Aparicio interview 2018.

62. Aparicio 2019.

63. Words visible on placards set on altar of "tobacco prayer ties," Aparicio 2019.

64. Implicit within Aparicio's work is the ancestral feminine energy that connects the philosophical vision and physiological understanding of the moon and her connection to the bodies of life-givers who have moon time or menstrual cycles.

65. Aparicio interview 2018.

66. Alvarez and Zepeda 2006: 128.

67. Mercado 2001: 29.

68. Guerrero interview 2013.

69. Alvarez and Zepeda 2006: 130.

70. Mendez interview 2010. For recent critiques of Indigenismo, see Alberto 2016.

71. Mendez interview 2019.

72. Mendez's life history and story of walking with Spirit is akin to essays, poetry, perspectives, and intellectual interventions held in Facio and Lara 2014. In particular, L. Perez's "Writing with Crooked Lines" and her discussion of Buddhism are significant for Mendez's art and trajectory.

73. Mendez recounted her intentional visit to the British Museum, which is known as a colonial institution that contains a significant collection of Indigenous art from various parts of the world, including precolonial Mesoamerica (Mendez interview 2012).

74. Böhm and Böhm 1991.

75. Stonewall activists like transgender Puerto Rican activist Sylvia Rivera, and Black lesbian feminist political essay writer and theorist Audre Lorde, are central to creating movements to give rise to alternative sexualities as a political struggle.

76. Mendez interview 2010.

77. Mendez interview 2010.

78. Mendez interview 2010.

79. Mendez interview 2010.

80. Taylor 2003: 17.

81. Taylor 2003: 17.

82. Taylor 2003: 17.

83. Böhm and Böhm 1991.

84. Böhm and Böhm 1991.

85. According to Böhm and Böhm 1991, "planetary conjunctions" are when "two planets observable from the Earth get in line and are nearly covering each other."

86. Böhm and Böhm 1991.

87. Also see Lopez 2017 and Alvarado 2017.

88. Mendez interview 2010.

89. "Here to Impress," Victoria Delgadillo, Victoriadelgadillo.com/here-to-impress/, accessed November 9, 2021.

90. Mendez interview 2019.

91. Mendez interview 2019

92. Victoria Delgadillo moderated the "Maestras" panel. Mendez also appeared on a later panel, "Challenging the Binary: Queerness in Printmaking" (www.selfhelp

graphics.com/45th-anniversary-exhibition-entre-tinta-y-lucha/, accessed January 19, 2020.

93. Dalila Paola Mendez, "Entre Tinta y Lucha," blog post, www.dalilamendez.com/single-post/2018/08/25/Entre-Tinta-y-Lucha, accessed November 9, 2021.

94. L. Pérez 2007: 284–85. Cervantes's artwork is discussed in L. Pérez 2007.

95. Mendez interview 2019.

96. In 2019, Mendez's *Balam Huipil Remix* was borrowed from LACMA to be in the *Cosmic Matriarchs Exhibition* at Taller Arte del Nuevo Amanecer (TANA) in Woodland, California. In addition to Mendez, the exhibit featured the artwork of Lilia "Liliflor" Ramirez and Suzy Hernandez, all of whom "through their respective works honor the earth, sacred elements, life-givers, and generations of birthing, healing, and love that align with ancestral rememberings" (Cosmic Matriarchs brochure, 2019).

97. See, for example, Herman 1997, Hanh 1992, Gonzales 2012a, Gonzales 2012b.

98. Sturken 1997: 8. Also see Foucault 1978, esp. 135–59, where Foucault explicitly speaks of racism, genocide, the "regulation of populations," and bio-power. An additional helpful essay is Foucault 1997.

99. On the western imperialist gaze, see Mohanty 2003.

100. Hahn 1992.

101. Soto 2010.

102. Taylor 2003: 82.

103. Sturken 1997: 3.

104. Gonzales 2003 is a powerful example of collective historical remembering in the form of oral story.

Chapter 4. Tracing Latina Lesbiana Historias of Resistance, Solidarity, and Visibility

1. Retter 1997, Córdova 2001.
2. Alexander and Mohanty 1997: xvi.
3. Calvo and Esquibel 2010: 217.
4. Calvo and Esquibel 2010: 218.
5. Anzaldúa 1998: 263.
6. H. Ramírez 2005.
7. Cruz 2019: 142.
8. Fanon 2004.
9. INCITE! 2016.
10. Ferguson 2004: 115.
11. Ferguson 2004: 115.
12. E. Pérez 2003: 129.
13. Gutiérrez 1993 problematizes the idea of the Chicano movement in the United States (1965–75). By drawing attention to the participation of students, Chicanas who argued for a feminist analysis, and queers who were not recognized, Gutiérrez emphasizes the multiplicity within the Chicano movement was often conceptualized as homogenous (62).

14. Sandoval 1991, 2000.

15. Castañeda 1992: 505.

16. The version cited here is from a reprint in Anzaldúa 1990, where the article is titled "Feminism and Racism: A Report on the 1981 National Women's Studies Association Conference." The original 1982 article is titled "The Struggle Within: Women Respond to Racism" and was part of the Occasional Paper Series of the Center for Third World Organizing.

17. Sandoval 1990: 60.

18. Sandoval 1990: 60.

19. Sandoval 1990: 62.

20. Sandoval 1990: 63. Also see Lorde 1984a on "Difference."

21. Sandoval 1990: 63.

22. Sandoval 1990: 67. My emphasis.

23. Lowe 1997 interview with Davis. Davis states: "Around the same time, numerous lesbians of color organizations emerged. In fact, the term lesbian of color acquired currency before women of color entered into our political vocabulary" (311).

24. Mohanty, Russo, Torres 1991: ix–x.

25. Sandoval 1990: 62.

26. Mohanty, Russo, and Torres 1991; Sandoval 1990.

27. Anzaldúa 1998: 264.

28. Esquibel 2006: 1.

29. Esquibel 2006: p. 2–3.

30. Muñoz 1999: 21–22.

31. Muñoz 1999: 22.

32. Esquibel 2006.

33. E. Pérez 2003, Leyva 1998.

34. Muñoz 1999; Ferguson 2004. Ferguson 2004: 110–37 builds on the Black lesbian feminism of Audre Lorde. Also significant to this discussion are J. Rodríguez 2003 and Soto 2010.

35. The 1999 anthology *Between Women and Nation: Nationalism, Transnational Feminism, and the State* is important to consider in this regard (Kaplan, Alarcón, and Moallem 1999), as is the 1988 Spanish version publication of *This Bridge, Esta Puente, Mi Espalda: Voces de Mujeres Tercermundistas en los Esatdos Unidos* (Moraga and Castillo 1988).

36. Calvo and Esquibel 2010: 217.

37. Beal 2005.

38. Muñoz 1999: 22.

39. Muñoz 1999.

40. Yarbro-Bejarano 1994: 9.

41. N. Alarcón 1990b: 356.

42. According to Short 1994, "*This Bridge Called My Back* was conceived in February 1979 by Gloria Anzaldúa at a women's retreat outside of San Francisco for which she had received a $150 scholarship to attend as the only woman of color" (3).

43. Call for Submission, Gloria Evangelina Anzaldúa Papers.

44. Call for Submission, Gloria Evangelina Anzaldúa Papers.

45. Chabram-Dernersesian 2007 notes that *This Bridge Called My Back* is "one of the foundational texts in Chicana/o cultural studies" (6).

46. Hurtado 1996. For further discussion, see Santa Feminist of Color Collaborative 2014.

47. Sandoval 2000: 42.

48. Moraga and Anzaldúa 2002: liii.

49. Sandoval 2000: 59.

50. Sandoval 2000: 61.

51. The original anthology had twenty-eight contributors, including a pair of sisters and a collective of Black women writers: Barbara Smith and Beverly Smith, and Combahee River Collective. The 3rd edition of *This Bridge Called My Back* released in 2002 by Third Woman Press contains a publisher's note by Norma Alarcón, additional writing by Celia Herrera-Rodríguez, and an extensive bibliography by Mattie Udora Richardson. It also included two new sections (Artwork and Art Folio) that feature seventeen artists of color, including Marsha M. Gómez's *Madre del Mundo*, Judith E. Baca's *Las Tres Marías*, and Ester Hernández's *Sun Mad*.

52. N. Alarcón 1990b: 363.

53. Moraga 2002: xlix.

54. Moraga and Anzaldúa 2002: 218. This anthology is not without its faults and limitations, as is the case with most texts. Among other instances of reflection, Moraga 2002 in her foreword to the 3rd edition writes about those that are "noticeably absent in the Bridge of 1981" (xvii).

55. Moraga and Anzaldúa 2002: 21.

56. Anzaldúa 2002b: 188.

57. Alexander 2005: 260. An earlier version of this article was published in Alexander et al. 2002.

58. Moraga and Anzaldúa 2002: 336.

59. Valerio 2002: 41.

60. Valerio 2002: 44.

61. Valerio 2002: 44.

62. Valerio 2002: 42, 45.

63. Valerio 2002: 45.

64. For other key scholarly works that critically explore the legacies of *This Bridge Called My Back*, see Duffield and Cespedes 2002 and Sudbury 2003.

65. D. Hernández and Rehman 2002: xxi. Another key anthology that reflect this intergenerational influence and legacy is INCITE! 2016.

66. Chabram-Dernersesian 2007.

67. Santa Cruz Feminist of Color Collective 2014: 34.

68. Quote is from Moraga and Anzaldúa 1983: 23. Ramos 1994; Trujillo 1991; Trujillo 1998; Anzaldúa 1990.

69. For example, the publishing of *This Bridge* ignited the start of the women of color–centered Kitchen Table Press after the original publisher (Persephone Press) folded. The press collaboration among various women of color writers, including Cherríe Moraga, Barbara Smith, Audre Lorde, and Mariana Romo-Carmona.

70. For more on "testimonio," see Latina Feminist Group 2001. Keating 2009 says about "autohistoria" that "Anzaldúa coined this term, as well as the term 'autohistoria-teoría,' to describe women-of-color interventions into and transformations of traditional western autobiographical forms. Deeply infused with the search for personal and cultural meaning, or what Anzaldúa describes in her post-*Borderlands* writings as 'putting Coyolxauhqui together,' both autohistoria and autohistoria-teoría are informed by reflective self-awareness employed in the service of social-justice work. Autohistoria focuses on the personal life story but, as the autohistorian tells her own life story, she simultaneously tells the life stories of others" (319).

71. Trujillo, ed. 1991: ix.

72. Trujillo interview 2011. It is significant that her 2003 novel, *What Night Brings*, features a young protagonist, Marci Cruz, who experiences domestic violence in her household and longs to be a boy.

73. Trujillo 1991 and 1998.

74. D. González 1992: 83.

75. D. González 1992: 83.

76. D. González 1992: 82.

77. D. González 1992: 82.

78. D. González 1992: 81.

79. D. González 1992: 81.

80. Trujillo 1991.

81. E. Pérez 2003.

82. Leyva 1998. Arrizón 2006.

83. An excerpt from tatiana de la tierra's 2007 tribute, "Yolanda the Powerful: In Memoriam-Yolanda Retter-Vargas, Presente!," accessed at USC ONE Gay and Lesbian Archives and published as de la tierra 2007. tatiana de la tierra's words speak to a legacy that Yolanda Retter lived as a Latina lesbian archivist and librarian. See also de la tierra 2012.

84. Yolanda Retter, interview conducted by Juanita Ramos, October 25, 2006. UCLA Chicano Studies Research Center Archives.

85. Retter interview by Ramos, 2006. In her dissertation, Retter 1999 emphasizes a focus on living as a "lifelong lesbian" who is aware of her women of color roots, including the imbalance wars and dictators bring, next to poverty and injustice in the United States. Retter 1997 documents the emergence of lesbian movements with an emphasis or intention to make visible lesbians of color and women of color.

86. Retter interview by author 2005. At UCLA Chicano Studies Research Center. I first learned of Retter's archivist and activist work through an extensive website fo-

cused on lesbian of color and women of color history. Retter met an untimely death in 2007.

87. Retter 1999.

88. Williams and Retter 2003. Also see Retter Vargas 2012.

89. See "Vargas, Yolanda Retter," proposal, Librarians Association of the University of California, https://lauc.ucop.edu/grant/vargas-yolanda-retter, accessed November 11, 2021.

90. de la tierra 2008: 95.

91. Castillo-Speed interview 2010.

92. Epstein 2017: 120.

93. Venegas 2018.

94. Venegas 2018.

95. Aguilar interview 2009.

96. Yarbro-Bejarano 1998. The black-and-white photos in fig. 9 are among the outtakes from Laura Aguilar's 1987 photo session with Yolanda Retter in Retter's home. Photographer Laura Aguilar shot these photos as part of her *Latina Lesbian* series. According to Christopher Velasco of the Laura Aguilar Trust, Aguilar created the series "in the 2000s when photographer Willie Middlebrook was teaching and helping Laura with using digital photography" (e-mail to the author, May 16, 2021). *Latina Lesbian* series, 1986–90, folder 1, box 6 (OS), Laura Aguilar Papers.

97. Aguilar interview 2009.

98. Aguilar interview 2011.

99. Christopher A. Velasco, e-mail to author, May 16, 2021.

100. Retter 1997 says about Connexxus: "From its inception in 1984 until its demise in 1990, the Connexxus board of directors was chaired by women of color, and the organization made serious efforts to create programming relevant to lesbians of color. It was most proactive in the Latina community" (336). "Connexxus sponsored photographer Laura Aguilar's Latina Lesbian series, portions of which traveled to various exhibition spaces including Los Angeles's City Hall" (336).

101. Yarbro-Bejarano 1998 and Epstein 2017.

102. For important examples of this visionary work, see Barker 2018, Fregoso 2003, and Lorde 1984b.

Epilogue

1. Anzaldúa 2002a and Gonzales 2012b.

2. "Exhibition Opening: Xicanx Futurity at Manetti Shrem Museum," Feminist Research Institute, UC Davis, https://fri.ucdavis.edu/events/exhibition-xicanx-futurity accessed December 21, 2021

3. Gonzales 2012b.

4. Román 2019 in her discussions of the temazkalli reveals that "the ceremony [of the temezcal] has the sole purpose of unifying bodymindspirit," 189.

5. Gonzales in Facio and Lara 2014: 224.

6. Hahn 2012 addresses how to deal with conflict by showing compassion, calling someone in, instead of calling them out in a violent accusatory form that is upheld as the "norm" in academia.

7. Gonzales 2012b: 235.

8. "De-Indianization, has been called 'mixture'[mestizaje], but it really was, and is, ethnocide." Bonfil Batalla 1996: 24.

9. Moraga 2011: 82. Original emphasis.

10. Gonzales 2012a: 27.

11. Hartley 2012.

12. Hartley 2012: 57.

13. Hartley 2012: 59.

14. Hartley 2012: 59.

15. R. Rodríguez 2014.

16. Moraga 2011. "Cherríe Moraga's *A Xicana Codex of Changing Consciousness*," book reading and panel discussion, Stanford University, January 17, 2012 (https://events.stanford.edu/events/301/30117/); panelists Cherríe Moraga, Celia Herrera Rodríguez, David Carrasco, and Dr. Loco. *New Fire* premiered January 13, 2012.

17. "Cihuatl" means "female" or "woman, feminine" in the Náhuatl language.

18. Cihuatl Productions, "Open Letter," Facebook, September 12, 2011, accessed September 12, 2011.

19. Cihuatl Productions, "Open Letter," Facebook, September 12, 2011, accessed September 12, 2011.

20. Celia Herrera Rodríguez is the illustrator for Moraga 2011 and the lead designer for *New Fire*, which Cherríe Moraga wrote and directed.

21. David Carrasco at "Cherríe Moraga's *A Xicana Codex*," panel discussion. See Moraga's epilogue in Moraga 2011 for more on eastern influence: "Xicana Mind, Beginner Mind."

22. Moraga 2011.

23. Moraga 2011: 191.

24. Moraga 2011: 191.

25. Moraga 2011: 191.

26. Gonzales in Facio and Lara 2014: 227.

27. Gonzales in Facio and Lara 2014: 233.

28. See, for example, "2,300 Migrant Children in Central American 'Caravan' Need Protection, UNICEF Says," UN News, October 26, 2018, https://news.un.org/en/story/2018/10/1024222

29. Celia Herrera Rodríguez, interview at Cache Creek Conservancy, https://cachecreekconservancy.org/tending-gathering-garden, accessed November 10, 2021.

BIBLIOGRAPHY

Archival Collections

Laura Aguilar Papers. M0829. Department of Special Collections. Stanford University Libraries, Stanford, CA. Virtual guide to archive: https://oac.cdlib.org/findaid/ark:/13030/tf1n39n516/entire_text/.

Gloria Anzaldúa Altares Collection. MS 308. Special Collections and Archives. University Library. University of California, Santa Cruz.

Gloria Evangelina Anzaldúa Papers. Nettie Lee Benson Latin American Collection. University of Texas, Austin.

Special Collections. UC Berkeley Ethnic Studies Library. Berkeley, California.

UCLA Chicano Studies Research Center Archives. UCLA, Los Angeles.

USC ONE National Gay and Lesbian Archives. University of Southern California, Los Angeles.

Artistic Media

Aguilar, Laura, photo. 1986–90. *Latina Lesbian.* Photographic series. Black and white photographs of Latina Lesbian community, sponsored by Connexxus Women's Center/Centro de Mujeres. In Laura Aguilar Papers.

——, photo. 1992. *Plush Pony.* Photographic series. Black and white photographs at working-class lesbian bar, documenting Mexican and Chicana butch/femme culture. In Laura Aguilar Papers.

——, photo. 2017. *Laura Aguilar: Show and Tell.* Exhibition curated by Sybil Venegas. Presented at the Vincent Price Art Museum at East Los Angeles College, September 2017–February 2018.

Aparicio, Gina. 2019. *Ipan Nepantla Teotlaitlania Cachi Cualli Maztlacayotl (Caught between Worlds, Praying for a Better Future).* Mixed-media installation. Displayed at *Xicanx Futurity* exhibition, Manetti Shrem Museum, Davis, California, January 29 through May 5, 2019. First iteration 2014.

Aparicio, Gina. 2005. *In the Spirit of the Ancestors.* Kiln-dried and painted clay. Clay sculpture. 25 × 18 × 27 inches.

Aparicio, Gina. 2004. *Cuica Maquixtia* (She Who Sings to Be Free, in Nahuatl). Clay sculpture. 27 × 19 × 7 inches.

Hernández, Ester. 1975. *La Virgen de Guadalupe Defendiendo los Derechos de los Xicanos.* Print sheet. 15 × 11 inches. Smithsonian American Art Museum.

Hidalgo de la Riva, Osa, dir. 1992. *Two-Spirit.* Documentary. 26 minutes. New York: Third World Newsreel. In Lak Ech. 2007. *Mujeres con palabra: Tú eres mi otro yo: you are my other me.* CD. 59:39 minutes. Xican@ Records & Film and Nomadic Sound System. Los Angeles, California.

Mendez, Dalila Paola. 2005. *Diosas Enamoradas.* Acrylic painting on canvas. 15 × 30 inches.

——. 2013. *Balam Huipil Remix.* Silk-screen serigraph. Hand-drawn. 30 × 42 inches. Los Angeles County Museum of Art.

——. 2017. *Diosas Enamoradas II.* Acrylic painting on canvas. 15 × 30 inches.

Moraga, Cherríe, dir. 2012. *New Fire: To Put Things Right Again. Theater Production.* Written and directed by Cherríe Moraga. Designed by Celia Herrera Rodríguez. January 9–29, 2012. Brava Theater and Cihuatl Productions, San Francisco.

Rodríguez, Celia Herrera. 2011. *Nepantlera: Remembering Gloria Anzaldúa.* Drawing. 11 × 15 inches. Reproduced in Moraga 2011.

——. 2019. *Cihuacoatl: Prayer for Our Future.* Part of *Acoyaliztli Tlachpana Xicana (To Elevate Ourselves in Prayer to the Open Road).* Mixed media. First displayed at *Xicanx Futurity* exhibition, Manetti Shrem Museum, Davis, California, January 29 through May 5, 2019.

Interviews Conducted by the Author

Aguilar, Laura. September 1, 2009, and September 29, 2011. Rosemead, California.

Aparicio, Gina. By phone, March 2013 and June 2018. Via Tallahassee, Florida, to Santa Cruz, California, and in Davis, California.

Castillo-Speed, Lillian. May 5, 2010. Berkeley, California.

Chavez, Pamela. August 25, 2009. Oakland, California.

Cordova, Jeanne. December 30, 2011. Los Angeles, California.

Czarrunchick, Nicolette. May 14, 2012. Santa Cruz, California.

de la tierra, tatiana. September 16, 2011. Long Beach, California.

Guerrero, Aurora. By phone, March 2013. Via New York City to Santa Cruz, California.

Hidalgo de la Riva, Osa. August 2009. Hayward, California.

Mendez, Dalila Paola. June 16, 2010, April 14, 2012, and December 2019. Berkeley and Los Angeles, California.

Mercado, Claudia. September 17, 2011. Los Angeles, California.
Ramos, Juanita. September 16, 2011. Long Beach, California.
Reti, Irene. 2010. Santa Cruz, California.
Retter, Yolanda. August 18, 2005. UCLA Chicano Studies Research Center, Los Angeles, California.
Trujillo, Carla. August 31, 2011. Berkeley, California.

Other Sources

Acosta, Katie. 2008. "Lesbianas in the Borderlands: Shifting Identities and Imagined Communities." *Gender and Society* 22, no. 5 (October 2008): 639–59.
Alarcón, Daniel C. 1997. *The Aztec Palimpsest: Mexico in the Modern Imagination.* Tucson: University of Arizona Press.
Alarcón, Norma. 1990a. "Chicana Feminism: In the Tracks of 'The' Native Woman." *Cultural Studies* 4, no. 3: 248–56.
——. 1990b. "The Theoretical Subject(s) of *This Bridge Called My Back* and Anglo-American Feminism." In Anzaldúa 1990, 356–69.
Alberto, Lourdes. 2016. "Nations, Nationalisms, and *Indígenas*: The 'Indian' in the Chicano Revolutionary Imaginary." *Critical Ethnic Studies* 2, no. 1 (Spring): 107–27.
Alexander, Jacqui. 2005. "Remembering *This Bridge Called My Back*, Remembering Ourselves." In *Pedagogies of Crossing: Mediations on Feminism, Sexual Politics, Memory, and the Sacred*, 257–86. Durham, NC: Duke University Press.
Alexander, M. Jacqui, and Lisa Albrecht, Sharon Day, and Mab Segrest, eds. 2002. *Sing, Whisper, Shout, Pray! Feminist Visions for a Just World.* Fort Bragg, CA: EdgeWork Books.
Alexander, M. Jacqui, and Chandra Talpade Mohanty, eds. 1997. *Feminist Genealogies, Colonial Legacies, Democratic Futures*. New York: Routledge.
Almaguer, Tomas. 1994. *Racial Fault Lines: The Historical Origins of White Supremacy in California*. Berkeley: University of California Press.
Alvarado, Karina Oliva. 2017. "Cultural Memory and Making by US Central Americans" *Latino Studies* 15, no. 4: 476–97.
Alvarez, Sandra, with Susy Zepeda. 2006. "Womyn Image Makers: A Colectiva of Queer Indígena Visionaries." In *Chicana Spectators and Mediamakers: Imagining Trans-Cultural Diversity*, edited by Osa Hidalgo de la Riva. Special issue, *Spectator: USC Journal of Film and Television Criticism* 26, no. 1 (Spring): 127–34.
Anaya, Rudolfo A. 1989. "Aztlán: A Homeland without Boundaries." In *Aztlán: Essays on the Chicano Homeland*, edited by Rudolfo A. Anaya and Francisco A. Lomelí. Albuquerque: Academia/El Norte Publications.
Anaya, Rudolfo, Francisco A. Lomelí, and Enrique R. Lamadrid, eds. 2017. *Aztlán: Essays on the Chicano Homeland.* Rev. and expanded. Albuquerque: University of New Mexico Press.
Anderson, Benedict. 1991. *Imagined Communities: Reflections on the Origin and Spread of Nationalism*. New York: Verso.

Anzaldúa, Gloria E. 1995. *Prietita and the Ghost Woman/Prietita y la Llorona*. San Francisco: Children's Book Press.

——. 1997. Foreword to *Cassell's Encyclopedia of Queer Myth, Symbol, and Spirit: Gay, Lesbian, Bisexual, and Transgender Love*. Edited by Randy P. Conner, David Hatfield Sparks, and Mariya Sparks, vii–viii. London: Cassell.

——. 1998. "To(o) Queer the Writer—Loca, Escritora y Chicana." In Trujillo 1998, 263–76. Berkeley, CA: Third Women Press.

——. 1999. *Borderlands/La Frontera: The New Mestiza.* 2d ed. San Francisco: Aunt Lute Books.

——. 2002. "Now Let Us Shift . . . the Path of Conocimiento . . . Inner Work, Public Acts." In Anzaldúa and Keating 2002, 540–78.

——. 2002b. "Speaking in Tongues: A Letter to Third World Women Writers." In Moraga and Anzaldúa 2002, 183–93.

——. 2007 (1987). *Borderlands/La Frontera: The New Mestiza.* 3d ed. San Francisco: Aunt Lute Books.

——. 2009a. "Border Arte: Nepantla, *el Lugar de la Frontera*." In Anzaldúa 2009b, 176–86.

——. 2009b. *The Gloria Anzaldúa Reader*. Edited by AnaLouise Keating. Durham, NC: Duke University Press.

——. 2015a. "Geographies of Selves—Reimagining Identity: *Nos/Otras* (Us/Other), *las Nepantleras*, and the New Tribalism." In Anzaldúa 2015b, 65–94.

——. 2015b. *Light in the Dark / Luz en lo Oscuro: Rewriting Identity, Spirituality, Reality.* Edited by AnaLouise Keating. Durham, NC: Duke University Press.

——. 2015c. "Now Let Us Shift . . . *Conocimiento* . . . Inner Work, Public Acts." In Anzaldúa 2015b, 117–59.

Anzaldúa, Gloria E., ed. 1990. *Making Face, Making Soul/Haciendo Caras: Creative and Critical Perspectives by Feminists of Color*. San Francisco: Aunt Lute Books.

Anzaldúa, Gloria E., and AnaLouise Keating, ed. 2002. *This Bridge We Call Home: Radical Visions for Transformation*. New York: Routledge.

Anzaldúa, Gloria E., Simon J. Ortiz, Inés Hernández-Avila, and Domino Perez. 2003. "Speaking across the Divide." *Studies in American Indian Literatures*, 2d ser., 15, nos. 3–4: 7–22.

Anzures, María. 1991. *Coyolxauhqui: Nuestra Madre Cosmica.* México, DF: Consejo Nacional de la Cultura Nahuatl Centro de Estudios Tepiteños.

Arrizón, Alicia. 2006. *Queering Mestizaje: Transculturation and Performance.* Ann Arbor: University of Michigan Press.

Avila, Elena, with Joy Parker. 2000. *Woman Who Glows in the Dark: A Curandera Reveals Traditional Aztec Secrets of Physical and Spiritual Health.* New York: Penguin.

Bacchetta, Paola. 2007. "Circulations: Thinking with Gloria Anzaldúa in Paris." In *Borderlands/La Frontera: The New Mestiza.* 3d ed. San Francisco: Aunt Lute Books.

Barker, Joanne. 2018. "Decolonizing the Mind." *Rethinking Marxism* 30, no. 2: 208–31.

Beal, Frances. 2005 (1970). "Double Jeopardy: To Be Black and Female." In *The Black Woman: An Anthology*, edited by Toni Cade Bambara, 109–22. New York: Washington Square Press.

Blackhawk, Ned. 2006. *Violence over the Land: Indians and Empires in the Early American West*. Cambridge, MA: Harvard University Press.

Blackwell, Maylei. 2003. "Contested Histories: *Las Hijas de Cuauhtémoc*, Chicana Feminisms, and Print Culture in the Chicano Movement, 1968–1973." In *Chicana Feminisms: A Critical Reader*, edited by Gabriela Arredondo, Aida Hurtado, Norma Klahn, Olga Nájera-Ramirez, and Patricia Zavella, 59–89. Durham, NC: Duke University Press.

——. 2011. *Chicana Power! Contested Histories of Feminism in the Chicano Movement*. Austin: University of Texas Press.

Böhm, Bohumiland, and Vladimir Böhm. 1991. "The Dresden Codex—the Book of Mayan Astronomy." Hermetic Systems. www.hermetic.ch/cal_stud/maya/boehm/boehm51.htm. Accessed November 4, 2021.

Bonfil Batalla, Guillermo. 1996. *México Profundo: Reclaiming a Civilization*. Translated by Philip A. Dennis. Austin: University of Texas Press.

Boone, Elizabeth Hill, and Walter D. Mignolo, eds. 1994. *Writing without Words: Alternative Literacies in Mesoamerica and the Andes*. Durham, NC: Duke University Press.

Boyd, Nan Alamilla. 2008. "Who Is the Subject? Queer Theory Meets Oral History." *Journal of the History of Sexuality* 17, no. 2: 177–89.

Brown, Lester B., ed. 1997. *Two Spirit People: American Indian Lesbian Women and Gay Men*. Binghamton, NY: Haworth.

Brown Childs, John. 2002. "Crossroads: Towards a Transcommunal Black History Month in the Multicultural United States of the Twenty-First Century." *Ecritures de L'histoire Africaine-Américaine*, 49–63.

——. 2003. *Transcommunality: From the Politics of Conversion to the Ethics of Respect*. Philadelphia: Temple University Press.

Calvo, Luz, and Catrióna Rueda Esquibel. 2010. "Latina Lesbianas, BiMujeres, and Trans Identities: Charting Courses in the Social Sciences." In *Latina/o Sexualities: Probing Powers, Passions, Practices, and Policies*, edited by Marysol Ascenio, 217–29. New Brunswick, NJ: Rutgers University Press.

Calvo, Luz, and Catrióna Rueda Esquibel. 2015. *Decolonize Your Diet: Plant-Based Mexican-American Recipes for Health and Healing*. Vancouver: Arsenal Pulp Press.

Cantú, Lionel. 2000. "*Entre Hombres*/Between Men: Latino Masculinities and Homosexualities." In *Gay Masculinities*, edited by Peter Nardi, 224–46. Thousand Oaks, CA: Sage.

Carrasco, Davíd. 2008. "Imagining a Place for Aztlán: *Chicanismo* and the Aztecs in Art and Resistance." In *The Aztec World*, edited by Elizabeth M. Brumfiel and Gary M. Feinman, 225–40. New York: Abrams.

Carrasco, Davíd, Leonardo López Luján, and Eduardo Matos Moctezuma. 2007. *Breaking through Mexico's Past: Digging the Aztecs with Eduardo Matos Moctezuma*. Albuquerque: University of New Mexico Press.

Carrigan, William D., and Clive Webb. 2003. "The Lynching of Persons of Mexican Origin or Descent in the United States, 1848 to 1928." *Journal of Social History* 37, no. 2: 411–38.

Castañeda, Antonia. 1992. "Women of Color and the Rewriting of Western History: The Discourse, Politics, and Decolonization of History." *Pacific Historical Review* 61, no. 4 (November 1992): 501–33.

———. 2001. "'Que Se Pudieran Defender (So You Could Defend Yourselves)': Chicanas, Regional History, and National Discourses." *Frontiers: A Journal of Women Studies* 22, no. 3: 116–42.

Castillo, Ana. 1994. *Massacre of the Dreamers: Essays on Xicanisma.* Albuquerque: University of New Mexico Press.

Chabram-Dernersesian, Angie, ed. 2007. *The Chicana/o Cultural Studies Forum*. New York: New York University Press.

Champagne, Duane 2014. "Are Ethnic Indians a Threat to Indigenous Rights?" *Indian Country Today*, December 27, 2014.

Cihuatl, Cuauhtli, and Gris Muñoz. "Maestra Cuauhtli Cihuatl: A Plática and Medicine Story, Part 3." *Ofrenda Magazine*, July 31, 2021. Interview by Gris Muñoz. www.ofrendamagazine.com/articles/a-platica-and-medicine-story-part-3.

Contreras, Sheila Marie. 2008. *Blood Lines: Myth, Indigenism, and Chicana/o Literature.* Austin: University of Texas Press.

Córdova, Jeanne. 2011. *When We Were Outlaws: A Memoir of Love and Revolution*. Midway, Florida: Spinsters Ink.

Cotera, María Eugenia, and María Josephina Saldaña-Portillo. 2015. "Indigenous But Not Indian? Chicana/os and the Politics of Indigeneity." In *The World of Indigenous North America*, edited by Robert Warrior, 549–68. New York: Routledge.

Cruz, Cindy. 2001. "Toward an Epistemology of a Brown Body." *Qualitative Studies in Education* 14, no. 5: 657–69.

———. 2019. "Reading *This Bridge Called My Back* for Pedagogies of Coalition, Remediation, and a Razor's Edge." *International Journal of Qualitative Studies in Education* 32, no. 2: 136–50.

Cruz-Malavé, Arnaldo, and Martin R. Manalansan IV, eds. 2002. *Queer Globalizations: Citizenship and the Afterlife of Colonialism*. New York: New York University Press.

Davis, Angela. Y. 1981. *Women, Race, and Class.* New York: Vintage.

de la tierra, tatiana. 2007. "Yolanda the Powerful." In *Chicana/Latina Studies: The Journal of Mujeres Activas en Letras y Cambio Social* 7, no. 1: 80–83.

———. 2008. "Latina Lesbian Subject Headings: The Power of Naming." In *Radical Cataloging: Essays at the Front*, edited by K. R. Roberto, 94–102. Jefferson, NC: McFarland.

———. 2012. "Gay, Bisexual, Transgender, Lesbian, Queer: Being There: Queer Latin@ Representation in the Library." In *Pathways to Progress: Issues and Advances in Latino Librarianship*, edited by John Ayala and Salvador Güereña, 93–102. Santa Barbara, CA: Libraries Unlimited.

Delgadillo, Theresa. 2011. *Spiritual Mestizaje: Religion, Gender, Race, and Nation in Contemporary Chicana Narrative.* Durham, NC: Duke University Press.

Denetdale, Jennifer Nez. 2007. *Reclaiming Diné History: The Legacies of Navajo Chief Manuelito and Juanita*. Tucson: University of Arizona Press.

Díaz Sánchez, Micaela. 2013. "Yemaya Blew that Wire Fence Down: Invoking African Spiritualities in Gloria Anzaldúa's *Borderlands/La Frontera: The New Mestiza* and the Mural Art of Juana Alicia." *Yemoja: Gender, Sexuality, and Creativity in the Latina/o and Afro-Atlantic Diasporas*, edited by Solimar Otero and Toyin Falola, 153–86. Albany: SUNY Press.

DiPietro, Pedro Javier [P. J.]. 2020. "Neither Human, nor Animals, nor Monsters: Decolonizing Transgender Embodiments." *Eidos* 34: 254–91.

Driskill, Qwo-Li. 2016. *Asegi Stories: Cherokee Queer and Two-Spirit Memory.* Tucson: University of Arizona Press.

Driskill, Qwo-Li, Chris Finley, Brian Joseph Gilley, and Scott Lauria Morgensen, eds. 2011. *Queer Indigenous Studies: Critical Interventions in Theory, Politics, and Literature.* Tucson: University of Arizona Press.

Duffield, Martha Arevalo, and Karina Lissette Cespedes. 2002. "Practicing Transgression: Radical Women of Color for the 21st Century." *Meridians: Feminism, Race, Transnationalism* 3, no. 1: 125–32.

Dunbar-Ortiz, Roxanne. 2014. *An Indigenous Peoples' History of the United States*. Boston: Beacon.

Epstein, Rebecca, ed. 2017. *Laura Aguilar: Show and Tell.* Los Angeles: UCLA Chicano Studies Research Center Press. Published in conjunction with an exhibition of the same title, curated by Sybil Venegas and presented at the Vincent Price Art Museum at East Los Angeles College, September 2017–February 2018.

Esquibel, Catriona Rueda. 2006. *With Her Machete in Her Hand: Reading Chicana Lesbians.* Austin: University of Texas Press.

Estrada, Gabriel S. 2007. "An Aztec Two-Spirit Cosmology: Re-sounding Nahuatl Masculinities, Elders, Femininities, and Youth." In *Gender on the Borderlands: The Frontier Reader*, edited by Antonia Casteñeda with Susan H. Armitage, Patricia Hart, and Karen Weathernmon, 10–14. Lincoln: University of Nebraska Press.

Facio, Elisa, and Irene Lara, eds. 2014. *Fleshing the Spirit: Spirituality and Activism in Chicana, Latina, and Indigenous Women's Lives.* Tucson: University of Arizona Press.

Falcón, Aida Guerra. 2009. "Temascal." In *Doña Queta y el legado de los habitantes de las nubes*, 26–35. Oaxaca, Mex.: Medicina Tradicional.

Fanon, Frantz. 2004 (1963). *The Wretched of the Earth*. Translated by R. Philcox. New York: Grove.

Ferguson, Roderick. 2004. *Aberrations in Black: Toward a Queer of Color Critique*. Minneapolis: University of Minnesota Press.

Forbes, Jack D. 1973. *Aztecas del Norte: The Chicanos of Aztlán*. Greenwich, CT: Fawcett.

———. 1981. *Africans and Native Americans: The Language of Race and the Evolution of Red-Black Peoples.* Urbana: University of Illinois Press.

———. 1992. *Columbus and Other Cannibals: The Wétiko Disease of Exploitation, Imperialism, and Terrorism.* New York: Seven Stories Press.

Foucault, Michel. 1978. *The History of Sexuality.* Vol. 1, *An Introduction*. New York: Vintage.

———. 1980. *Power/Knowledge: Selected Interviews and Other Writings, 1972–1977*, edited by Colin Gordon. New York: Pantheon Books.

———. 1997. "17 March 1976." In *Society Must Be Defended: Lectures at the Collége de France, 1975–1976*, 239–63. New York: Picador.

Fregoso, Rosa Linda. 2003. *MeXicana Encounters: The Making of Social Identities of the Borderlands*. Berkeley: University of California Press.

Fregoso, Rosa Linda, and Angie Chabram. 2006. "Chicana/o Cultural Representation: Reframing Alternative Critical Discourses." In *The Chicana/o Cultural Studies Reader*, edited by Angie Chabram-Dernersesian, 26–32. New York: Routledge.

Galarte, Francisco. 2014. "On Trans* Chican@s: Contesting, Interrogating, and Transforming Chicana/o Studies." *Aztlán: A Journal of Chicana/o Studies* 13, no. 2: 118–39.

———. 2020. "Transgender Studies and Latina/o/x Studies." *Oxford Research Encyclopedia of Literature*, March 2020. https://doi.org/10.1093/acrefore/9780190201098.013.349.

Galeana, Martha. 2012. *Coyolxauhqui: Another Scientific Book for Indigenous Societies. A Partera's Perspective.* N.p.: CreateSpace Independent Publishing Platform.

Garcia, Alma M, ed. 1997. *Chicana Feminist Thought: The Basic Historical Writings.* New York: Routledge.

Garcia, Santiago Andrés. 2021. "Contesting Trauma and Violence through Indigeneity and a Decolonizing Pedagogy at Rio Hondo Community College." *Journal of Latinos and Education* 20, no. 4: 376–96. https://doi.org/10.1080/15348431.2019.1603749.

Gluck, Sherna Berger, in collaboration with Maylei Blackwell, Sharon Cotrell, and Karen S. Harper. 1998. "Whose Feminism, Whose History? Reflections on Excavating the History of (the) U.S. Women's Movement(s)." In *Community Activism and Feminist Politics: Organizing across Race, Class, and Gender*, edited by Nancy Naples, 31–56. New York: Routledge.

Gómez, Laura E. 2007. *Manifest Destinies: The Making of the Mexican American Race*. New York: New York University Press.

Gómez, Reid. 2003–4. "They Killed the Word." *Studies in American Indian Literatures* 15, no. 3/4 (Fall/Winter): 64–95.

Gómez-Barris, Macarena. 2009. *Where Memory Dwells: Culture and State Violence in Chile.* Berkeley: University of California Press.

Gonzales, Patrisia. 2003. *The Mud People, Chronicles, Testimonios and Remembrances*. San José, CA: Chusma House.

———. 2012a. "Calling Our Spirits Back: Indigenous Ways of Diagnosing and Treating Soul Sickness." *Fourth World Journal* 11, no. 2: 25–39.

———. 2012b. *Red Medicine: Traditional Indigenous Rites of Birthing and Healing*. Tucson: University of Arizona Press.

———. 2014. "Native American Healing with Patrisia Gonzales." HerbTV. www.youtube.com/watch?v=3LSF2bNFIZw. Posted May 20, 2014.

González, Deena J. 1991. "Malinche as Lesbian: A Reconfiguration of 500 Years of Resistance." *California Sociologist* 12, nos. 1–2 (Winter–Summer 1991): 91–97.

———. 1992. "Masquerades: Viewing the New Chicana Lesbian Anthologies." *Out/Look*, Winter, 80–83.

Gonzalez, Maria C. 2002. "This Bridge called NWSA." *NWSA Journal* 14, no. 1: 71–82.

Gorocica, Cristina. 2019. "Coyolxauhqui Canto." In *Voices from the Ancestors: Xicanx and Latinx Spiritual Expressions and Healing Practices*, edited by Lara Medina and Martha Gonzales, 296–97. Tucson: University of Arizona Press.

Grande, Sandy. 2008. "Red Pedagogy: The Un-Methodology." In *Handbook of Critical and Indigenous Methodologies*, edited by Norman Denzin, Yvonna Lincoln, and Linda Tuhiwai Smith, 1–29. https://dx.doi.org/10.4135/9781483385686.n12.

Gray, Herman, and Macarena Gómez-Barris, eds. 2010. *Toward a Sociology of the Trace*. Minneapolis: University of Minnesota Press.

Grewal, Inderpal, and Caren Kaplan, eds. 2006. *An Introduction to Women's Studies: Gender in a Transnational World*. 2d ed. Boston: McGraw-Hill Higher Education.

Griswold del Castillo, Richard. 1990. *The Treaty of Guadalupe Hidalgo: A Legacy of Conflict*. Norman: University of Oklahoma Press.

Grosfoguel, Ramón, Nelson Maldonado-Torres, and José David Saldívar. 2005. "Latin@s and the 'Euro-American Menace': The Decolonization of the U.S. Empire in the Twenty-First Century." In *Latin@s in the World-System: Decolonization Struggles in the Twenty-First Century U.S. Empire*, edited by Ramón Grosfoguel, Nelson Maldonado-Torres, and José David Saldívar, 3–27. New York: Routledge.

Guidotti-Hernández, Nicole M. 2011. *Unspeakable Violence: Remapping U.S. and Mexican National Imaginaries*. Durham, NC: Duke University Press.

Gumbs, Alexis Pauline. 2011. "Seek the Roots: An Immersive and Interactive Archive of Black Feminist Practice." *Feminist Collections* 32, no. 1 (Winter): 17–20.

Gutiérrez, Ramón A. 1991. *When Jesus Came, the Corn Mothers Went Away: Marriage, Sexuality, and Power in New Mexico, 1500–1846*. Stanford, CA: Stanford University Press.

———. 1993. "Community, Patriarchy, and Individualism: The Politics of Chicano History and the Dream of Equality." *American Quarterly* 45, no. 1: 44–72.

———. 2004. "Internal Colonialism: An American Theory of Race." *Du Bois Review* 1, no. 2: 281–95.

Halfmoon, Mark, with Gina Aparicio, Monica Enriquez, Aurora Guerrero, and Dalila Paola Mendez. 2006. "Voices." Panel. At *Regenerations*, the 13th Annual Women of Color Film Festival. Santa Cruz Community Television. Santa Cruz, CA. August 3, 2006.

Hall, Stuart. 1996. "The Problem of Ideology: Marxism without Guarantees." In *Stuart Hall: Critical Dialogues in Cultural Studies*, edited by David Morley and Kuan-Hsing Chen, 25–46. New York: Routledge.

Hanh, Thich Nhat. 1991. *Peace Is Every Step: The Path of Mindfulness in Everyday Life*. New York: Bantam Books.

———. 1992. *Touching Peace: Practicing the Art of Mindful Living*. Edited by Arnold Kotler. Drawings by Mayumi Oda. Berkeley, CA: Parallex.

Hartley, George. 2010. "The Curandera of Conquest: Gloria Anzaldúa's Decolonial Remedy." *Aztlán: A Journal of Chicano Studies* 35, no. 1 (Spring): 135–61.

———. 2012. "Chican@ Indigeneity, the Nation-State, and Colonialist Identity Formations." In *Comparative Indigeneities of the Américas: Toward a Hemispheric Approach*, edited by M. Bianet Castellanos, Lourdes Gutiérrez Nájera, and Arturo J. Aldama, 53–66. Tucson: University of Arizona Press.

Herman, Judith. 1997. *Trauma and Recovery: The Aftermath of Violence from Domestic Abuse to Political Terror.* New York: Basic Books.

Hernández, Daisy, and Bushra Rehman. 2002. *Colonize This! Young Women of Color on Today's Feminism.* New York: Seal.

Hernández, Roberto. 2005. "Running for Peace and Dignity: From Traditionally Radical Chicanos/as to Radically Traditional Xicanas/os." In *Latin@s in the World-System: Decolonization Struggles in the Twenty-First Century U.S. Empire*, edited by Ramón Grosfoguel, Nelson Maldonado-Torres, and José David Saldívar, 123–38. New York: Routledge.

Hernández-Avila, Inés. 2003–4. "Indigenous Intersections." Indigenous Intersections in Literature: American Indians and Chicanos/Chicanas." *Studies in American Indian Literature* 14, no. 3/4 (Fall/Winter): 1–6.

——. 2006. "Ometeotl Moyocoyatzin: Nahuatl Spiritual Foundations for Holistic Healing." In *Teaching Religion and Healing*, edited by Linda L. Barnes and Inés Talamantez, 127–38. New York: Oxford University Press.

Hidalgo de la Riva, Osa. 2006. Introduction. In *Chicana Spectators and Mediamakers: Imagining TransCultural Diversity*, edited by Osa Hidalgo de la Riva. Special issue, *Spectator: USC Journal of Film and Television Criticism:* 26, no. 1 (Spring): 7–12.

Hurtado, Aída. 1996. *The Color of Privilege: Three Blasphemies on Race and Feminism.* Ann Arbor: University of Michigan Press.

INCITE! Women of Color Against Violence, eds. 2016. *Color of Violence: The INCITE! Anthology.* Cambridge, MA: South End Press.

Joysmith, Claire. 2007. "Coatlicue-Poet, *Nepantlera* and *Curandera Cultural*." In *Borderlands/La Frontera: The New Mestiza* by Gloria E. Anzaldúa. San Francisco: Aunt Lute Books.

Kaplan, Caren, Norma Alarcón, and Minoo Moallem, eds. 1999. *Between Women and Nation: Nationalism, Transnational Feminism, and the State*. Durham, NC: Duke University Press.

Keating, AnaLouise. 1996. *Women Reading, Women Writing: Self-Invention in Paula Gunn Allen, Gloria Anzaldúa, and Audre Lorde*. Philadelphia: Temple University Press.

——. 2000. "Quincentennial: From Victimhood to Active Resistance: Inés Hernández-Ávila y Gloria E. Anzaldúa (1991)." In *Gloria E. Anzaldúa: Interviews = Entrevistas*, edited by AnaLouise Keating, 177–94. New York: Routledge, 2000.

——. 2008. "'I'm a Citizen of the Universe': Gloria Anzaldúa's Spiritual Activism as Catalyst for Social Change." *Feminist Studies* 34, no. 1/2: 53–69.

——. 2009. "Introduction: Reading Gloria Anzaldúa, Reading Ourselves . . . Complex Intimacies, Intricate Connections." In Anzaldúa 2009b, 1–15.

——. 2013. *Transformation Now! Toward a Post-Oppositional Politics of Change.* Urbana: University of Illinois Press.

——. 2014. "Mesoamerican Mythmaking as Queer(ed) Visionary Hermeneutics." In *The Cambridge History of Gay and Lesbian Literature*, edited by E. L. McCallum and Mikko Tuhkanen, 529–47. New York: Cambridge University Press.

——. 2015. "Editor's Introduction: Re-envisioning Coyolxauhqui, Decolonizing Reality: Anzaldúa's Twenty-First Century Imperative." In Anzaldúa 2015b, ix–xxxvii.

——, ed. 2000. *Gloria E. Anzaldúa: Interviews = Entrevistas.* New York: Routledge.

——, ed. 2005. *Entre Mundos/Among Worlds: New Perspectives on Gloria Anzaldúa.* London: Palgrave Macmillan.

Kennedy, Elizabeth L. 2006. "Telling Tales: Oral History and the Construction of Pre-Stonewall Lesbian History." In *The Oral History Reader*, edited by Robert Perks and Alister Thomson, 271–82. 2d ed. New York: Routledge.

Lara, Irene. 2005a. "Bruja Positionalities: Toward a Chicana/Latina Spiritual Activism." *Chicana/Latina Studies* 4, no. 2 (Spring): 10–45.

——. 2005b. "Daughter of Coatlicue: An Interview with Gloria Anzaldúa." In Keating 2005, 41–55.

——. 2008. "Goddess of the Américas in the Decolonial Imaginary: Beyond the Virtuous Virgen/Pagan Puta Dichotomy." *Feminist* Studies 34, nos. 1/2: 99–127.

Lara, Irene, and Elisa Facio. 2014. "Introduction: Fleshing the Spirit, Spiriting the Flesh." In *Fleshing the Spirit: Spirituality and Activism in Chicana, Latina, and Indigenous Women's Lives*, edited by Elisa Facio and Irene Lara, 3–18. Tucson: University of Arizona Press.

Latina Feminist Group. 2001. "Introduction: *Papelitos Guardados*: Theorizing Latinidades through Testimonios." In *Telling to Live: Latina Feminist Testimonies*, edited by The Latina Feminist Group, 1–24. Durham, NC: Duke University Press, 2001.

León-Portilla, Miguel. 1988. "Mesoamerica 1942, and on the Eve of 1992." 1992 Lecture Series. Working Papers, No. 1. College Park: University of Maryland.

Leyva, Yolanda Chávez. 1996. "Breaking the Silence: Putting Latina Lesbian History at the Center." In *The New Lesbian Studies*, edited by Bonnie Zimmerman and Toni A. H. McNaron, 141–51. New York: Feminist Press.

——. 1998. "Listening to the Silences in Latina/Chicana Lesbian History." In Trujillo 1998, 429–34.

——. 2002a. "The Revisioning of History es una gran limpia: Teaching and Historical Trauma in Chicana/o History." *La Voz de Esperanza* 14, no. 7 (September): 10–12.

——. 2002b. "The Revisioning of History es una gran limpia: Teaching and Historical Trauma in Chicana/o History, Part 2." *La Voz de Esperanza* 15, no. 8 (October): 4–6.

Lopez, Floridalma Boj. 2017. "Mobile Archives of Indigeneity: Building la Communidad Ixim through Organizing in the Maya Diaspora." *Latino Studies* 15, no. 2: 1–18.

——. 1984a. "The Master's Tools Will Never Dismantle the Master's House." In *Sister Outsider: Essays and Speeches by Audre Lorde*, 110–13. Berkeley, CA: Crossing Press Feminist Series.

——. 1984b. "Uses of the Erotic: The Erotic as Power," In *Sister Outsider: Essays and Speeches* 53–59. Berkeley, CA: Crossing Press Feminist Series.

Lowe, Lisa 1997. "Angela Davis: Reflections on Race, Class, Gender in the USA." In *The Politics of Culture in the Shadow of Capital*, edited by by Lisa Lowe and David Lloyd, 303–23. Durham, NC: Duke University Press.

Lugones, María. 2008. "The Coloniality of Gender." *Worlds and Knowledges Otherwise* 2 (Spring): 1–17.

Luna, Jennie M. 2012a. "Building a Xicana Indigena Philosophical Base." *APA Newsletters: Newsletter on Hispanic/Latino Issues in Philosophy* 11, no. 2: 9–16.

——. 2012b. "Coming Home to Danza." In *Speaking from the Heart: Herstories of Chicana, Latina, and Amerindian Women*, edited by Rose Borunda and Melissa Moreno, 68–70. Dubuque, IA: Kendal Hunt.

Luna, Jennie, and Gabriel S. Estrada. 2020. "Trans*lating the Genderqueer -*x* through Caxcan, Nahua, and Xicanx Indígena Knowledge." In *Decolonizing Latinx Masculinities*, edited by Arturo J. Aldama and Frederick Luis Aldama, 251–74. Tucson: University of Arizona Press.

Luna, Jennie, and Martha Galeana. 2016. "Remembering Coyolxauhqui as a Birthing Text." *Regeneración Tlacuilolli: UCLA Raza Studies Journal* 2, no. 1 (June): 7–32.

Marez, Curtis. 2001. "Signifying in Spain, Becoming Comanche, Making Mexicans: Indian Captivity and the History of Chicana/o Popular Performance." *American Quarterly* 53, no. 2: 267–307.

Mariscal, George, ed. 1999. *Aztlán and Viet Nam: Chicano and Chicana Experiences of The War*. Berkeley: University of California Press.

Martínez, María Elena. 2004. "The Black Blood of New Spain: Limpieza de Sangre, Racial Violence, and Gendered Power in Early Colonial Mexico." *William and Mary Quarterly*, 3d ser., 61, no. 3: 479–520.

——. 2008. *Genealogical Fictions: Limpieza de Sangre, Religion, and Gender in Colonial Mexico*. Stanford, CA: Stanford University Press.

Martinez, Samuelin. 2017. "Traditional Healing Praxis Re-membering, Re-rooting, and Re-connecting: A Native Re-vitatlization Plan." In *Cultura y Bienestar: Meso-American Based Healing and Mental Health Practice Based Evidence*, edited by Ricardo A. Carrillo and Concepcion Saucedo Martinez, 183–226. CreateSpace Independent Publishing Platform.

Martinez-Cruz, Paloma. 2011. *Women and Knowledge in Mesoamerica: From East L.A. to Anahuac*. Tucson: University of Arizona Press.

Medina, Lara, and Martha Gonzales, eds. 2019. *Voices from the Ancestors: Xicanx and Latinx Spiritual Expressions and Healing Practices*. Tucson: University of Arizona Press.

Mercado, Claudia 2001. "Womyn Image Makers: Las Nuevas Doñas?" *Tongues Magazine* 1: 29–30.

Mesa-Bains, Amalia. 1991. "*El Mundo Femenino*: Chicana Artist of the Movement—A Commentary on Development and Production." In *Chicano Art: Resistance and Affirmation, 1965–1985*, edited by Richard Griswold del Castillo, Teresa McKenna, and Yvonne Yarbro-Bejarano, 131–40. Los Angeles: Wight Art Gallery.

Mignolo, Walter D. 1996. "Linguistic Maps, Literary Geographies, and Cultural Landscapes: Languages, Languaging, and (Trans)nationalism." *Modern Language Quarterly* 57, no. 2 (June): 181–97.

——. 2007. "Introduction: Coloniality of power and de-colonial thinking." *Cultural Studies* 21, nos. 2–3: 155–67.

Miller, Susan. 2008. "Native America Writes Back: The Origin of the Indigenous Paradigm in Historiography." *Wicazo Sa Review* 23, no. 2 (Fall): 9–28.

———. 2009. "Native Historians Write Back: The Indigenous Paradigm in American Indian Historiography." *Wicazo Sa Review* 24, no. 1 (Spring): 29–45.

Miner, Dylan. 2012. "Aztlán, Anishinaabewaki, Ixachilan: Radical Hemispheric Indigeneity and the Liberation of Art through the Graphic Work of Carlos Cortéz Koyokukatl." In *Comparative Indigeneities of the Américas: Toward a Hemispheric Approach*, edited by M. Bianet Castellanos, Lourdes G. Najera, and Arturo J. Aldama, 289–306. Tucson: University of Arizona Press.

———. 2014. *Creating Aztlán: Chicano Art, Indigenous Sovereignty, and Lowriding Across Turtle Island.* Tucson: University of Arizona Press.

Miranda, Deborah. 2010. "Extermination of *las Joyas:* Gendercide in Spanish California." *GLQ: A Journal of Lesbian and Gay Studies* 16, no. 1/2: 253–84.

Miranda, Deborah, and AnaLouise Keating. 2002. "Footnoting Heresy: E-mail Dialogues." In Anzaldúa and Keating 2002, 202–7.

Mitchell, Pablo. 2010. "Making Sex Matter: Histories of Latina/o Sexualities, 1898 to 1965." In *Latina/o Sexualities: Probing Powers, Passions, Practices, and Policies*, edited by Marysol Ascenio, 38–47. New Brunswick, NJ: Rutgers University Press.

Mohanty, Chandra Talpade. 2003. "Under Western Eyes: Feminist Scholarship and Colonial Discourses." In *Feminism without Borders: Decolonizing Theory, Practicing Solidarity*, 17–42. Durham, NC: Duke University Press.

Mohanty, Chandra, Ann Russo, and Lourdes Torres, eds. 1991. *Third World Women and the Politics of Feminism.* Indianapolis: Indiana University Press.

Moraga, Cherríe L. 1993. "Queer Aztlán: The Re-formation of Chicano Tribe." In *The Last Generation: Prose and Poetry*, 145–74. Boston: South End Press.

———. 2000 (1983). *Loving in the War Years: lo que nunca pasó por sus labios*. Expanded 2d ed. Boston: South End Press.

———. 2002. "From Inside the First World: Foreword, 2001." In Moraga and Anzaldúa 2002, xv–xxxiii.

———. 2011. *A Xicana Codex of Changing Consciousness: Writings, 2000–2010.* Drawings by Celia Herrera Rodríguez. Durham, NC: Duke University Press.

———. 2017. "Queer Aztlán: The Re-Formation of Chicano Tribe." In *Aztlán: Essays on the Chicano Homeland*, edited by Rudolfo Anaya, Francisco A. Lomelí, and Enrique R. Lamadrid, 253–72. Rev. and expanded ed. Tucson: University of New Mexico Press.

Moraga, Cherríe, and Gloria Anzaldúa. 1983 (1981). *This Bridge Called My Back: Writings by Radical Women of Color*. 2nd ed. New York: Kitchen Table: Women of Color Press.

Moraga, Cherríe L., and Gloria E. Anzaldúa. 2002. *This Bridge Called My Back: Writings by Radical Women of Color.* 3d ed. Berkeley, CA: Third Woman Press.

Moraga, Cherríe, and Ana Castillo, eds. 1988. *Esta puente, mi espalda: Voces de mujeres tercermundistas en los Estados Unidos.* Translated by Ana Castillo and Norma Alarcón. San Francisco: ISM Press.

Morgensen, Scott Lauria. 2011a. *Spaces between Us: Queer Settler Colonialism and Indigenous Decolonization*. Minneapolis: University of Minnesota Press.

——. 2011b. "Unsettling Queer Politics: What Can Non-Natives Learn from Two-Spirit Organizing." In *Queer Indigenous Studies: Critical Interventions in Theory, Politics, and Literature*, edited by Qwo-Li Driskill, Chris Finley, Brian Joseph Gilley, and Scott Lauria Morgensen, 132–52. Tucson: University of Arizona Press.

Muñoz, José Esteban. 1999. *Disidentifications: Queers of Color and the Performance of Politics.* Minneapolis: University of Minnesota Press.

——. 2009. *Cruising Utopia: The Then and There of Queer Futurity*. New York: New York University Press.

Omi, Michael, and Howard Winant. 1994. *Racial Formation in the United States: From the 1960s to the 1990s.* 2d ed. New York: Routledge.

Pérez, Emma. 1998. "Irigaray's Female Symbolic in the Making of Chicana Lesbian *Sitios y Lenguas* (Sites and Discourses)." In Trujillo 1998, 87–101.

——. 1999. *The Decolonial Imaginary: Writing Chicanas Into History*. Bloomington: Indiana University Press.

——. 2003. "Queering the Borderlands: The Challenges of Excavating the Invisible and Unheard." *Frontiers: A Journal of Women Studies* 24, no. 2/3: 122–31.

——. 2005. "Gloria Anzaldúa: La gran nueva mestiza theorist, writer, activist-scholar." *NWSA Journal, 1–10. Indiana University Press.*

——. 2020. "Letter to Gloria Anzaldúa." *Aztlán: A Journal of Chicano Studies* 45, no. 2: 161–68.

Pérez, Laura E. 2007. *Chicana Art: The Politics of Spiritual and Aesthetic Altarities.* Durham, NC: Duke University Press.

——. 2008. "Hybrid Spiritualities and Chicana Altar-Based Art: The Work of Amalia Mesa-Bains." In *Mexican American Religions: Spirituality, Activism, and Culture*, edited by Gastón Espinosa and Mario T. García, 338–58. Durham, NC: Duke University Press.

Perks, Robert, and Alister Thomson, eds. 2006. Introduction to *The Oral History Reader.* 2d ed. New York: Routledge.

Pulido, Laura. 2018. "Geographies of Race and Ethnicity III: Settler Colonialism and Nonnative People of Color." *Progress in Human Geography* 42, no. 2: 1–10. https://doi.org/10.1177/0309132516686011.

Quijano, Anibal. 2000. "Coloniality of Power, Eurocentrism, and Latin America." *Nepantla: Views from South* 1, no. 3: 533–80.

Ramírez, Catherine S. 2002. "Alternative Cartographies: *Third Woman* and the Respatialization of the Borderlands." *Midwestern Miscellany* 30: 47–62.

Ramírez, Horacio N. Roque. 2005. "A Living Archive of Desire: Teresita La Campesina and the Embodiment of Queer Latino Community Histories." In *Archive Stories: Facts, Fictions, and the Writing of History*, edited by Antoinette Burton, 111–35. Durham, NC: Duke University Press.

Ramirez, Renya. 2002. "Julia Sanchez's Story: An Indigenous Woman between Nations." *Frontiers: A Journal of Women's Studies* 23, no. 2: 65–83.

Ramos, Juanita, ed. 1994. *Compañeras: Latina Lesbians*. New York: Routledge.

Rebolledo, Tey Diana. (2006). "Prietita y el Otro Lado: Gloria Anzaldúa's Literature for Children." *PMLA* 121, no. 1: 279–84.

Reti, Irene. 2005. "Living in the House of Nepantla." In Keating 2005, 57–59.
———. 2017. *House of Nepantla: Living with Gloria Anzaldúa.* N.p.: Juniper Lake Press.
Retter, Yolanda. 1997. "Lesbian Spaces in Los Angeles, 1970–90." In *Queers in Space: Communities, Public Places, Sites of Resistance*, edited by Gordon Brent Ingram, Anne-Marie Bouthillette, and Yolanda Retter, 325–36. Seattle: Bay Press.
———. 1999. "On the Side of Angels: Lesbian Activism in Los Angeles, 1970–1990." PhD diss., University of New Mexico.
Retter Vargas, Yolanda. 2012. "Preservation of LGBT History: The One Archive." In *Pathways to Progress: Issues and Advances in Latino Librarianship*, edited by John Ayala and Salvador Güereña, 169–76. Santa Barbara, CA: Libraries Unlimited.
Retzloff, Tim. 2007. "Eliding Trans Latino/a Queer Experience in U.S. LGBT History: José Sarria and Sylvia Rivera Reexamined." *Centro Journal* 19, no. 1 (Spring): 298–318.
River Rose Apothecary. 2014. "Plant Allies for Self-Healing Series, Part 1: Building Relationships with Plantcestors and Ancestors (Foundations of Working with Plants as Medicine)." Conference, Oakland, CA, November 1, 2014. www.riverroseapothecary.com.
Rodríguez, Juana María. 2003. *Queer Latinidad: Identity Practices, Discursive Spaces*. New York: New York University Press, 2003.
Rodríguez, Roberto Cintli. 2014. *Our Sacred Maíz Is Our Mother: Indigeneity and Belonging in the Americas*. Tucson: University of Arizona Press.
Rodríguez, Roberto, and Patrisia Gonzales. 1998. "The Treaty of Guadalupe Hidalgo Still Relevant Today." *Diálogo* 3, no. 1, 25–27.
Román, Estela. 2012. *Nuestra medicina: De los remedios para el aire y los remedios para el alma.* Bloomington, IN: Palibrio.
———. 2019. "El Temazkal, a Place for Rest and Purification." In *Voices from the Ancestors: Xicanx and Latinx Spiritual Expressions and Healing Practices*, edited by Lara Medina and Martha Gonzales, 188–90. Tucson: University of Arizona Press.
Roscoe, Will. 1991. *The Zuni Man-Woman.* Albuquerque: University of New Mexico Press.
———, ed. 1988. *Living the Spirit: A Gay American Indian Anthology.* Compiled by Gay American Indians. New York: St. Martin's Press.
Rowe, Aimee Carrillo. 2017. "Settler Xicana: Postcolonial and Decolonial Reflections on Incommensurablity." *Feminist Studies* 43, no. 3: 525–36.
Ruiz, Vicky. 2008. *From Out of the Shadows: Mexican Women in Twentieth-Century America.* New York: Oxford University Press.
Saldaña-Portillo, Maria Josephina. 2003. "Toward an American 'American Studies': Postrevolutionary Reflections on Malcolm X and the New Aztlan." In *The Revolutionary Imagination in the Americas and the Age of Development*, edited by M. Saldaña-Portillo, 259–90. Durham, NC: Duke University Press.
Salvídar-Hull, Sonia. 1999. Introduction to *Borderlands/La Frontera*, by Gloria E. Anzaldúa. 2d ed. San Francisco: Aunt Lute Books.
Sandoval, Chela. 1990 (1982). "Feminism and Racism: A Report on the 1981 National Women's Studies Association Conference." In Anzaldúa 1990, 55–70.

——. 1991. "U.S. Third World Feminism: The Theory and Method of Oppositional Consciousness in the Postmodern World." *Genders* 10 (Spring): 1–24.

——. 2000. *Methodology of the Oppressed.* Minneapolis: University of Minnesota Press.

Santa Cruz Feminist of Color Collective. 2014. "Building on 'the Edge of Each Other's Battles': A Feminist of Color Multidimensional Lens." *Hypatia* 29, no. 1: 23–40.

Seidman, Steven, ed. 1996. *Queer Theory/Sociology*. Malden: Blackwell.

Shohat, Ella 2001. "Area Studies, Transnationalism, and the Feminist Production of Knowledge." *Signs* 26, no. 4: 1269–72.

Short, Kayann. 1994. "Coming to the Table: The Differential Politics of *This Bridge Called My Back*." *Genders* 20: 3–44.

Smith, Andrea. 2005. *Conquest: Sexual Violence and American Indian Genocide.* Boston: South End Press.

——. 2006. "Heteropatriarchy and the Three Pillars of White Supremacy: Rethinking Women of Color Organizing." In *Color of Violence: The INCITE! Anthology*, edited by INCITE! Women of Color Against Violence, 66–73. Cambridge, MA: South End Press.

——. 2010. "Queer Theory and Native Studies: The Heteronormativity of Settler Colonialism." *GLQ: A Journal of Lesbian and Gay Studies* 1, no. 1–2: 41–68.

Smith, Linda Tuhiwai. 1999. *Decolonizing Methodologies: Research and Indigenous Peoples.* New York: Zed Books.

Soto, Sandra, K. 2010. *Reading Chican@ Like a Queer: The De-Mastery of Desire*. Austin: University of Texas Press.

Spivak, Gayatri C. 1999. *A Critique of Postcolonial Reason: Toward A History of the Vanishing Present*. Cambridge, MA: Harvard University Press.

Sturken, Marita. 1997. *Tangled Memories: The Vietnam War, the AIDS Epidemic, and the Politics of Remembering*. Berkeley: University of California Press.

Sudbury, Julia. 2003 "Toward a Holistic Anti-Violence Agenda: Women of Color as Radical Bridge-Builders." *Social Justice* 30, no. 3: 134–40.

Taylor, Diana. 2003. *The Archive and The Repertoire: Performing Cultural Memory in the Americas*. Durham, NC: Duke University Press.

Tello, Jerry. 2018. *Recovering Your Sacredness: Ancestral Teachings for Today's Living.* Hacienda Heights, CA: Sueños Publications.

Thiong'o, Ngũgĩ wa. 1986. *Decolonising the Mind: The Politics of Language in African Literature*. London: James Curry.

Torres, Eliseo. 2006. *Healing with Herbs and Rituals: A Mexican Tradition.* Albuquerque: University of New Mexico Press.

Trujillo, Carla. 1991. "Chicana Lesbians: Fear and Loathing in the Chicano Community." In *Chicana Lesbians: The Girls Our Mothers Warned Us About*, edited by Carla Trujillo, 186–94. Berkeley, CA: Third Woman Press.

——, ed. 1991. *Chicana Lesbians: The Girls Our Mothers Warned Us About*. Berkeley, CA: Third Woman Press.

——, ed. 1998. *Living Chicana Theory.* Berkeley, CA: Third Woman Press.

Tuck, Eve, and K. Wayne Yang 2012. "Decolonization Is Not a Metaphor." *Decolonization: Indigeneity, Education, and Society* 1, no. 1: 1–40.

Vakalahi, Halaevalu F., and Saundra Hardin Starks. 2011. "Health, Well-Being and Women of Color Academics." *International Journal of Humanities and Social Sciences* 1, no. 2 (February): 185–90.

Valerio, Max Wolf. 2002. "It's in My Blood, My Face—My Mother's Voice, the Way I Sweat." In Moraga and Anzaldúa 2002, 41–46.

Venegas, Sybil. 2017. "Take Me to the River: The Photography of Laura Aguilar." In Epstein 2017, 9–17.

———. 2018. "Connected to the Land: The Work of Laura Aguilar." *Artbound*, April 11, 2018, 1–13. kcet.org/shows/artbound/connected-to-the-land-the-work-of-laura-aguilar.

Warner, Michael, ed. 1993. Introduction to *Fear of a Queer Planet: Queer Politics and Social Theory*, vii–xxi. Minneapolis: University of Minnesota Press.

Waziyatawin. 2008. *What Does Justice Look Like? The Struggle for Liberation in Dakota Homeland.* St. Paul, MN: Living Justice Press.

Waziyatawin and Michael Yellow Bird, eds. 2005. *For Indigenous Eyes Only: A Decolonization Handbook.* Santa Fe, NM: School of American Research Press.

Weber, David J., ed. 1973. *Foreigners in Their Native Land: Historical Roots of the Mexican Americans*. Albuquerque: University of New Mexico Press.

Williams, Walter L. 1986. *The Spirit and the Flesh: Sexual Diversity in American Indian Culture.* Boston: Beacon.

Williams, Walter L, and Yolanda Retter, eds. 2003. *Gay and Lesbian Rights in the United States: A Documentary History.* Westport, CT: Greenwood.

Wolfe, Patrick. 2006. "Settler Colonialism and the Elimination of the Native." *Journal of Genocide Research* 8, no. 4: 387–409.

Yarbro-Bejarano, Yvonne. 1994. "Gloria Anzaldúa's *Borderlands/La Frontera*: Cultural Studies, 'Difference,' and the Non-Unitary Subject." *Cultural Critique*, no. 28 (Autumn): 5–28.

———. 1998. "Laying It Bare: The Queer/Colored Body in Photography by Laura Aguilar." In Trujillo 1998, 277–305.

———. 1999. "Sexuality and Chicana/o Studies: Toward a Theoretical Paradigm for the Twenty-First Century." *Cultural Studies* 13, no. 2: 335–45.

Zentella, Yoly. 2009. "Developing a Multi-Dimensional Model of Hispano Attachment to and Loss of Land." *Culture and Psychology* 15, no. 2: 181–200.

Zepeda, Lizeth. 2018. "Queering the Archive: Transforming the Archival Process." *disClosure: A Journal of Social Theory* 27 (July): 94–102.

Zepeda, Susy. 2014. "Queer Xicana Indígena Cultural Production: Remembering through Oral and Visual Storytelling." *Decolonization: Indigeneity, Education and Society* 3, no. 1: 119–41.

INDEX

SUSY J. ZEPEDA is an assistant professor at the University of California, Davis.

TRANSFORMATIONS: WOMANIST, FEMINIST, AND INDIGENOUS STUDIES

Teaching with Tenderness: Toward an Embodied Practice *Becky Thompson*
Building Womanist Coalitions: Writing and Teaching in the Spirit of Love
Edited by Gary L. Lemons
Hungry Translations: Relearning the World through Radical Vulnerability
Richa Nagar, in journeys with Sangtin Kisan Mazdoor Sangathan and Parakh Theatre
Shared Selves: Latinx Memoir and Ethical Alternatives to Humanism *Suzanne Bost*
Shapeshifting Subjects: Gloria Anzaldúa's Naguala and Border Arte *Kelli D. Zaytoun*
Queering Mesoamerica Diasporas: Remembering Xicana Indígena Ancestries
Susy J. Zepeda

The University of Illinois Press
is a founding member of the
Association of University Presses.

University of Illinois Press
1325 South Oak Street
Champaign, IL 61820-6903
www.press.uillinois.edu

FSC
www.fsc.org
MIX
Papier | Fördert
gute Waldnutzung
FSC® C083411

Zeitfracht Medien GmbH
Ferdinand-Jühlke-Straße 7
99095 Erfurt, Deutschland
produktsicherheit@kolibri360.de